the
wait

LOVE, FEAR, AND HAPPINESS ON THE HEART TRANSPLANT LIST

Jennifer Bonner with Susan Cushman

Foreword by Jane Hamilton

ISBN 13: 978-1- 63489-113- 4
eISBN: 978-1- 63489-114- 1

Library of Congress Catalog Number: 2018931159
Printed in the United States of America
First Printing: 2018

22   21   20   19   18   5   4   3   2   1

Cover design by Emily Mahon
Interior design by Kim Morehead

The poem "Obsession" from *The Ride Home* by Judith Hemschemeyer was reproduced with permission from the author.

Wise Ink Creative Publishing
837 Glenwood Ave.
Minneapolis, MN 55405
www.wiseinkpub.com

To order, visit www.itascabooks.com or call 1-800-901-3480. Reseller discounts available.

To Bob and Barbara Bonner,
and all families affected by congenital heart disease

"I dwell in possibility."

—Emily Dickinson

Table of Contents

Foreword

IT'S OFTEN SAID that within every person there is a story, a book. Certainly "anybody who has survived childhood," as Flannery O'Connor once famously remarked, "has enough information to last him the rest of his days." And yet, while we all of course rack up experiences, not everyone has the capacity, the insight, or the endurance to shape her life into something comely and meaningful and with forward motion—that is to say, to make a cohesive narrative, to produce a book.

In these pages, Jennifer Bonner, at the tender point of young womanhood—the girl vibrantly thrumming, the fully fledged adult within reach—understands that her diary will very likely be read by her family, and maybe others, too. She knows full well that she might not live long enough to get a new heart, and that if she does she might die in surgery or soon after. Despite her understanding, the diary is an essential place for her to chronicle her feelings, her fears, and her thoughts, her pages private and in the moment. She's both young and wise beyond her years, coltish yet calm in her knowing. And funny. About a boy she likes: *He's sleeping without his shirt on. Oh Lord.* Her appetite for life, her hunger for beauty, for meaning, for love, for joy radiates from these entries. How often she falls in love, how deeply she thinks about art, how insightful she is about her friends and family, how vulnerable and also how strong she is. It could be argued that she made the most of what she was granted, and yet we wish for her and for us, too, that she had had more time. (In 1988 she's already deeply concerned about global warming and, remarkably tuned in, she predicts the election of a Trumpian character. She describes Elvis as *a great puppet, a skulking wreck hiding in worthless luxury under a miraculously lucrative image. Good thing he's dead. He could probably get elected President.* What prescience!)

Here she is faced with her mortality, writing about a hospital stay: *This surgery has been very relaxing in some ways—it's given a name and face to the formless terror of life.* And a few entries later, *Oh please let me have my heart transplant by winter, so I can go to the winter ball and dance all night.* The diary turns harrowing and poignant.

Susan Cushman has eloquently and clearly framed Jennifer's diary, providing context about the heart transplant procedure and Jennifer's childhood in a remarkable family. Jennifer indeed had a book in her. I'm so grateful she wrote as much as she did and that Cushman and the Bonners have brought her words and her art to life. The old miracle is at work: in black ink Jennifer's love shines bright.

—*Jane Hamilton*
July 2017

Guide To People in The Diary Entries

CARLETON STUDENTS

Art Majors

- Gretchen, a close friend
- Andy, Nat, and Dan, all a year ahead of Jen
- Beth, in Jen's class, a rival of sorts
- Riccardo
- Sue H., who spent the summer of '88 in Northfield and stayed with Jen when her parents were away
- Kevin T.

Others

- J.B., Jen's boyfriend at Carleton until late fall of '87
- Sean, a younger friend from Jen's high school forensics team
- Devin, a history major
- Traci, Jen's sophomore-year roommate
- Maggi and Rich, friends who stayed with Jen the summer of '88

- Sue S., Jen's roommate in the fall of '87
- Joseph
- Sarah, a close friend who left Carleton during the spring of '88
- Pat, a dorm floormate Jen's sophomore year
- Jay, a history major who became a good friend during the fall of '88
- Bryce, a friend of Devin's who got to know Jen in the spring of '88
- Sarah K.
- Matt, a friend whose physique Jen admired
- Kris, another friend who stayed with Jen the summer of '88
- Rick and John R., history majors who rented a Northfield apartment the summer of '88
- John P., a music history major who roomed with Jay
- Julie A.
- Sue L.

OTHER FRIENDS

- Alex, Jen's boyfriend during her senior year of high school
- Kurt, a younger friend from the high school forensics team who attended St. Olaf
- Tricia, a close friend in high school who shared "The Others" fantasy
- Susie, a friend since grade school
- Sue, a friend from grade school

CARLETON FACULTY

- Fred Hagstrom, an art professor and printmaker, and his wife, Sandra Spadaccini (Sometimes referred to as S.)
- Allison Kettering, an art history professor
- Joe Byrne, an art professor and painter
- Ed and Toni Sostek, an English and theater arts professor and his wife, Jen's dance instructor
- Raymond Saunders, a visual artist and visiting faculty member of the art department
- Tisdales, a faculty family; Bob Tisdale was an English professor
- Chang-tai Hung, a history professor
- Jewelnel Davis, the Carleton chaplain

MEDICAL

- Susan Schultz, psychotherapist
- Elizabeth Braunlin, pediatric cardiologist at the University of Minnesota (U of M)
- Stuart Jamieson, chief of cardiothoracic surgery at the U of M and a heart-lung transplant surgeon
- Aldo Castaneda, U of M surgeon who performed Jen's first heart operation in 1967
- Gordon Danielson, cardiothoracic surgeon at Mayo who performed Jen's open-heart operations when she was thirteen
- Mark Mellstrom, the Bonner family doctor in Northfield
- Sara Shumway, Jen's U of M heart transplant surgeon

Part One

A Girl with Blue Lips

IN A MINNEAPOLIS hospital in 1966, two parents greet their firstborn, not yet aware of the anomalies that hobble their daughter's tiny heart. Born a decade earlier, or in most places other than the city her parents newly called home, she would have died. Many other babies with heart complications like hers who entered the world before medical advances could save them had died before her.

This is the story of that girl's journey and her wait for a new heart when she reached adulthood. The medical story that made hers possible began long before she was born.

HELEN TAUSSIG LINED her workspace at Johns Hopkins with containers of preserved hearts from children she had known and been unable to save. As a pediatrician specializing in heart problems in the 1930s, she could do little to help many of her patients. Though she hadn't much more to offer than an oxygen tent, at least she could try to understand what was wrong with their hearts.

Often, she learned whether her diagnosis was correct only

after her patient died. Then she correlated her examination and conclusions with the postmortem findings. She filled notebook after notebook with her observations, eventually creating what became the first textbook about pediatric heart disease.

Taussig had wanted to be a surgeon, but that was out of the question for a female of her era. Harvard allowed her to take medical school classes, but she realized the university did not intend to award her a degree. She completed her training at Johns Hopkins. There, after proving her aptitude, she established a heart clinic for children.

At the time, listening to the heart with a stethoscope was the most important part of heart evaluation. Taussig began losing her hearing in her early thirties. First she tried an amplified stethoscope, but after her hearing worsened, she learned to interpret heart activity by resting her fingertips on a patient's small chest. She used tactile information to help her puzzle through what was wrong.

As she studied the wide range of congenital heart defects, Taussig also cared for the dying children and consoled their parents. She observed firsthand the short, distressed lives of blue babies, who suffered from multiple defects and a lack of oxygen. Low oxygen content in the babies' blood imparted a bluish color to their skin, a condition known as cyanosis, and deprived their brains and other organs of an element essential to life.

Searching for ways to help, Taussig realized that some of these children lived longer than expected. Why was that? As she considered the possibilities, she consulted her array of hearts.

A human fetus receives maternal blood rich in oxygen through the umbilical cord. That oxygen-rich blood partially bypasses the lungs, which are not yet needed, through a small blood vessel called the *ductus arteriosus*. This blood vessel typically closes soon after birth.

When the *ductus arteriosus* doesn't close on time, it usually causes problems. A baby with a normal heart can develop heart failure. A baby with abnormal heart structure has a different situation. In some of these babies, blood reaches the lungs to pick up oxygen only through the *ductus arteriosus*. Taussig realized that certain blue babies survived just as long as the fetal blood vessel remained open.

After Harvard's Robert Gross performed the first operation to close a *ductus arteriosus* in 1938, Taussig arranged a meeting. She wanted to know if he could create a structure that functioned like the *ductus* to help blue babies. Gross rejected the idea as impossible, and she returned to Baltimore to seek help closer to home.

LIFE WAS ESPECIALLY good for Bob and Barbara Bonner in the fall of 1966. They had recently returned to the University of Minnesota after a year in London, made possible by Bob's Fulbright scholarship. Now a PhD candidate in the history department, Bob had already accepted a job offer, which came unexpectedly in London's afternoon post, at Carleton College. Although he had looked forward to competing for an academic position at the upcoming American Historical Society meeting, his advisor told him the spot at nearby Carleton was too good to pass up.

Bob started writing his dissertation in September. He made such rapid progress that he took time off to help a colleague campaign for a state senate seat.

Barbara was happily in flux. She had moved on from her undergraduate work in psychology, mostly spent studying rats rather than people, to a masters program in library science. After blissful hours in the churches and museums of London, she contemplated a switch to art history. Still, she loved combing the stacks of the old Walter Library at the U of M, locating books to be transferred to the new West Bank campus.

THEY GREW UP in Western towns, Bob in Powell, Wyoming, and Barbara in Belle Fourche, South Dakota. Each town held fewer than four thousand people and provided welcoming spaces for children. But soon after they began dating at the University of Wyoming, it was clear they wouldn't return to either one.

Every love story begins with the infinitesimal chance that the couple would meet at all. Stanford University invited Bob to attend on the basis of his college entrance exams. But he was unprepared for such a rigorous university and, after two years, joined the army. At Fort Riley in Kansas, he found his footing as chief of pay section for the First Battle Group of the Eighteenth Infantry. When his enlistment was up in 1959, he joined the junior class at the University of Wyoming, which included Barbara.

Barbara spent much of her free time at her town library and always knew she would attend a nearby state university. The University of Wyoming became the obvious choice, since the town of Laramie featured her (soon to be history) high school boyfriend and the nearby Medicine Bow mountains. She first met Bob when he rolled into the campus bookstore late one afternoon—he had torn himself away from beers with his buddies after realizing he needed a few books for class.

A year later, Bob asked Barbara on a coffee date. Over a scuffed café tabletop, he described his vision of the future: graduate school, then life as a history professor living in a particular kind of house—one with a library. For the first time since meeting him, Barbara was intrigued.

THAT WONDERFUL FALL, three years into their marriage, the Bonners did not yet have a book-filled house. In an apartment near campus, they lived comfortably enough on Bob's $2,200 dissertation-year stipend, the equivalent of $16,800 in 2017 dollars, and what Barbara made working part-time at the university library. Their eagerly anticipated first child was due in early February. Given their student health plan, Barbara would deliver at the university hospital, but there was no reason to think they would need the sophisticated medical services the University of Minnesota could provide.

When undergraduates leave for the winter holidays, a wonderful sense of quiet settles on a university community. But on the morning of December 24, the Bonners were scrambling—Barbara was having regular contractions five weeks before her due date. Bob rushed out to buy little T-shirts and diapers and spent $100 on hastily gathered baby supplies, a significant sum for two students.

Barbara's contractions were the real thing. In midafternoon, Jenny arrived, weighing a little over five pounds. She looked beautiful to the Bonners, with auburn hair and a slightly dusky complexion. The next day felt glorious as sunlight streamed through the hospital windows and Lions Club members went from room to room, delivering big fruit baskets.

The Christmas of 1966 became the only day unclouded by worry that the Bonners have known as parents. It was just as well no one talked to them right away about the unusual findings on their daughter's newborn exam. On December 26, a pediatric cardiologist told them about Jenny's loud heart murmur.

The dusky skin hue Bob and Barbara admired came from cyanosis that was almost certainly caused by heart abnormalities. Jenny would be moved to an incubator in the intensive care unit. The new parents were too shaken to press for many details. Later, while talking with the nurses, Barbara learned that babies like Jenny usually did not live long—a few days, or possibly weeks.

The doctors began to determine what exactly was wrong. At five days of age, now under five pounds, Jenny underwent her first invasive medical study: a heart catheterization, which showed how blood flowed through her heart and suggested what her heart structure might be.[1] The cardiologist inserted a flexible catheter into a blood vessel in her groin and guided it to her heart. There it measured pressures and blood flow in the heart chambers and great arteries (the pulmonary artery and the aorta). The catheterization revealed that Jenny had several heart defects that, fortunately, worked together, at least for the moment, to keep her alive.

A normal heart sends blood on a predictable journey—to the lungs, where it picks up oxygen, then out to the body, where it delivers oxygen. Jenny's heart couldn't pump blood along the usual path: right heart, lungs, left heart, body. Instead, blood swirled inefficiently inside her heart, hitting a dead end where there was ordinarily a valve and escaping through openings between heart chambers where there should have been solid walls.

First, she had a rare condition in which the position of her ventricles was switched. The ventricles are the lower pumping

---

1 In 1966, cardiac ultrasound was many years away from being useful in diagnosing newborn heart abnormalities noninvasively.

chambers of the heart—the heart's workhorses. In normal hearts, the left one is larger and stronger, and it pumps oxygen-rich blood to the far reaches of the body. Blood from the right ventricle makes just a short trip to the lungs to gather oxygen. In Jenny's case, the smaller chamber had to pump blood the much longer distance, against higher pressure. The mismatch of her ventricles with their roles in her circulation was not her most serious problem at birth. But this condition, known as "congenitally corrected transposition of the great arteries," became crucially important later in her life.

Jenny's heart also had unnatural openings. The first, an opening between her ventricles, or a ventricular septal defect, allowed oxygen-poor blood returning to her heart from her body to mix with oxygen-rich blood returning from her lungs. As a result, the blood her heart sent to her body had far lower levels of oxygen than normal, making her a blue baby. This hole was so large that her heart functioned as if it had only one ventricle. The second, an atrial septal defect, was an opening in the wall that separated her upper heart chambers. Though much smaller than the ventricular defect, the atrial opening contributed to the inefficiency of Jenny's heart.

But even these major abnormalities were not responsible for Jenny's most pressing problem: getting blood to her lungs for oxygenation. Her pulmonary valve, the heart valve that allows blood flow from the heart to the lungs, hadn't formed. This is called pulmonary atresia. To get to her lungs, Jenny's blood traveled through the *ductus arteriosus*, the small blood vessel that previously grabbed Helen Taussig's attention.

Like the umbilical cord, the *ductus arteriosus* is essential to a fetus but unnecessary to a newborn. For Jenny, given her other heart abnormalities, blood flow through the *ductus arteriosus* was life-saving. Once this blood vessel closed—and her doctors could not accurately predict when that might happen—she would die.

To her parents, Jenny looked stunned when she returned to the ICU after the heart catheterization. They knew about theories that babies didn't feel pain like older children and adults, and wondered if she had received any pain medication. Stunned themselves by the test results, the Bonners returned their baby supplies.

After Jenny had been in the hospital for about a week, Bob and Barbara began to think about the hospital bill. They checked with the business office and learned that the charges were already $10,000, roughly four times their annual income. The bearer of bad news quickly told them not to worry—they could get assistance through Hennepin County to cover Jenny's medical bills.

As it turned out, Jenny needed those little T-shirts after all. After a month in an incubator getting formula through a feeding tube, she went home with Bob and Barbara. Their Prospect Park apartment was ten minutes from the University of Minnesota Hospital and the pediatric cardiology clinic. The medical team evaluated Jenny every week, and whenever her parents had concerns.

As the weeks passed, Jenny grew, and her complicated heart circulated her blood the best it could. The *ductus* remained open. At three months, she developed a double chin of retained fluid, a sign of progressing heart failure. Her bluish skin darkened when she drank from a bottle because her heart couldn't send out the additional oxygen needed by working muscles. She didn't move as vigorously as a healthy three-month-old—no arm-waving or leg-kicking for her. When she was four months old, her doctors decided to intervene.

Turning Blue Lips Pink

ALDO CASTANEDA BEGAN his medical career at the University of Guatemala Medical School. Fluent in Spanish and English, he performed simultaneous translation at a pediatric conference in Guatemala and even managed to make the audience laugh at the end of a long Scandinavian joke. That speaker helped Castaneda land a spot in the surgical training program at the University of Minnesota in 1958, where he remained for the next fourteen years. In 1967, Castaneda and C. Walton Lillehei, the pioneer of open-heart surgery, shared responsibility for pediatric heart surgery at the U of M.

According to Castaneda, "The entire field of open-heart surgery was created with congenital heart disease in mind." Heart defects are among the most common serious problems at birth, affecting approximately one percent of newborns—including Jenny. But Jenny was too small for Castaneda to attempt corrective surgery that would establish normal anatomy for her heart. At that time, the best he could do was a palliative procedure that created a reliable route for blood to reach her lungs.

A report on the Waterston shunt first appeared in a little-known Czech medical journal in 1962. Four years later, just months before Jenny was born, two American medical papers described the same type of shunt, which established a connection between the ascending aorta and the right pulmonary artery. This approach was a surgical option for a baby less than six months old. When Castaneda brought Jenny to the University Hospital operating room, he performed a procedure that was relatively new to surgeons in the United States.

The shunt took over the role of the *ductus arteriosus*. With each heartbeat, some of Jenny's blood traveled out the aorta to her body, and some went to her lungs to pick up more oxygen. But the shunt would last far longer than the unpredictable fetal blood vessel.

Although it was a straightforward operation, the shunt had to be the right size for Jenny, who was younger than an ideal candidate. If the shunt diameter was too small, blood clots might block it; if it was too large, high blood flow could damage her lungs. But the Waterston procedure was lower risk than doing nothing, and it could be reversed during later corrective surgery. It would give Jenny time to grow, and cardiovascular surgeons time to develop better techniques for repairing complex defects. Her other heart problems would have to wait.

WHAT HAD HELEN TAUSSIG done after Robert Gross dismissed her idea about how to help blue babies? She approached Alfred Blalock after he became Chief of Surgery at Johns Hopkins in 1941. Blalock was an innovative thinker who proved that shock was due to blood loss, a discovery that saved countless lives during World War II. He listened with interest and asked Vivien Thomas, his gifted lab technician, to develop what became the first operation that gave some blue babies a chance.

A barely alive fifteen-month-old girl received the first Blalock-Thomas-Taussig shunt in 1944. She did well for two months before succumbing to a complication related to her heart disease, not the operation. Soon other surgeons adopted the shunt and it became a preferred approach for some blue babies. (The Waterston procedure that Jenny underwent two decades later was developed for younger infants.) But shunt survivors, and many others with congenital defects, eventually needed structural repairs inside the heart to create a semblance of normal anatomy.

The earliest open-heart procedures addressed simple problems that a surgeon could fix in under six minutes. This was how long a heart could be stilled without the patient suffering serious brain damage. Sometimes, surgeons would open a patient's heart and find problems more extensive than expected, which they could not address in the allotted time.

By the 1950s, Owen Wangensteen, Surgery Chief at the University of Minnesota, had created an ideal setting for curious, inventive young physicians, including C. Walton Lillehei, Norman Shumway, Christiaan Barnard, and Aldo Castaneda, all of whom became leaders in cardiovascular surgery. The U of M training program stood out because it offered extended surgical laboratory time and encouraged innovation.

The early heart surgeons worked in a setting that was equal parts liberating and grim. Without an intervention, many of their patients would soon die. Because death was imminent, surgeons could justify trying new approaches. A death on the operating table, or in the days to follow, provided a learning opportunity within a tragedy that was already in motion.

It was grim because they made mistakes and because there was so much death. Some surgeons became discouraged as they faced desperate parents and moribund children whom they couldn't help. Castaneda described Lillehei as "an emotionally hardy iconoclast" who had the fortitude to keep trying new ideas. Like Taussig, he kept current failures in perspective as he worked to help families of the future.

Surgeons needed more time to repair a heart. To get that time, they needed a way to oxygenate and circulate blood while they operated on the person's heart. The earliest attempts at mechanical heart-lung bypass killed most of the patients. Looking for a safer approach, Walt Lillehei devised a process he called "cross-circulation," in which an adult, usually a parent, served as a child's human heart-lung machine. After encouraging tests connecting the circulations of small and much larger dogs in the lab, he was ready for his first human trial in 1954. A one-year-old who would die soon without heart surgery was admitted. Lillehei asked Wangensteen for permission to proceed. The famous (at least in surgical circles), brief note he received simply said, "By all means, Walt, go ahead. Good luck."

That operation became the first successful open-heart repair of a complex defect. In all, Lillehei did forty-five cross-circulation cases, proving that more complex repairs could be done. He abandoned the circulation technique as too risky for the healthy adult after one mother suffered a debilitating stroke from an air embolism. The way forward would be with a machine.

In 1955, biomedical engineers and surgeons at the University of Minnesota and Mayo Clinic developed different versions of heart-lung bypass pumps. Both versions successfully served in open-heart operations, allowing surgeons to complete complex procedures that gave patients additional years of life. For a brief time, the U of M and Mayo were the only institutions in the world performing open-heart surgery.

Richard DeWall, a resident in the surgery program, designed the smaller, more practical U of M pump. Wangensteen believed that medical advances should be freely shared and soon the DeWall oxygenator made open-heart surgery possible elsewhere. At the Texas Heart Institute, Denton Cooley's team quickly adopted and then modified the DeWall pump. By the end of 1956, the Texas group had carried out more than a hundred open-heart operations, the most in the world. But even with these advances, many years would pass before surgeons could correct heart defects in young infants like Jenny.

As Wangensteen prepared for retirement in 1966, many assumed Lillehei was his natural successor as chief of surgery. Around the time of Jenny's birth, the hospital buzzed with a new rumor—the medical school dean had chosen John Najarian, a specialist in kidney transplantation and immunology from the University of California. The dean wanted a strong administrator with new skills. Though Wangensteen objected, the decision held.

Castaneda later reflected, "Even the cleaning lady in Minnesota could have told them that Walt was not a good candidate . . . You could walk into his office, and there were these piles of old records. His desk was full of death certificates that hadn't been signed for months."

LIKE MOST FAMILIES at the U of M hospital, the Bonners knew little about the upheaval in the Surgery Department. When Jenny returned for the Waterston shunt in April of 1967, Aldo Castaneda happened to be her surgeon, rather than Lillehei. Meeting with the Bonners, Castaneda downplayed his own considerable skill, saying the anesthesiologist did the hard part. Lillehei left the U of M late in the year for Cornell University.

As the Bonners prepared to return home after Jenny's successful operation, a trusted resident physician told them, "Don't worry. In ten years there will be an artificial heart." The Bonners' optimism, however, was tempered by conflicting medical advice—that they should have another child if they really wanted to be parents.

Had Bob not been recruited early to join the Carleton faculty, he might have been away interviewing for jobs as his infant daughter stubbornly spun her predicted days of life into weeks and then months. Instead he was home every day. Determined to document Jenny's existence, Bob took pictures all the time, following Barbara around the apartment as she cuddled their baby and sang to her. The photos showed that Jenny's appearance and behavior changed dramatically after the operation. Soon, her bright eyes no longer obscured by puffy eyelids, she held her head up, doing a baby pushup in her crib. Another shot showed the movement—a blurred, waving arm—missing from her early photos.

One morning, Barbara awakened to her daughter singing to the mobile that hung above her crib. By fall, the grin of an entertained, intelligent child emerged. Barbara says, "Here we had this baby who wasn't supposed to live more than a few days, and every morning when we went to lift her out of her crib, she was just beaming."

IN SEPTEMBER, WITH little more than a plastic infant seat and their Siamese cat Sybil, the Bonner family moved to Northfield, an hour south of the Twin Cities, where Bob began teaching

English history at Carleton College. His dissertation, one-third complete when Jenny was born, had advanced no further. "I was virtually disabled from working on it, completely dislocated from my topic," he says. Barbara's graduate work had halted as well. And at the time of the move, fully occupied with Jenny's care, she was pregnant with their second child.

Tim Bonner arrived on February 1, 1968, after a long labor and with a large hematoma on his head. He seemed healthy at birth, with high Apgar scores. That summer, under a September deadline, Bob holed up in his office to complete his overdue thesis. Barbara spent her days with their frail toddler and enigmatic infant.

Tim was an inactive baby with little facial animation. He hardly slept, and what sleep he got had no recognizable pattern. His tear ducts didn't work well, and he often seemed dazed, interested only in nursing. He revealed his personality then, chuckling when he saw his mother's breast, even though he struggled with breathing and swallowing during this favorite activity.

The Bonners refrained from comparing Jenny and Tim to other children, but by the time Tim was six months old they were sure he had developmental delays. Their family doctor referred Tim to a pediatrician and then a neurologist. Both told the Bonners he had profound developmental abnormalities, and they suggested Tim live at Faribault State Hospital, which had opened in 1879 for Minnesota's "idiotic and feeble-minded children." Instead, Bob and Barbara brought Tim home to give him the best life they could. They were used to living day-to-day with Jenny's uncertain health, and they would do the same with Tim.

In the late 1960s, few services existed for handicapped children living at home. Children and adults with severe deficits were expected to live in an institution; these societal norms did not change until after the national 1975 Education for All Handicapped Children Act. The Bonners were largely on their own raising Tim at home, relying on their wits and a network of friends.

Refusing to be oppressed by the long-term challenges their family faced, they focused on whatever joy each day brought. Tim banged his head on the floor when he was frustrated, but he nursed with endearing enthusiasm and laughed when Bob played on the floor with him. Jenny required constant help to get around outside the house, but her spirit and artistic imagination lifted the family.

Bob and Barbara's own childhoods were marred by a parent's alcoholism—and, in Bob's case, harsh discipline—but the Bonners were determined to escape their family legacies. They treasured and tirelessly nurtured their own children and showed a long line of Carleton students what it meant to be a parent. They didn't set out to be role models for so many. Their house was an abundant place, filled with conversation, laughter, food, music, and art, so students joined the family whenever they could.

The Bonners were an appealing faculty couple—only half a generation older than the students, good-looking despite Bob's eyewear of the time, each with an irrepressible personality. Bob's voice carried when he expressed enjoyment of a delectable bite of food or a guest at the door. Barbara's pleasure in life's offerings was quieter but no less intense. She met an apt phrase or bit of found beauty with swift and unshakeable appreciation.

Even the regular babysitters had only a rudimentary understanding of the challenges the family faced. They were a unified couple, and their children added greatly to their happiness.

Impressed by all the creative toys and children's books, a

newcomer to the Bonner household asked Barbara if she ran a nursery school. It was a reasonable question. Barbara orchestrated an all-day-and-into-the-night school for two. Jenny was both student and assistant teacher—the Bonners started seeing her as the sun to Tim's moon. From a young age, she knew how to entertain herself. She quickly moved from singing to the mobile above her bed to grasping a colored marker and applying it to paper. After Tim arrived, it came naturally for Jenny to entertain him as well.

Jenny, Barbara, and Tim

For the babysitters, Jenny was a dream child—smart, funny, cooperative, and likely to stay put. Tim moved slowly but got into trouble fast. Once, after he dumped a large canister of flour on the kitchen floor, Barbara let the kids play with it for the rest of the afternoon. After all, winters were long and the house was their playground.

The living room floor began each day an uncluttered expanse. By midafternoon, evidence of intricate play covered its surface—papers decorated and twisted into three-dimensional forms, toys (and makeshift toys) scattered, books all about, pillows strewn, a girl still intent on her latest building of wooden blocks.

Barbara supplemented their home environment with weekly trips to the Northfield library, a complicated outing with two handicapped children. She carried each child up the front steps and then down a curving staircase to the children's room in the basement, leaving one briefly as she transported the other, and reversing the process when they went home.[2]

A 1971 photo of Jenny and Tim shows two preschoolers on the floor behind a chair, heads together over a book, looking like typical little kids. They were anything but. Jenny emerged from her rocky infancy with her psyche and intellect clearly intact, but the Bonners didn't know what to expect of her physical capabilities. In 1973 they optimistically bought a house near Carleton with bedrooms upstairs, where Jenny had to be carried to her room. They had little practical help from her medical team. Physical and occupational therapists wouldn't be included in treatment plans for children with congenital heart problems until much later. Barbara says, "We were always trying to find the border between what she could and couldn't do."

Tim's abilities were an even deeper mystery. He had no diagnosis. When he was two, the only abnormality on genetic

---

2 The front steps of this and other Carnegie libraries symbolized the "elevation provided by learning." In 1985, the Northfield public library was expanded and renovated to provide handicapped access.

analysis was nonspecific "chromosomal debris." Bob and Barbara briefly considered having a third child. Doctors said they carried a high risk of having another child with impairments, and the Bonners realized they couldn't take care of another child anyway, disabled or not.

Tim took his first steps at three and a half, and he didn't start talking until after that. His motor skills, especially fine skills, were woeful—to this day he wears only slip-on shoes—but his sense of humor developed ahead of other children his age. This became key in his relationship with Jenny, who looked for ways to make him laugh. Tim had trouble engaging with the world, and as Jenny created new portals for him, she benefited as well. At home she didn't feel handicapped, with Tim as her audience and her inspiration.

Watching *Sesame Street* helped Tim learn to count and recognize words. His TV shows were often in the background as Jenny worked on her projects. But, like any younger sibling, Tim could be very disruptive, interrupting or destroying what Jenny had created. They had the same conflicts about privacy, personal space, and possessions as most brothers and sisters. When they got a little older, Jenny put a sign on her bedroom door directed at Tim: "KEEP OUT! —This means you!" And he knew it.

Every day of reasonable weather, Barbara took them to the park, where Tim played in the sand and Jenny wandered, smelling the flowers and taking in the more expansive surroundings. Pushing them first in a clunky double stroller and then on swings, Barbara got by far the most exercise during these outings.

In March of 1972, the Bonners returned to London for Bob's first sabbatical and a summer off in their favorite city. This time, they had two kids to carry wherever they went. Some couples might not have attempted a nine-month stay abroad with hand-icapped children, but Bob and Barbara embraced the opportunity. Jenny was five and Tim had just turned four. They lived once again in Goodenough House, subsidized housing in central London for visiting international scholars, with a nursery school next door.

Jenny at Goodenough House in London

Early in their stay, the National Health Service gave Jenny and Tim large strollers that the Bonners could bring on London buses or the Underground. As they roamed London, both kids learned to say a very British "Oh dear, oh dear" in the face of unexpected events—an improvement over a time the year before, when Tim kicked over Jenny's juice in a hospital cafeteria and she exclaimed, "Goddammit!" to the mild shock and hearty amusement of a nearby table of nuns.

That fall, Bob and a Carleton English professor taught a history and literature seminar to thirty-two students in the college's London Program. After the program ended, the Bonners returned to Northfield, and they brought the strollers with them. Jenny used hers in lieu of a wheelchair for years to come.

HUMAN HEART TRANSPLANTATION had been around for about as long as Jenny herself. In June of 1966, six months before her birth, Adrian Kantrowitz prepared to perform the first heart transplant at Maimonides Hospital in Brooklyn. Two other cardiovascular surgeons—Norman Shumway at Stanford University and Richard Lower at Stanford and then the Medical College of Virginia—had worked since the late 1950s on surgical approaches to transplant a human heart.

Unlike the other two surgeons, Kantrowitz was particularly interested in helping babies born with severe heart defects. He believed the transplanted heart could grow along with the child and that an infant's immune system might accept the new heart more readily than a fully developed adult immune system.

Jenny and a six-week-old boy at Maimonides were born with the same heart defects—pulmonary atresia, atrial and ventricular septal defects, and the same version of transposition of the great arteries. As the Bonners would soon hear about Jenny, his parents learned he was not expected to live long.

The infant Kantrowitz proposed as the heart donor was born without critical parts of the brain and skull, a condition known as anencephaly. This infant would inevitably die in the very near future. Kantrowitz obtained permission from both sets of parents, but the Maimonides hospital administration intervened. They would not allow the surgical team to remove the heart of the anencephalic baby until after it had stopped beating.

In his lab, Kantrowitz successfully stopped, restarted, and

then transplanted animal hearts, but he could not restart this tiny human heart. The six-week-old boy who would have been the recipient was recalled from anesthesia and died soon after of heart failure.

Kantrowitz wrote later, "In the early heart transplantation attempts, the challenges of surgical technique, rejection, and infection never were the only obstacles. Ethical issues were at least as daunting . . . According to the definition of clinical death that was generally accepted at the time, the donor was not considered dead until the heart had stopped beating . . . I felt that we could in good conscience remove the donor's heart while it was still beating because an anencephalic infant has no chance of surviving. However, colleagues at Maimonides Medical Center insisted we allow the donor's heart to stop naturally before removing it."

In October 1967, Shumway and Lower spoke at the American College of Surgeons meeting. In separate presentations, each said he was prepared to start clinical trials of human heart transplantation.

Lower devised an ingenious approach that preserved portions of the heart recipient's own upper chambers, making it easier to connect the great vessels to the donor heart. A South African man named Christiaan Barnard, who first performed cardiac surgery at the U of M, spent three months at Lower's animal lab to learn the heart transplant procedure.

Despite having far less experience with transplants than the other three surgeons, Barnard successfully transplanted the first human heart on December 3, 1967.[3] He instantly became an international celebrity. Kantrowitz and Shumway followed with

---

3 In 1964 a gravely ill heart patient at the University of Mississippi received a chimpanzee's heart and died soon after.

their first heart transplants soon after. Though the transplant teams honed their surgical approaches in animal labs, they were far less prepared for postoperative problems.

Barnard's patient survived eighteen days, Shumway's fifteen days, and Kantowitz's less than one day. Richard Lower soon performed his first transplant, but his program was put on hold when he was sued for wrongful death, having transplanted the heart of a recent work-accident victim who appeared brain-dead, but whose heart still beat. (Lower "won" the case when it went to trial four years later.)

For a few years, there was great public enthusiasm for heart transplants, despite the troublingly brief survival of most heart recipients. Philip Blaiberg, Barnard's second heart transplant patient, became the compelling exception, living nineteen months after the procedure. In May of 1968, encouraged by Blaiberg's ongoing survival, Denton Cooley began transplanting hearts at St. Luke's Hospital in Houston. Cooley transplanted twenty-one hearts over the next year.

Other medical centers ramped up their own heart transplant programs. By 1970, sixty-four medical teams around the world had performed a heart transplant, but most did only one or two. The results were almost all disastrous, with few heart recipients living long enough to justify the procedure. The medical community increasingly supported a heart transplant moratorium. Minnesota senator Walter Mondale proposed a federal commission to regulate medical research, including transplants.

At Stanford, Shumway achieved better survival rates, methodically learning as much as he could from each patient. In November 1970, presenting at a symposium on organ transplants, he said,

After an early and almost hysterical acceptance, transplantation of the heart has seemingly fallen into therapeutic disrepute. Perhaps the fact that only twenty-three of one hundred fifty-five patients undergoing heart transplantation worldwide are now alive has something to do with this repudiation. At any rate, eleven of these twenty-three current survivors are in the Palo Alto series, and heart transplantation at the Stanford University Hospital continues as part of an expanded program for the treatment of far-advanced cardiac disease.

Shumway went on to report Stanford's results, including work on immunosuppression to prevent rejection of the transplanted heart. He also noted that Barnard's important contribution was

equating brain death with death of the donor. [4] Since time immemorial, absence of the heartbeat had been the accepted criterion of death, but in modern cardiac surgery the heart is electively arrested in many hospital centers every day . . . the ancient concept of a so-called "moment of death" gave way to extensive revision . . . all parts of the body do not die at the same time. The brain dies first, then the heart, liver, kidneys, and so on . . .

Shumway concluded by advocating for those with end-stage heart disease.

---

4 In South Africa, at the time of Barnard's first heart transplant, the donor could be legally declared dead on the basis of no brain activity, even if the heart was still beating. Within a year of Barnard's transplant, a Harvard committee published criteria for brain death. In the United States, the Uniform Determination of Death Act, drafted in 1981 for states to approve, clearly recognized brain death as a legitimate basis for declaring a person dead.

These patients will again ask what can be done, and they
will not accept the contention that they are doomed and
that no therapeutic resource remains. They will be relatively young patients with some knowledge of the ongoing status of heart transplantation, and the terrible
tendency to let patients die without an all-out effort will
not be acceptable to them.

Life magazine's September 17, 1971, cover story, "A New and Disquieting Look at Transplants," detailed the rise and fall of Cooley's early transplant program in Houston. It included a photo of
six happy-appearing heart recipients, five men and one woman,
all dead only months later. A cardiologist told how he turned
against the procedure as he lost patient after patient. Cooley
said he didn't regret trying to help the "desperately ill," but by
the time of his *Life* interview, along with almost all other heart
transplant surgeons, Cooley supported the moratorium.

Shumway continued to work on how to control infection
and prevent the recipient's immune system from rejecting the
new heart. He was determined that a new heart could be a hopeful option for people with end-stage heart failure.

Senator Mondale did not get his commission on medical research, but ongoing discussion led to a practical way for willing
individuals to become organ donors. After the Uniform Ana-
tomical Gift Act was passed, states began allowing individuals
to indicate they wished to be organ donors on their driver's license. By 1972, all fifty states adopted this method.

AFTER RETURNING HOME from London in late 1972, Jenny eagerly joined her kindergarten class partway into the school year.

But she had low social standing and few options for new friends, despite her companionability and intelligence. Unprepared for the physicality of school activities, she couldn't participate in recess or gym class. She rode the short school bus for handicapped kids.

Jenny watched the comings and goings of neighborhood kids for years—but she was rarely among them. She never had the strength or aerobic capacity to go to a playground, much less independently to the larger neighborhood, where kids become closer friends and establish a pecking order.

When Jenny was ten, like many girls her age, she started a diary. She didn't mention any health problems. But if you fan the pages of an early diary from back to front, "I LOVE SCOTT" gradually appears in the upper right-hand corner. She was undeterred when she heard he was unhappy that she liked him. "I know he doesn't hate me, because if you hate someone, and you've both missed the bus, you wouldn't say, 'Don't worry Jenny. I'll call my mom and she'll take us home.'"

Around that time Jenny filled out an "All About Me" sheet at school. Her answers to three questions reveal some of what she felt about her physical self.

The thing I like best about how I look: <u>I don't know.</u>

One thing that really scares me is <u>when somebody jumps on me.</u>

If you could have any wish in the whole world, what would you wish for? <u>That I could run.</u>

Jenny at age ten

Her heart performed best, and she was most comfortable, when her body was at rest. Away from home, she needed to be carried, pushed, or driven. If somebody did jump on her, she couldn't do much to defend herself. She certainly couldn't run away, or run just for the fun of it. At school she rode in the British stroller between classes, pushed by schoolmates, either a trusted older friend or anyone who was available and presumably willing. Some days, she came home and reported that a kid who propelled her was "a snot."

As she grew older, she found it harder to depend on others for locomotion. She hated when a grade school teacher slung her over a shoulder to hustle her outside during fire drills. Rough handling wasn't Jenny's only grievance against this particular teacher; at home she got private revenge by sketching the teacher as a squawking hybrid, a fowl-human.

Jenny knew from a young age that she was different, and she became friends mostly with other children seen as different. One day during grade school, Jenny and three others sat at the Bonner kitchen table, talking about what made each of them stand out.

Jenny began, "People stare at me because my lips are blue." Another girl said, "And I'm black."

"I'm too short," a boy contributed.

Jenny spoke for her brother, who was at the table but couldn't name his remarkable feature. "And Tim is retarded."

Satisfied with their analysis, they returned to their snacks.

Despite being different, Jenny enjoyed elementary school. Her closest friend, Mallory, was happy to forego physical play for imaginative activities. Outside school they practiced magic tricks and created elaborate scenarios and costumes, learning to sew in the process. They wrote a neighborhood newspaper, priced at fifteen cents, with a regular feature interviewing people about how to make Northfield a better place. They included recipes, fashion tips, ideas for having fun, help-wanted ads for chores at the Bonner house, and advice. "Be nice to everyone you know. People are only human. People do make mistakes. This is something you should think about."

MEETING TIM'S NEEDS became increasingly challenging for the Bonners. Like many of the parents of remarkable children interviewed in Andrew Solomon's *Far From the Tree*, they were "dedicated to extending the optimal conditions they had achieved at home into the larger community . . ."

Tim knew his alphabet and could count in English and Spanish. After doing well in a "trainable" kindergarten special education class, he transitioned to an "educable" first-grade special education class.

Then the school system mainstreamed him in second grade. But his teacher didn't integrate him, and except for two boys who befriended him, he sat isolated in the back of the room. He couldn't use the school bathroom. Recess in the open space of the playground terrified him. Sometimes, at the end of the day, he hurled himself off the school bus screaming. The school psychologist told Barbara that he intended to lock Tim in a bathroom for a few days until he learned to use the toilet.

Yet at home, Tim generated humor and hugs. One weekend night after he was in bed, his parents sat at the top of the stairs, out of his sight. They listened as he reprised his day, humming music from *Peter and the Wolf* and interspersing quotes from his family. It became clear he was Peter. He gave Jenny and Barbara the lighter flute and oboe tunes, and Bob the authoritative notes of the bassoon.

Lacking a diagnosis or treatment plan for Tim, the Bonners were becoming desperate about his situation. Their young family doctor, recently trained at the University of Minnesota, recommended the Children's Rehabilitation Center at the University. When they brought Tim to the Rehab Center, the director said, "Children like this are unable to structure time or space." These were such fundamental deficits the Bonners had been unable to recognize them.

Around that time, a friend loaned Barbara *The Siege* by Clara Claiborne Park. As she read about a family with an autistic child, Barbara realized that Tim shared problems with the child in the book. If Tim were autistic, that might explain some of his distress in the world.

The Bonners learned about autism, including the now-discredited theory[5] that autism is caused by "refrigerator mothers." The University of Minnesota had moved beyond this idea, recognizing that Tim's problems began with perceptual defects. Three times a week, Barbara drove Tim to the U of M so that occupational, speech, and physical therapists experienced with autistic children could work with him.

The clinic recommended that Tim spend the summer of 1976, when he was eight, as a rehabilitation patient at University Hospital. Meanwhile, his parents chased tips about schools for him. They investigated several programs in Minneapolis and St. Paul, but didn't like the way staff members talked about Tim.

One of the rehab staff at the U of M suggested the individualized day school for handicapped students at St. Joseph's Home for Children in Minneapolis, which combined classroom instruction with occupational therapy. Bob and Barbara saw that St. Joseph's didn't insist on labels and worked with whatever mix of problems students presented. In the fall, Tim started commuting every day from Northfield to Minneapolis.

FROM A YOUNG age, Jenny loved to make lists and was a natural with the humor inherent in ordering items. She often began her to-do lists with "Get organized"—an item she could cross off as soon as she completed the list. Each Christmas, her wish list ranged more widely. At age twelve, she noted in her diary:

This is a list for self improvement.

---

5 Proposed by Leo Kanner in 1949 and later championed by Bruno Bettelheim. Parents of autistic children, especially mothers, were described as lacking warmth.

Don't swear so much.

Don't eat so much junk food.

Try to make some money.

Don't sit inside listening to the radio all day.

Try to forget Scott.

Stop acting weird in front of everybody.

Try to take care of your body.

Later that year, she reviewed what she valued most:

> Here are some things that make life worth living. Not necessarily in order.
> 1. Scott (soon I might cross him out)
> 2. Roast beef
> 3. Dad's barbequed chicken
> 4. Love (except boy-girl love; I'm getting nowhere there)
> 5. Friends
> 6. Education
> 7. Talent
> 8. Family
> 9. God
> 10. A roof (and a nice one too) over my head

Jenny's daily record stayed remarkably coherent through the years. Though only a preteen, she knew what would stay important to her. Curiously, she did not include "Health" on this list, perhaps because she had found life could be worth living without it.

Art Is My Psychiatrist

IN 1979, AS JENNY turned thirteen, the physical constraints she'd always lived with became more isolating. Her classmates were going through puberty, but her body wasn't visibly maturing. Instead of gaining adolescent strength and overconfidence, she became weaker. She had headaches every day and came home from school in glum confusion.

That year, at her annual cardiology checkup in December, she expressed complaints for the first time. Ray Anderson had practiced and taught pediatric cardiology at the U of M since 1951; now he neared retirement. He knew the Waterston shunt, placed when she was four months old, had served far longer than expected.

In the years since Jenny's birth, many blue babies survived infancy only because of palliative procedures such as the Waterston. But problems arose later because normal anatomy was not established. Cardiac surgeons like Aldo Castaneda, now surgeon-in-chief at Boston Children's Hospital, worked to correct complex congenital heart defects earlier and earlier in life. Jenny was born in time for a gifted heart surgeon to keep her alive but too soon for that same surgeon to perform a more ideal operation.

Anderson, skilled at cardiac catheterization, carefully re-evaluated Jenny's heart. His findings suggested the wide opening between her ventricles might now be repaired, given the advances in open-heart surgery. Since Castaneda was no longer at the U of M, Anderson referred the Bonners to Gordon Danielson at the Mayo Clinic in Rochester, Minnesota.

Ninety miles apart, Mayo and the University of Minnesota competed and cooperated with each other. Many patients traveled far from home to reach one of these heart centers. The Bonners luckily lived between them, less than an hour's drive away from either one.

Danielson had successfully operated on patients with Jenny's rare congenital heart condition. He told the Bonners he felt 90 percent certain he could improve the delivery of blood to her lungs and the rest of her body. He would create a new conduit to replace the Waterston shunt. Then he'd try to divide her lower heart chamber into two ventricles so that oxygen-poor blood would no longer mix with oxygen-rich blood, diluting the oxygen content of blood pumped out to her body.

The surgery was high risk—there was no getting around it. But not replacing the shunt was increasingly risky as well. That Jenny might live a more normal life after this procedure elated Bob. Barbara worried, seeing the magnitude of both risks.

Now fairly routine, heart-lung bypass allowed surgeons to perform complicated surgery on a still and bloodless heart. Surgical teams safely oxygenated and also cooled blood outside a patient's body. The returning blood lowered body temperature, protecting the patient's heart and other organs during the operation. Because cooling reduced metabolism, vital organs required less oxygen to remain healthy during the procedure.

As Jenny got to know the heart team at Mayo, the first mention of health problems appeared in her diary. "Today I went to Rochester for a checkup. I'm going back tomorrow for another checkup. Wednesday I check into the hospital and Thursday I have my surgery." In the same entry she went on to say how cute a certain boy was when he washed his hair, and that she blew six dollars on pinball.

ON THE MORNING of Jenny's surgery, knowing the operation would last at least six hours, her parents wandered around the hospital and tried not to think too much about what was happening in the operating room. There, Dr. Danielson had entered Jenny's chest. After working his way through scar tissue from her previous operation, he evaluated her unusual cardiac anatomy and made preparations for the heart-lung bypass to begin. Then he stopped Jenny's heart with a chemical solution and started his repair.

Danielson placed a conduit that sent blood from the right side of Jenny's heart to the artery serving her lungs, bypassing the dead-end where a pulmonary valve would ordinarily have been. He was able to close the huge opening between her ventricles as well as the smaller opening between the upper chambers of her heart. Then he took down the Waterston shunt. It was time to warm Jenny and restart her heart.

Meanwhile, the Bonners returned to the surgery waiting room, where they listened to seemingly routine announcements that told one group after another that their family member was off heart-lung bypass and that they could meet with the surgeon. As the afternoon dragged on, Bob and Barbara turned to each other and wondered out loud how the announcement would differ if the operation hadn't gone as planned.

Soon they heard a voice overhead directing them to a room next to the hospital chapel. Danielson had completed his repair, but the surgical team couldn't get Jenny's heart to resume beating. They would keep trying. Barbara sat where she was and prayed; Bob entered the chapel to implore somebody or something to give Jenny the strength to live.

Forty-five minutes later, when they learned Jenny's heart was beating normally, the Bonners were overcome with relief, not knowing they were just beginning their most terrifying year as parents. Later on, that time haunted Jenny as well. She survived the operation, but many months would pass before she recovered.

One summer morning, back in Northfield, Jenny remained in her room with the door closed. When she finally appeared, she handed Barbara a shoebox. It contained a doll she had sewn from an old sheet and stuffing, wearing a hospital gown. A line of stitches traversed the doll's chest, and sprouting pipe cleaners represented chest tubes. Over its face was a mask representing a ventilator. The doll lay on a sheepskin (so it wouldn't get bedsores). There was also a TV set made from a small jewelry box. Jenny removed the mask and then the chest tubes. The doll, now wearing a terry-cloth robe and scuffs, was able to sit up and play solitaire. Jenny told Barbara, "Art is my psychiatrist."

JENNY DID NOT WRITE in her diary for months. Then, in November, she began to acknowledge her hospital experiences through cartoons, memories of a song frequently played in the intensive care unit, and blithe recaps of a series of hospital admissions.

Cartoons about a young teen in the hospital

My operation in April went just fine . . . In June I started feeling bad. What happened was that my valve was leaking so they rushed me to the hospital where I was diagnosed with a "torrential leak" . . . On July 17th I had another operation. Dr. Danielson replaced my bad valve with this thing that goes thump-click-thump-click and everyone can hear it if it's quiet.

Jenny's diary entries didn't reflect that she knew how close she had come to dying just a few months earlier. But the near miss was never far from her parents' minds as she prepared to go back to the OR in July. This time, Danielson was relaxed and smiling when he met them near the recovery room. He had placed a mechanical heart valve and restarted Jenny's heart relatively easily. Ten days later, she returned home.

But even with her new valve, Jenny suffered from symptoms of heart failure and, later, pneumonia. She coughed all fall and had trouble eating and sleeping. At night, she kept a bell by her bed to ring when she needed one of her parents to pound her chest to loosen mucus so she could breathe more easily.

In December, she gamely announced plans to publish a book of letters and cartoons. But on Christmas night, as Jenny fought for breath, the Bonners called an ambulance to take her to St. Mary's Hospital, ordinarily fifty-five minutes away in Rochester. Lights and a siren should have sped the trip, but the ambulance driver took a wrong turn, adding crucial minutes to the drive. When Jenny arrived in severe respiratory distress, an emergency room physician quickly placed a breathing tube down her throat.

On February 2, 1981, Jenny described her ordeal matter-of-factly. "I just got out of the hospital from pneumonia. I went in on Christmas night in an ambulance, went home with false wellness Jan. 1, stayed 4 days, went back, came home yesterday. Back on low sodium diet. Shit."

Soon after that, Jenny's cardiologist tried a new medication, a vasodilator that she could take temporarily to reduce her heart's workload. A vasodilator causes blood vessels to expand, leading to lower blood pressure within them. After languishing in ill health for more than a year, within days Jenny sat up and said, "I'm starving—bring me some food."

She was fourteen years old and weighed eighty-two pounds. She had an artificial heart valve that she and others could hear, and she would be on an anticoagulant for the rest of her life. (Because mechanical heart valves can cause blood clots, an anticoagulant was necessary to protect her from a heart attack or stroke.) But from then on, she made a steady recovery.

After enduring the bleakness of hospital food and a low-salt diet, she learned to cook with herbs and spices. She created her first full meal for her parents' anniversary in 1981. A pear flambé followed the rack of lamb main course. Then Jenny turned the torch on the Irish coffee. As Barbara remembers, "It seemed like everything was flaming. She was so tired afterwards, we had to carry her upstairs to her bedroom."

In the months before her April 1980 operation, Jenny had spent her free time resting on the couch—listening to music, or reading—barely able to lift her head for a visitor. Then, and during her long recovery, her friends didn't know how they could help or even how to spend time with her when she was so weak. She missed much of seventh and eighth grade, attending school intermittently, but somehow completed enough home-work to keep up with her classes. When she finally felt better, only a small group of friends waited for her to rejoin them. Per-haps that made it easier to start over socially, as she shed her sick-kid role and got ready for high school.

But in the recesses of her mind, Jenny couldn't quite leave the hospital behind. She wondered what triggered hospital memories: "maybe the light." She remembered a fragment from *Brideshead Revisited*: "just so, years later, it is a bit of gilding, or a certain smell, or the soft tick of a clock, that recalls one's mind . . ."

Whenever she heard the song "Shining Star," played so of-ten in the intensive care unit, it brought "feelings up out of my subconscious that I can't even name." As an adult, she described them as "the feel of wind on my face and hands as I covered my eyes and pretended I wasn't swinging past the yawning abyss of death." She had to grow up before she found the language to describe the fear she felt in childhood.

And what of Tim during this harrowing time for the family?

During four years at St. Joseph's, Tim had made steady progress with his living and learning skills. His parents and older sister continued to provide reassuring routines at home. After his progress plateaued, staff at St. Joseph's had recommended that Tim return to Northfield to begin middle school in the fall of 1980. When the rest of his family had no choice but to spend extended time in Rochester, Carleton faculty families and Northfield neighbors maintained the routines so crucial to him and stayed at the Bonner home when Bob or Barbara couldn't be there. And Tim found a way to help Jenny during her hospital stays. He knew which cassette tapes held the music she would want to hear, and he made sure his parents brought them to her.

IN ADDITION TO cardiac surgeons, others made progress during the 1970s that impacted Jenny's long-term prognosis. Early in the decade, a Swiss researcher collected soil samples while vacationing in Norway. He was hoping to isolate fungi that might produce a useful antibiotic. Instead he found a fungus that released a different kind of substance—one that prevented a body's immune system from rejecting that which was foreign to it. He discovered cyclosporine, which became a breakthrough antirejection drug. Twelve years passed before the FDA approved cyclosporine for human use, but early reports of its effectiveness reenergized the heart-transplant field.

Many drugs that are effective in humans come from fungi. In *The Man Who Touched His Own Heart*, Robb Dunn describes why fungi might release an antirejection drug. This particular fungus, *Cordyceps subsessilis*, procreates inside the body of beetles. After somehow influencing the occupied beetle to climb a tree, the fungus grows through the beetle's exterior. From an elevated position in a tree, the fungi spores become airborne and spread widely. All along, the fungus has been releasing the substance we know as cyclosporine so the beetle's immune system does not recognize and attack its invader.

Back at the University of Minnesota, surgeons had been successfully transplanting kidneys since 1963, and John Najarian, the new chief of surgery, was a transplant expert. But the U of M hadn't joined the race to set up an early heart-transplant program in the late '60s. The University was doing its own work on the rejection problem. And U of M cardiologists became leaders in heart-failure research, optimizing medical treatment and laying the groundwork for a heart transplant program.

The U of M was ready to perform its first heart transplant in 1978. The case went well in the operating room, but the patient developed postoperative complications and died a few months later. The second patient survived only eight days after surgery. Then, the U's third heart transplant became a landmark success. The heart recipient, a young woman with a hereditary disease of the heart muscle, surprised even the most optimistic members of her transplant team as she passed post-transplant milestones. She ultimately lived for another twenty-eight years, and the U of M firmly established its heart-transplant program among the world's best.

But even after the rejection problem was solved, or at least somewhat solved, everyone involved in heart transplants recognized the biggest problem—there would never be enough donor hearts for all the people who needed one.

DURING THE LONG hospital days at Mayo, Jenny often wished for a puppy. When she came home for good, the Bonners got a beagle puppy, not anticipating that his brains would follow his nose or that he would bark incessantly at anyone who walked by the house.

One day, Jenny took Chester, the puppy, on a seven-block walk to the veterinary clinic for a vaccination. Barbara says, "We didn't think about how Jenny had grown up with no chance to explore the town and no sense of direction. We just assumed she could do it. She didn't have the muscles, and she kept having to stop and sit down because of leg cramps. She got confused at an angled intersection. She and Chester did eventually get there, although we had to drive to the clinic and bring them home."

New aerobic capacity couldn't bestow coordination, strength, or endurance. How surprised Jenny's skeletal muscles must have been when, after fourteen years of quiet coexistence with the rest of her, she asked them to do new things. She had far less muscle mass than her peers and not much muscle memory, and she had spent most of a year convalescing. Lacking physical stamina, she always depended on others to transport her and was unconcerned with whether a right or left turn brought her to a destination. Jenny knew her town, and yet she didn't. Now she had to learn physical independence as a teenager.

The Bonners set up a mini gym for her, with leg weights and two-pound dumbbells. She and Bob walked together, gradually increasing their distance. When she developed shin splints, Bob helped her through them, relying on his experience as a distance runner.

At school later that year, she fell in gym class and knocked out a front tooth, once perfectly aligned from years of braces. Her mouth bled heavily, in part because of the anticoagulant she took. Both Bonner parents were out of town—Bob was coaching the Carleton tennis team and Barbara was at Special Olympics with Tim—so a neighbor rushed Jenny to the dentist. Jenny had looked forward to participating in gym, but she had no way to gauge what she could do. Bob says, "Jenny didn't know how to fall. No other child her age would have knocked out a tooth that way."

Jenny grew up feeling like a study of one, unique in her community. When her heart could power her body well enough to try new things, she had no precedents to follow. She knew that she and her brother had experienced childhoods that were far from the norm.

Most children can run soon after walking and bounce up quickly after a fall. With long experience of sometimes rough play, they don't care if somebody jumps on them. They develop balance by climbing trees, hopping on one foot, or sliding across the ice on snowboots. They learn to ride a bicycle around the age of six. Helped by an excited parent or willing older sibling, they ride close to the ground and go solo after a handful of lessons.

Jenny and Barbara thought a bicycle would be a good way for her to get around town, and they worked on it together. Jenny wrote, "I am riding my bike better now. I am less scared every time I ride." But she couldn't master it. Perched high off the ground on a full-sized bike, she felt vulnerable and lacked the strength and confidence to go fast enough to balance a moving two-wheeler.

She briefly tried to learn Bob's favorite sport. "The bad part of the day started when Dad was trying to teach me how to play tennis. I did not do well and he was not very pleased. I know it was because I'm not good at that sort of thing but I partially blamed it on him; his face was anything but encouraging."

Bob doesn't remember the tennis lesson, but freely admits he didn't understand her situation. "I should have been more sensitive. I should have understood she couldn't suddenly do all these things."

As JENNY'S HEALTH improved in 1981, the Bonners looked forward to time away from the tedium and terror of the hospital. For Barbara, two breast cancer operations bookended Jenny's year in and out of Mayo. Then Bob became sick. After his brief hospital stay, Jenny wrote, "Dad came home from the hospital today. He has diverticulosis so now he has medicine too. Blue Cross is sending out hit men for our family."

What more could go wrong? Quite a lot, it turned out, mostly for Tim. In addition to his other problems, he'd had seizures since age ten, only partially controlled by medication. Jenny often looked out for him from a nearby vantage point. Barbara could be working in the garden and Jenny would yell out the window, "Mom, Tim's having a seizure."

Bob and Barbara had never been happy with Tim's medical care, starting with the consultants who suggested institutionalizing him when he was a baby. The Bonners thought medical professionals weren't meticulous with him, as if they didn't see his life having much value.

In late 1982, Barbara brought Tim to a new Northfield surgeon to have an ingrown toenail treated. He found that Tim's blood pressure was dangerously high and that an unrecognized infection had destroyed one of Tim's kidneys. It is hard to imagine the pain Tim must have been unable to express as his kidney became necrotic.

A doctor at Mayo, uncertain about working with Tim,

offhandedly told the Bonners he might live another fifteen years with one kidney, given his other urinary tract problems that were just being diagnosed. At Children's Hospital in Minneapolis, they consulted Ron Glasser, who arranged surgery to remove the dead kidney. But nothing was ever medically straightforward for Tim. His preoperative evaluation revealed significant scoliosis that had somehow not been detected earlier. He would need a spinal fusion soon after his nephrectomy.

Tim's kidney was removed at Children's Hospital in the spring of 1983, and that fall, he underwent spinal fusion at Gillette Children's Hospital in St. Paul. There a resident physician failed to prescribe Tim's seizure medication. Soon after awakening from anesthesia, Tim had a grand mal seizure. He returned to the operating room, where his surgeon reset a steel rod that had been dislodged during the seizure. As a precaution, he also extended Tim's cast to immobilize his neck as well as his torso.

Fifteen-year-old Tim, still wearing diapers, spent five months in a body cast, not fully understanding why. Among other inconveniences, the cast kept his head level so he couldn't look down to see where he was walking. For someone who hated change in his routines, wearing the cast must have seemed like an endless trial.

Jenny empathized with Tim and wrote a jubilant diary entry when his cast was removed. "Tim got his cast off!!! A month early too. Wow. Our house is in celebration. I got the first real hug from him in a long time." A few years later she noted, "Tim makes your heart feel so peaceful when he hugs you."

Jenny entered high school underweight and prepubescent but with a well-developed intellect. Any of her three heart operations, near-fatal pneumonia, or years growing up with cyanotic heart disease could have left her with cognitive deficits. Instead, she was a top student.

After being an invalid for so long, Jenny took pleasure in her intellectual abilities. "I got my PSAT scores back today, overall in the 99th %tile. Mom and Dad were proud of me. This time it was funny: Dad was freaking out (well, dads don't freak out, but you know) and Mom wasn't surprised."

Jenny also distinguished herself in art, theater, and speech competitions. And, as she continued to express her thoughts in her diary, she was learning to be a writer. She had a lot to draw upon in her creative pursuits. A psychological assessment at fifteen described Jenny's "extremely rich Rorschach," showing her to be "psychologically healthy, unusually resourceful and possibly precociously mature."

After years of semi-isolation, she had to find ways to jump into the high school scene. About one social circle she wrote, "Somehow I feel out of place in that group. I feel welcome and everything—it's just like there's something under the surface. Like I act too strangely or something. But when I feel that way I want to act strangely."

Jenny found it hard to let new acquaintances—or even her handful of loyal friends, together since grade school—know what she had been through. "It's not that I have so much to say. I've kept it in so long."

Noticeably thin, she wasn't developed enough to be considered fashionably slender. Some of her female contemporaries had completed puberty years earlier. She finally got her menstrual period when she was almost sixteen and quickly realized facial eruptions came along with it. Still, she was glad.

Jenny finally found a way to exercise after so many inactive years. "I'm taking ballet with Toni Sostek. Finally, maybe I'll be able to use my body." A family friend and professional dancer, Toni first worked with Jenny in the Bonner kitchen to establish the basic conditioning that ballet classes would require. With a counter edge serving as a ballet barre, Toni casually delivered the patient, pressure-free, enjoyable instruction that Jenny needed.

Ballet classes provided physical training and became a source of pride. "Great ballet class today. It's so much fun when I start getting it and my body starts responding." She wrote later, "Mom said Toni says I dance really well, and Toni doesn't just say things like that."

Still, she needed to listen to her body more intently than her classmates did. "I scared myself to death in ballet today. It's the first time I've danced in two weeks, so naturally it was hard. The grande battements were especially tiring and toward the end, I felt my heart muscle sort of pull. I stopped right then and went and sat down. I didn't dare dance the rest of the day."

In high school, she wished she could forget about all the things that made her different. "Sometimes, as I get more and more integrated into a 'normal' lifestyle, it hits me how much more I have to worry about than most people. I just get sick of being so imperfect. Nobody's perfect, but most people have a better shot at it than I do. I have a bright pink scar right down my chest, a false tooth, and all these stupid little pills and a medical alert bracelet I can never take off and hundreds of little scars all over my body. I know I have a wonderful life, but once in a while it just gets to me."

Consider How Far We've Come

JENNY HAD LONG been entranced by options for romance. Most days in her self-examined life, she noted, at least in passing, her current possibilities for love. From middle school on, she practiced the art of The Crush. Over the years, she became an expert. And Jen was practical, developing her first crush on her neighbor Scott, whom she saw often. She could feel the magic on a regular basis.

It seemed more longing poured out than came her way. She was too unusual to be one of the popular kids, but she liked them anyway and considered any high school boy to be fair game as a crush object. She studied chemistry with a less-academically-gifted boy and looked for a signal, any signal, that he liked her back. She waited for a date or even a phone call but settled for smiles and shared homework.

During this time, she communed with another girl about imaginary, romantic beings—"The Others." Each girl channeled an eternal couple, male and female souls who remained together through many previous lives. The males could inhabit a local boy and reveal what he was thinking. The female eternal beings resided in Jenny and Tricia. This conceit gave Jenny more than one someone to think about and occupied her diary for more than a year. And why not? She was lovelorn in the real world.

"The Others" wrote letters to her and occasionally argued with each other, always reassuring Jenny her crush was reciprocated. This sustained fantasy made sense for a handicapped girl, who must have been comforted by the idea she could persist in a series of human bodies, given the challenges of the body she was currently using.

At some point in Jenny's high school years, Barbara posted a newspaper column on the refrigerator about ridding one's life of stress. She was amused by Jenny's artful response: a cartoon showing their family as four caterpillars crossing the highway with semitrucks bearing down on them.

Most of the time, Jenny was happy in high school, thinking she had progressed a long way in a short time. "Last night of sweet 16. Before I start getting bummed about never being kissed, let's consider how far we've come. Last year I knew of no guys liking me. Now I'm talking to boys without even thinking about it. A guy asked me for my picture. I am actually beginning to fill my bra (AA, oh well, one can't have everything). I am dancing. I have legs. I can drive. I can walk respectable distances. I got higher scores on my PSAT than some other Carleton faculty kids. I have one or two guys possibly liking me. I've learned how to paint. Wow. Not bad. If I can achieve this in one year, just wait 'til I'm 18."

Despite her childhood frailty, Jenny was remarkably self-confident. She liked who she was and was surprised to find her peers didn't all feel the same way. Her parents had a lot to do with this, but some of her assurance came from Tim's reliance on her, undiminished from their preschool days. She was always the sun to at least one person.

A driver's license gave Jenny an expanded sense of freedom. Behind the wheel of a 1980 Volkswagen Dasher, she was an equal of others her age. Though this was the family car, Jenny embraced it as her own. She and Tim, riding shotgun, became a common sight around town as they drove, listening to his favorite music. Barbara says, "The car was a wonderful carapace for them."

New friends in high school came mainly from Jenny's extracurricular activities, particularly the forensics team that traveled together to speech competitions. Jenny specialized in humorous speeches, including one about her medical trials, and she relished the pressure of competition. After being so ill, she was relaxed and confident competing in something that was not a matter of life and death.

During her junior year, a young, charismatic forensics coach arrived and quickly came to appreciate the quirky energy Jenny brought to the team. For the year-end Forensics Follies, Jenny wrote an extended parody based on "The Raven"—and still, more than two decades later, a member of her team could readily produce a copy.

Jenny relied on her writing ability because she couldn't easily engage in casual games others took for granted. At a forensics picnic, she played ultimate frisbee, but quickly wore out. "The trouble is nobody understands why I get tired. They think I'm normal."

Frisbee was better than the volleyball game at another forensics party. "I was all psyched to play frisbee but everyone ended up playing volleyball which I am dreadful at, so I started feeling a little worthless." Ever resourceful, Jenny began carrying a frisbee around so she wouldn't be subjected to volleyball again.

Jenny loved acting in theater productions too, even though she got the part of Mrs. Higgins instead of Eliza in *My Fair Lady*. While she enjoyed the cast parties, she wasn't as close to the theater crowd as she was to the forensics team, especially after "an audition with a guy who looked at me like I was a sewer vole."

Jenny in high school

Jenny went on to win a National Merit Scholarship—so she could have her pick of almost any college or university when the time came to choose. As she thought about one day leaving home, Jenny realized she grew up with an unusually close relationship with her parents.

Bob and Barbara transported her in their arms for many years, and Jenny continued to rely heavily on them as a young adolescent, even to travel a block or two away from home. The family spent countless hours together as Jenny explored her own tastes in books, art, music, and cooking. "It will be nice to leave home and not depend on their opinions so much."

Before her senior year in high school, Jenny attended the Carleton summer writing program. She saw that she would flourish not just in a college but also in the intense residential student life of the academically challenging Carleton College. Most of her friends in the program hoped to attend Carleton. Jenny realized Carleton was her first choice too—and a sensible one, as it was close to the two medical centers that kept her alive.

During the writing program Jenny met Alex—the boy who became her first boyfriend. At first, Jenny was unsure how she felt about him. "I don't know. I don't want to scare him off. If he wants to get a crush on me, it'd be just great though."

After the program ended, they began a tentative long-distance romance during their senior year of high school. Alex lived in Duluth, Minnesota, a three-hour drive from Northfield. When Alex visited and she faced a boyfriend in the flesh, Jenny was uncertain. "I'm trying to decide if I'm ready to kiss him. I don't want to go too fast and lose everything. I'd rather have him as a friend for life than a flash-in-the-pan romance. I don't know much about relationships, but I do know that romance can definitely change them. Real love is so different than just imagining. In my head, I'm making out all over the place with a guy and I'm bored. With Alex, all we did was hug and I was scared to death."

The first kiss finally arrived when she was eighteen. She analyzed it. "Kissing's strange. It's not at all like my pillow (surprise, surprise, but that's all I had to go by). Lips are soft and they taste a lot different than muslin, and I could feel his teeth a little bit."

After graduating from high school, Jenny dropped her childhood name and became Jen. That summer, she worked for the Carleton food service. Though she missed Alex, her diary made increasing mention of a guy named J.B., a coworker soon to be a Carleton sophomore. Once classes started, with Alex not too far away at Macalester College in St. Paul, Jen and J.B. started seeing each other. In November she officially broke up with Alex.

Jen's relationship with J.B. was complicated and intense from the beginning. She resisted giving him control over the relationship. Not wanting to be rushed into sex, she sought her mother's advice. "I do want to talk to Mom. She was very emphatic about me not taking sex lightly, and I'm not. But I'd like to discuss it with her, because I worry I'm not seeing all the angles."

Jen and Barbara had this discussion over the long Thanksgiving weekend. "After talking to Mom all weekend about sex, I think I'm going to wait on it. J.B. and I are pretty young to risk pregnancy. And we have a lot of stuff to keep us occupied. I hope he's not too disappointed."

Only a resilient mother-daughter duo could have spent a holiday weekend in this way. (She makes no note of her father's activities that weekend.) Jen and Barbara met as equals when they appreciated art, and much of Jen's self-confidence came from the woman who had always encouraged and respected her opinions. In her diary, Jen often considered the pros and cons of a possible course of action, and she readily engaged in this process with her mother.

The next spring, her cardiologist said she could safely take birth control pills. "Here I am, going on another pill. It all feels very tenuous and risky. I wonder if it's worth it."

Jen loved J.B. but worried about getting pregnant and didn't know if her heart could sustain a healthy pregnancy. She kept thinking it through. "What would we do? I suppose ideally I would carry the baby to full term and give it up for adoption. But what if I got sick, or the baby wasn't 'perfect' (good adoption material)?"

Jen always asked good questions.

Her relationship with J.B. didn't keep her from having crushes. A crush on a dorm floormate named Pat stayed kindled for much of sophomore year. At the start of the next academic year, she noted,

Only one strange thing in my life now. A Prof Crush. I told Fred[6] that I worshipped him today. I do—for his ink wiping abilities—and I explained this. I have no idea what he thought though. This is so much better than my last crush. Fred is: a tall skinny artist with 1) a wife, 2) bad posture, 3) receding/receded hairline, 4) bad teeth, and 5) no body, who is at least 10 years older than I. I drank wine with [some friends] the other night and discovered that all the women in the Art Dept. have crushes on Fred. I thought I was unique! Sob! Oh well. Pointless crushes are good though. Because it could never work, you can't get too depressed, but you still have someone to think about.

JEN AND HER parents hadn't especially noted Stuart Jamieson's arrival at the University of Minnesota in 1986. Coming from Norman Shumway's department at Stanford, Jamieson was one of the few surgeons in the world who had performed a heart-lung

6 Fred Hagstrom, an art professor

transplant. His recruitment was a coup for John Najarian, who wanted to return the U of M to the forefront of cardiothoracic surgery, where it had been in the 1950s. For Jamieson, it was a chance to build his own program and to run the new Minnesota Heart and Lung Institute. Jamieson also said that Minnesota's central location in the US offered excellent access to donor organs, which had to arrive within six hours.

Whenever Jamieson performed a transplant, it made the news, including glowing follow-up stories on the patients' progress. Over the next year plus, he performed seven heart-lung transplants and two lung transplants, along with many other heart operations. All of Jamieson's transplant patients did well after surgery.

As FALL TERM drew to a close in 1987, Jen was a junior, about to turn twenty-one. An art major, she rued the imminent dispersal of her close friends within the department. "I can't believe it's the end of term already. We're all sad because of people leaving next term, or not taking any more Art, or being in different classes. It really is the end. On Friday we went to *Maurice* in Edina and stayed out at Perkins 'til 4:00 in the morning. The last stand of the Little Double Date that couldn't. We've all become such good friends that we'd agree it's fun enough without sex."

Jen and J.B. were breaking up too. She wrote that he wanted her "to be a different person; a Jen he's created that's impressive like a talking dog, that's small enough to fit inside him." After two tumultuous years, they finally pulled themselves apart. By mid-December, Jen was on her own.

With finals and the breakup behind her, Jen began the short walk from her family home to her job on campus. Although moving at her usual slow pace, she felt uneasy; uneasiness turned into terrifying shortness of breath. Chest heaving, she crumpled at her destination and called home for help. So much had been going on, she almost forgot about her heart.

Like traffic noise a city dweller can ignore, Jen's heart problems were a background annoyance she learned to tune out. But now her heart had set off an alarm she couldn't deny. The night of her collapse she wrote, "I'm a cauldron of feelings and most of the stuff's been in there so long it's no longer recognizable. I have a wall inside me that hurts. It's terrifying to feel your physical heart flutter under a heartache. Here I sit, I can't even cry."

A day later, arriving with his nearly grown child at the Mayo cardiology clinic, Bob decided to show respect for her autonomy. Knowing Barbara would have stayed at Jen's side, he remained in the waiting room after her name was called. Seated once again in a not-quite comfortable institutional chair, he willed time— but not too much time—to pass.

A historian more intimate with cardiology than he cared to be, Bob could describe all the defects built into Jen's heart, the operations she'd endured, and the limitations she'd overcome. Though he knew her present state was serious, he was unprepared for her tears when he was called to join her. He was furious when he realized the attending physician, who was not Jen's usual cardiologist, had delegated a resident to give her the bad news.

PART TWO

The Transplant Bomb

12/16/87

The bomb dropped today and broke my wall to pieces. My ejection fraction, the amount of blood my heart pumps out each beat, is down to half my normal half of normal. They have begun to consider my equipment not serviceable. My world fell in today. My normal life, my hopes of old age, not gone, but forced through a sieve. My perceptions, once again forced to change, make allowances. Surmount odds. Beat risks. My heart is stone, rolling over challenges, crushing them, my feelings safely hid inside . . .

Transplant. They told me I should start the machinery. "Best to start while you're stable." I don't need it yet—but I will. Here I've been bouncing along letting myself think I was almost normal. Considering my drugs a chore, not a key that unlocks a prison. "Not even allowed that luxury!" I scream. But who is normal? And are they any happier? Who cares whether your curse is heart disease or alcoholism or bad parents or the inability to care? Who cares whether you die at 120 or 22?

This is my deal. I've seen enough to know I'm lucky. So I play it for all it's worth. I'll have fun along the way—I already have. Mozart could've written more, but he could've written less.

It's still hard to shake the anxiety. I feel vaguely like throwing up—and it's not the pills. I've walked in a nightmare today. But this is my life. I've accepted myself. Fuck my heart—how many "normal" people can say, truly, that they like themselves? Still, it'd be nice to live long enough to also become the greatest artist in the world.

12/21/87

Life's flattened out again. Tomorrow I go to the doctor's at the University of Minnesota. Next Monday may be my last appt. at Mayo. The end of an era. I'm back where I started now—at the 2nd best transplant center in the world. Stanford's done more, they said, but they're not so much better that it'd be worth moving out there. I've accepted that Transplant is a viable future option. I'm even accepting the fact that I've been scheduled for another heart catheterization in the near future.

I had my 2nd appt with Susan Schultz, my therapist today. She's really nice. I feel good after I talk to her. I still wish she'd give me The Answers, but I'm beginning to accept she won't. Therapy is good. I'm glad to be in it again.

12/23/87

Tomorrow I turn 21. I just had the best birthday dinner of lamb and chocolate chip pound cake with Gretchen.[7] It was great to have Gretchen down—I really love talking to her. She makes me feel sane. She brought me fudge and good paper.[8]

My body knows when my heart's failing. And it gets scared.

I just hate it. My life's surreal. I had so much fun tonight, and in the bath, I felt like I was waking up. I felt like I'd managed to distract myself for a few hours. I miss my normal life. I'm going to have to live at home next term. But with my new heart, I'll be able to be so much more normal—I'll be able to climb hills. And play basketball!

12/28/87

Tomorrow I go into the hospital for tests. Today I moved out of the dorm. I think I'm completely miserable about this, but it takes too much energy to break down, so I

---

7 A fellow art major at Carleton who was home in the Twin Cities of Minneapolis/St. Paul for the holiday break

8 For painting

just keep going. Who was it that wrote about being a juggernaut, rolling over everything in her path? That's what I am now. I'm fully assembled. It's been interesting to watch the change. I'm a bitch to talk to—tongue as sharp as a razor and humor too. Not so much a bitch as a smart-ass. I learned early that if you could make people laugh you don't have to deal with things seriously.

Someone's set up a "prayer circle" for me. After all my religious thinking I don't know if it does anything for me, but I know people care and that's what matters.

I can still almost see my old self before this started, and feel a twinge of sadness. But the shield comes up quickly: What is life anyway?

12/30/87

Hospital time. The U is very different from St. Mary's Hospital in Rochester. Almost all the changes are positive—the people are much warmer. I have done the impossible: I have met cute guys. My doctor (Edwards) is cute. The guy who wheeled me down for my EKG, Dirk, is funny. Not cute, but real nice. He came by to say good night last night and visited me today.

The really cute one is Daniel. He took me to my CAT scan[9] tonight. He has blonde curly hair and brown eyes and is slightly balding. He came to say good night, but

---

9 Computerized axial tomography, now more commonly called a CT scan

he's not working tomorrow. Aw.

Haven't had time to write or paint or anything. I did one watercolor last night. This is the first I've written of anything. Gretchen's come by twice and has kept me company.

I'm sitting in my bed, looking out at Minneapolis. Beautiful view at night, sparks of light in the rose-black sky. The walls are beige—restful, but offset by wood and curtains—so not annoyingly beige. The room is peaceful—most of the hall noise must be shut out by the door. Not that I could forget where I am. When in doubt, look at the tags on my wrist and feel the unmistakable hardness of a mechanical bed beneath me. Even the window's glassed in venetian blinds and the industrial (though stylishly patterned) curtains keep my location firmly in mind.

In six hours, I will have my fourth heart catheterization.[10] I'm sleepy—I'm not sure if the cath is keeping me awake. But when I think cath, I think pain and so to justify the pain, I think of why I need the cath. Then I can't sleep. My heart feels like it's beating underwater. I've been without food or drink for two hours and I'm starving.

Maybe I'm not scared any more. I'll write until I'm too

---

10 The procedure could diagnose and treat certain heart conditions. In Jen's case, the heart catheterization would show details about her current heart and lung function.

tired to be scared. Every time I hear my heart do that, I start worrying that I won't last 'til I get my new heart. I've accepted the idea of the new heart.

I think.

But it still depresses the hell out of me. I'll be able to do more with a new heart. But I thought I was doing fine with the old one.

I can't believe I'm facing surgery again. Like a WWI veteran being drafted for WWII. Or maybe they weren't required? Maybe they only volunteered to go in again. I sure as hell didn't. As we drove up here, I thought, "This is the same route we'll take for surgery," and wondered what it will feel like . . . I'll be awake—dressed—conscious—in the car—in the emergency room—talking to people—communicating with doctors. Consciously going into surgery. You go into the hospital because it's a good idea and then they haul you out of bed before you know what's happening. But this—delivering oneself up to the knife. It's almost too much to ask. Oh—even the first surgery (that I remember), when they didn't take me until 11:00 a.m.—Dad and I played foosball at the hospital that morning while we were waiting.

It was unreal. I wasn't awake. The sunlight was streaming in the window and the room was filled with orange and yellow dust motes floating around us when they came for me. How else could I not have noticed Dad's tension? How else could I not have guessed the reason why I beat him twice at foosball? I wasn't conscious. It wasn't real. Here, you are in a real situation and are expected to drop it as soon as the beeper from the transplant office goes off. [11] They should give us Valium to take as soon as it goes off, so we'll be sufficiently doped out when we get to the hospital.

---

11 The heart transplant team issued beepers to patients on the transplant list so they could be reached if they weren't at home when a heart became available. In 1988, few people outside the medical profession carried beepers.

Fear and Seriousness

1/1/88

I'm home now. The cath was hell, absolute hell. But the news was good—the pressures were low enough.[12] I don't have my beeper yet, but I think any other problem they might find is surmountable. This was the big test and I passed it.

I just finished a six-page letter to J.B. about our relationship. I'm pretty sure he'll read it, but I'm not too sure how he'll react. I was honest, but I may have dwelt too much on his faults for his taste. Oh well, he can burn it for all I care—it's done me a world of good to have written it.

For the first time this whole notebook, I'm stress-free! No worry about my heartbeat and no trauma with J.B. And no school. Sigh.

---

12 If Jen had high pressures in her lungs, she would not be a heart transplant candidate.

1/4/88

J.B. called again tonight. He just got the letter and wanted to make me feel bad. I didn't. It was fortunate that he called then, however, because otherwise I would have assumed the roses I had just gotten were from him. But he assured me he wouldn't waste the time and money, so I was relieved. I was mad afterwards that I wasn't more cutting, but I think the reserved, ironic style is more mature.

So back to the roses: three red roses were here when I got back from the clinic with a card that read, "Anyone needs flowers in the hospital. I love you." No signature. Who the hell??? I have a lot of girlfriends who love me, but roses? Gretchen might, but is she the type to say, "I love you"? Does she love me? I pray it's not Riccardo.[13] He's just sweet enough to do it, but sweet though he is, I don't love him. Alex has a girlfriend (whew). Maybe it's Edwin. I could handle that. "Love" seems a little strong. I know—it's Steve Martin! Maybe it's Dr. Edwards. Dirk? Daniel? Oh hell. Well it's not J.B. Maybe I'll find out tomorrow.

Saw Dr. Braunlin[14] today. She was jubilant about the cath. Everyone up there is so nice. I feel like I'm visiting old friends and I've only been with the program two weeks. If I do get rich, I should leave them all my money—except I'll still be paying for what I'm getting from

---

13 Another art major
14 Elizabeth Braunlin, Jen's pediatric cardiologist at the U

them now. Four years of Carleton isn't half what this costs. Okay, maybe it is—but not much more.

Met Dr. Jamieson today. Woo! He's hot. Of course, I'm sure he's married. Two things the doctors all have in common at the U: 1) they're cute, and 2) they're married. I haven't fallen for a single guy in months!

1/5/88

I've started reading again and it's saving me. I'm reading about a man who survived Auschwitz and his message[15] is helping me overcome the fear that keeps suffocating me whenever I slip or push myself too much.

I went to Boliou[16] today. I thoroughly wore myself out. I talked to Fred. He was so sweet (of course). I'm going to have an independent study with him. He's going to help with printmaking, so I don't get tired. He's so careful— it's like having a second Daddy.

Yes, it does worry me that I have such a crush on a paternal figure.

A long day. The terror begins again. I am so weak, I can barely speak. How I can write, I don't know. It starts with a stomachache; a vague, hungry feeling. Then my heartbeats grow louder, and under my many sweaters, I

---

15 Likely referring to Viktor Frankl's *Man's Search for Meaning*
16 Art and art history hall

feel the ventricle shudder with its bloated function. The anxiety centers there, on my sternum, spreading out to enclose my heart and lungs within its narrow fingers. I would sleep, but my mind is not tired. My body may be exhausted, but my eyes will remain open and my mind alive, connected to some tiny electrical wire, running through my shoulders and down my breastbone. I suppose I shall remain like this for most of my wait.

My mind is a prisoner, praying for the energy to hold a pen or a drypoint,[17] or speak with a friend, or even go somewhere in the car. Right now, the journey to the bathroom is on the edge of my abilities.

The fingers stir my stomach and squeeze my heart. I know their touch now, and can almost convince myself I'm not in danger, that all this rest is helping, making me stronger. But still, my throat constricts as well, and a deep breath to relax is almost pointless—the fingers have pulled my diaphragm tight as a drum. A breath cannot loosen it.

I want to cry from the fear. I want to get up and do something to prove I'm alive. But I must lie here, a prisoner of fear I have already over-tired myself today. I have no margin. I also have no idea of what lies beyond this margin. Would I simply drop dead? Would it merely hasten the process? If so, have I already hastened the process?

17 A sharp tool used in a printmaking process

1/7/88

Gretchen is the most wonderful person in the entire world. She is the nicest, sanest, most mature person I have ever met. She came by again today, just to say hi and talk. It's euphoric almost in the sense of a love affair to have someone you like, respect, and enjoy come by, not because they need you, but just because they like your company. I still get nervous, because I'm used to friends who need me, that I'll lose her, because I don't have a hold on her in that way. The wonderful thing is learning that the hold we have on each other is much stronger than any hold of need. Now if I can only meet a guy like that . . .

I went to my first support group today. Aside from the ex-University coach who wouldn't shut up and kept talking about how cute his nurses were, I met some very nice people. Some people were very sick. I have a long way to go before I start worrying. I met the dynamite woman who my parents met last week, whose heart has stopped two times, and a sweet little man from Hawaii who's in the hospital with breathing problems. Afterwards, a really nice, rough-faced man ran over to me and asked how old I was. He was there with his fifteen-year-old daughter from Rapid City, for her one-year check up. I didn't like what I saw of her, but he looked like he had weathered a lot and looked wonderful.

1/8/88

I encountered one of the worst reactions to my situation. A faculty wife came bounding out of the paint studio and gushed all over me while I was trying to talk to my friends. I've managed to become a local celebrity, one of the pilgrimages good people take to pay pity. Bleah!

It was especially hard, because what I crave now is seriousness. Seriousness and honesty. I do have friends who are capable of this, but not many. I haven't talked to any of them today. Fred is serious, but I don't "talk" to him. He's more of a Prof than a friend. Still, I value his seriousness more highly than anything. He understands my situation and is being very helpful, but he doesn't give an inch on his standards. That's a relief, in the midst of everyone else lowering requirements left and right. I still wish I could talk to him, though.

I find it hard to deal with people now. I don't want to dwell on what I'm going through, but I never forget about it either. And no one knows what to say. Small talk (the necessary but mostly evil glue of society) is just plain insupportable.

I just went to *Buckaroo Banzai*. What a fun movie! My energy level's way up now, but I came home anyway, because that's the wise thing to do.

Before that, I went to Boliou because I needed to get out of the house and talk to somebody serious. I was in luck.

Andy was there, painting with no shirt on. Ooh baby. He hadn't heard anything about me, so I sat down and told him. That set the tone for our conversation and we talked about all things serious for about an hour. His sister is retarded and his dad has crippled hands.

He was good to talk to, even if he is a little too grounded in the Art Speak Pronounce-Any-Half-Baked-Idea-As-Law style. He's intelligent enough to get out of that once in a while. And he has a sexy back.

1/10/88

The fear came back. Last night I had a bad dream about darkness and being scared. Today I felt chest pain and had to come home from Boliou. I've been reading about the survivors of concentration camps and there's one thing I feel in common with them, however slight it may be, and that is the choice of whether to fight to live or give up and die. I could give up and still live—the odds aren't as against me as theirs. But I'd have much less of a chance. And I also might go mad. When horrible things happen, you can either lose your soul or grow. I could interpret this as yet one more sign that I'm just not meant to be on this earth! Obviously I haven't, but that is not an automatic decision. You continue to be besieged by whatever is your enemy. In my case, terror. My physical condition, its waxing and waning affects this, but my main enemy, especially when I turn out the light, knowing full well that I am not that sick, and certainly expected to last the night, is the constant, living fear that I will, in fact, die. So big is this fear that this is the first time I've even written out its object. It's not rational—when is fear rational? So it's hard to combat. I'm glad I'm finally processing this through my subconscious; it makes me much less anxious to go to sleep.

1/11/88

I feel the aftermath of terror today. I know I can do things: paint, drive a car, go to Boliou, write. But it never leaves, this seriousness. I don't know if it's depression. Good music can still make me happy. I certainly don't feel helpless. But I feel bleak. The sky is gray, and the dark dead branches against it match my mood exactly. I wonder if spring will cheer me up or make me feel out of place.

I don't want to be depressed. Oh—I'm quite able to be cheerful for people. But this starkness is always there. I guess it's the situation. I'm in decline. I will die unless I get a transplant. And I never know when that will be. And that in itself is a hard thing. It's a bleak situation. And a bleak process. But I don't want to go around with this tortured look on my face. That invites evil things like pity. Oh God, who invented pity? Who, in their right and self-respecting mind, wants to be pitied? I just want to be loved, respected, and left the hell alone.

1/12/88

Not a month ago, I lost my shit because they said I might have to have a transplant. Now I'm just about ready to go insane. They said I might not need one. Braunlin says the measurements from the cath are good. So good, in fact, that I have to have a stress test on Thursday to measure my stamina—at rest I am, while certainly not normal, quite a bit healthier than most transplant candidates. Hey— maybe it's a miracle—maybe I'm getting better. I asked Braunlin if I could improve. She said, "I won't say 'never.'" I take that to mean "Yes, but it's highly unlikely." So what, I wait to get sick enough to wait for a heart? Yippee Skip! Waiting for a heart was nerve-wracking enough. Waiting to get sick . . . ?! I just pray that, should they give me the "good news," that they'll give me something more con- crete than "You're moderate; continue what you're doing and call us when you can't breathe." AAAAAAAUGH!

If I could go back to school, that'd be fine.[18] But unless I've got a really bad case of the Psychosomatics, I don't think it's possible. So, I'm on hold from regular life and now I might be on hold from the transplant program. I will be on hold from reality soon, if life doesn't straight- en out just a LITTLE bit. I can fight anything. I'm a great fighter. But in limbo, there's nothing to fucking fight.

BY THE TIME Jen was referred back to the U of M, the heart-trans- plant program was well established. It was not a given that the program would accept her. The year before, only half of the 141

---

18 Jen was auditing classes, not taking them for credit.

people referred to the U of M actually went on its heart transplant list. Some had other treatment options or refused transplantation. Others had too many other health problems. A small number had hearts that were too healthy for replacement. The rest chose another program, had grossly inadequate insurance, or died before the evaluation could be completed.

Over several days, the transplant team gathered information on Jen's heart function and how healthy the rest of her was. Her results were somewhat better than expected and were a reason for her cardiologist to celebrate briefly. But overall, Jen was physically impaired enough to need the transplant, likely to die fairly soon[19] without it, and able to comply with a post-transplant regimen. She went on the waiting list.

While there was short-lived uncertainty about whether the transplant program would accept Jen, the Bonners never questioned the need for it. It was clear to them that Jen was sick and getting sicker. Since they lived nearby, the U of M made geographic sense, and the hospital staff had served them well in the past. Today, prospective transplant families would probably be online, verifying for themselves that a heart transplant was the only option, comparing results of medical centers, and reading about other patients' transplant experiences. In the 1980s, less information was available and families acquired it from their own transplant program.

When Jen joined the program, the U of M had recently opened a new hospital overlooking the Mississippi River. Most of the patient care moved to the new hospital, with only the pathology department, Labor and Delivery, and some administrative offices temporarily left behind.

---

19 To join the transplant program, candidates had to have less than a 50 percent chance of surviving the next year.

In the old hospital, several buildings were connected over time, resulting in floor numbers that didn't match, and a maze of discontinuous halls and stairways that visitors and staff had to learn. Barbara remembers viewing a video about heart transplants in a "ramshackle, cordoned-off space" in the old hospital—not the most reassuring setting for learning about a high-tech procedure.

The family attended heart transplant support group meetings run by a social worker. The support group brought people who were waiting for a transplant together with those who already had a new heart. The Bonners looked for encouragement and information at these gatherings, but there were so many unknowns and different experiences, and the girl closest to Jen's age was clearly not thriving post-transplant. Jen and her parents attended meetings sporadically.

Bob says, "Jen was in the program and we would do whatever was asked of us. We didn't pore over every possible outcome or ask a lot of questions. Like the time right after she was born, we simply moved ahead with hope."

Bob, Jen, Tim, and Barbara on Tim's twentieth birthday in 1988

1/16/88

I think the thing that pisses me off the most about heart surgery or any other physical problem is the segregation. People were staring at me at the Prairie House[20] tonight. Did they recognize my picture from the paper? Maybe we just looked too Carleton or something, but I couldn't help wondering. Do I stare at them because they're alcoholics? Or recently divorced? Or old and alone? At least it's not as thoroughly preposterous as skin color—I'm having a radically different experience than they, but I'm no different.

Yes, I've finally made the switch in my mind. I've been hanging out with my friends all day and just being Jen Bonner. I haven't even felt the urge to talk on and on about the transplant. I have returned to equilibrium. It's such a relief. People may think I'm different, but I know I'm not a patient, I'm a person.

1/17/88

I dreamt I had a baby last night. I was sick, though, so I hadn't seen her. Mom was keeping her in this little white garage with a gas heater somewhere. I knew she was J.B.'s, but I didn't want to tell him. Mom called her Akika, but assured me I could rename her when I wanted. I had hardly been pregnant—the baby just appeared. She was sick too . . . lying still and comfortable, but with terrible circles under her eyes. I picked her up and at

---

20 An inexpensive café on the outskirts of Northfield

first she protested, not knowing me. She didn't really cry, she spoke to me. We settled down on the couch and gradually she started purring. I wanted to nurse her, but it had been so long that I was dry. I took her back to the house; I was going to keep her in my room. Everyone at home referred to her as "Jen"—a little me. I was thinking of naming her Elizabeth. I was trying to figure out how to tell people about her, because everyone thought I was so brave for going through heart surgery, but if they knew I was an unwed mother, some of them would no longer respect me. I was also trying to adjust to the fact that my future held a child in it, always. She would be with me whatever I did and I would have to learn to live with that.

1/19/87

Beth[21] called me Jenny today. This has got to stop. The next time I'm alone with Fred, I've got to tell him. I'm already a little annoyed with him anyway. First he's calling me "champ" and acting like I'm so god-darned special, and then he's ignoring me. I thought Independent Study meant individual instruction, criticism, a chance to talk to Fred about my work more than once or twice a term. Every time I come down, I get five minutes of cursory attention—which I have to drag him from Beth to get. I don't want to be jealous. I'm pretty much over the Prof crush thing. But I'm not getting what I wanted from the class.

---

21 An art major in Jen's class

I really would like to sit and talk with Beth once. She has never allowed me to get close, which was the original and only grievance I have had against her. But she also has the habit of conforming completely to a specific Prof's ideas, loves, and personal quirks in a class. In Sculpture, she did feminist, process-oriented work. In Printmaking, she does abstract, experimental, process-oriented work. In Jr. Seminar with a ceramics professor she talks about craft as art form. Is she incredibly lucky? Is she really a genius? Is she just a raging con artist? I don't like her stuff. It doesn't seem to contain her. It looks like something done by a student, fooling around to please her Profs.

1/20/88

Dad and I are beginning to worry about Mom. Every time our family wellbeing is threatened, she goes down farther. I don't know how far she is from bottom now. I started worrying when she began talking about running away. Now any time she thinks we're picking on her (otherwise considered normal banter in our family) she says she's just going to leave and go someplace quiet. I've tried to gently suggest therapy, but I'm not sure how she took it. Dad and I can build boxes to put our troubles in, so we can face the world with calm. Mom doesn't build boxes. Everything in her spills and swirls around and shows out her eyes and her voice when she talks.

I meditated too well tonight. Now I'll never get to sleep.

Charlotte Black Elk[22] will be here on Friday and Saturday. I'm taking her class. I would love to meet her—I don't know what I'd say, but I would just love to meet her.

1/22/88

I met Charlotte Black Elk today. I went up after class and kind of gushed out my feelings at her. I guess I rather built up a relationship between us based on my experiences seeing her. She doesn't have the energy to open up to every fan, so I don't have the right to expect anything of her. I guess it's just a growing experience.

Kurt and Sean[23] stopped by today. They had heard about my health and brought chocolate. Sweeties! I still have the same whisper of a crush on Kurt. He's applied to Carleton. Sean's in—he went early decision. Yay! It'd be great if Kurt came too. He's probably too young to be a good thing, but what if he matured . . . ? Maybe we could just date? Maybe I'm getting desperate?

I'm having exciting dreams finally. I used to wonder why I didn't—I wasn't frustrated! Gretchen and I watched *Romancing the Stone* and *Jewel of the Nile*. Oh! The love scenes . . . it was almost painful to watch. At this point, I could go for some women-oriented porn. Except I hate watching it—I want to feel it. Grrrr!

---

22 A spiritual and cultural leader of the Lakota Sioux tribe

23 Friends from Jen's high school forensics team. They were freshmen when Jen was a senior.

1/23/88

My heart's got that fluttery feeling. I'm sure I'm just anxious. How is it that I never *feel* that anxious when my heart does this?

 Friends came over tonight with a movie—*Young Doctors in Love*. Fortunately it wasn't too offensive, but I didn't laugh for the first 5 or 10 minutes. I don't want to be an oversensitive person whom no one can say "heart" in front of, but tasteless jokes about doctors fucking up in surgery are not something I need to seek out.

I know it wasn't meant in a bad way, but it did seem remarkably insensitive. At least it didn't have any transplant jokes.

I feel lonely again.

I'm going to go crazy. How can a mind create such feelings? Sometimes I'm just tense. Right now, I feel like there's cool water inside my left arm and chest. Then I feel little needles in my left or right breast. Or I just lie awake and listen to my heart flutter against my ribs and sometimes in my throat. I know there's nothing wrong, but what else do you think about at night? The lack of boys in your life? I've been thinking about that too. Sometimes I think about art and then I want to get up and draw. Why am I so awake?

1/26/88

I've started going to Jr. Seminar now. This is my second week and I'm talking about leading a discussion on Dadaism—I don't know much about it and Dadaism brings up issues I would very much like to address, such as "Where Do We Draw the Line Between Art and Bullshit?"

The Jr. Seminar is great though. We all get together and fight about important issues in art today. Sometimes it's frustrating, but it's so much fun to be out and involved with my classmates and thinking about things. Gretchen offended some people today by showing two slides of Christo and labeling them "obsessive wrapping behavior" (deemed by the feminist artists to be a strictly female characteristic). Riccardo and I hit the floor laughing.

I talked to Beth last night and it was good. She was very nice and serious to talk to. Obviously we disagree on some points, but if she would talk to me more often I would like to become friends.

I've worn myself out at Boliou two days in a row. It's all kinds of fun, but it's strange too. I'm so proud to be carrying out some semblance of normal activity, but at the same time, it's so much less, so restricting, hard.

And I still don't know what to think about at night.

1/28/88

Gretchen and I were discussing the relationship of Zen to Art. She's writing a paper on this and wanted me to read it. It's given me a lot to think about in the nerve-wracking face of the Jr. Show. Though this is not a contest, one of us will get $1000 based on our stuff.[24] I really can't handle it. My ego is still so involved in my work. I've always been the "best" artist in my class. I've always just assumed I was the best. I have dealt with not getting A's from Fred, but I have not dealt with Beth getting them. She's the only one whose success I really don't understand. I hate process art. I try so hard to express an idea and I can't stand the thought of someone just farting around "out on a limb" getting ranked above me. I don't mind—in fact one *should* go out on a limb to express an idea. Gretchen and I assume (though I must admit I still hope for me) Beth will win. She's the most "avant-garde" of all of us and that seems to be what counts. I won't let myself change my style for the show, but I do feel the urge to work in that direction.

But no, what I learned tonight is that to become enlightened, one must "die the great death." Fred's B+ was my first slap in the face. Not winning the Jr. Seminar would be very, very good for me. I could overcome my jealousy of Beth and I would have the humility to approach my work as I should: as something I do, that needs constant

---

24 Ursula Hemingway Jepson, an artist who attended Carleton, donated funds for the annual Junior prize. She was Ernest Hemingway's sister.

practice and improvement, that is a part of me, but not my ego; something I do for myself, not my reputation or others' approval.

But as I write this, I feel so wise for thinking it. I have a long way to go.

1/29/88

I cured myself of my anxiety over the Jr. Show. I went through my portfolio. If I win, it will be an act of God. Not that I'm completely out of the race; I just reminded myself that I am not a genius. That a lot of my stuff is crap. Or, if not crap, valid student work—that should never be shown to anyone. I feel a little calmer now. Not that it'll help me sleep—I'll just spend full time on beeper scenarios.

I cut up my *Love Medicine* print with a blowtorch to-day.[25] Or at least I started. I have to talk to Beth about the mechanics of it—it's more difficult than I thought. If you can't beat the avant-garde, join 'em, I guess.

1/30/88

Tricia and Susie[26] were just over for heartthrob double feature: *Dirty Dancing* and *La Bamba* . . .

---

25 A way to "deconstruct" a work of art

26 Friends since grade school

I miss having a boyfriend. I wonder if I should call Kurt, or if that'd be silly. I don't want to act out of pure desperation. Right now what I really want is to go dancing. That, I'll have to wait for, regardless.

I still have those tickets to First Ave.[27] I hope they last.

1/31/88

Tomorrow is Tim's 20th birthday. The day after that he moves to Laura Baker.[28] I wonder how betrayed he'll feel. Maybe he was the dog in my dream last night. I was trying to get my dog into the car but halfway in she had cut her back—just sliced it open really deep on the car door. I picked her up out of the car and carried her to a vet. I wasn't worried about her dying, but I didn't want her to hurt.

I saw Devin[29] today. I was in the library and Devin came over and asked me how I was. He had heard—I wonder who from? I wonder about him. Am I just being desperate? Well, I was rather interested last term. He did squeeze my foot today and he is interesting. My folks and I talked about what character flaws were allowable and what were not. Devin knows how to work and that's a big plus in his favor. He's not outrageously cute, but

---

27 A music club in downtown Minneapolis

28 A residential facility for developmentally disabled people a few blocks from the Bonner home

29 A history major in Jen's class

he is not ugly. He's really bright and really obnoxious. And has a 4.0. Dad likes him, I think he reminds him of himself. Maybe that's why I like him too.

Well, at least I have someone to think about.

IN HIS LATER teens, as a respite for his parents, Tim had spent an occasional weekend or overnight at Laura Baker School for people with disabilities, three blocks from his home. By the time the Bonners learned that Jen needed a heart transplant, their family fortitude and informal community support had nearly reached their limits. When an opportunity arose for Tim to live full-time at Laura Baker, the Bonners welcomed it as a way for Tim to reside nearby as an adult.

Tim celebrated his twentieth birthday at home. Concerned about how he would handle the transition, Bob, Barbara and Jen each talked to him about it, with no clear sign that he understood. He still couldn't organize space and time in his mind. After the birthday dinner, Bob tucked Tim in bed, reminding him that he would move to Laura Baker in the morning. Tim threw his arms around his dad's neck and said, "But not tonight." The next morning Jen drew a pencil portrait of her brother taking a pensive last bath at home.

Laura Baker staff recommended that family members keep their distance for a time, while Tim adjusted to new surroundings. As the year went on, and Jen pushed herself emotionally and physically to confront questions about life, love, and art, she had little in reserve for the brother who had helped define her. But she remained at the center of his life.

`Tim in the bath

Thriving Under Pressure

2/2/88

Tim's gone. He seems well settled at Laura Baker. His roommate's a snot, but Tim's good at ignoring annoying people, so I think he'll do all right.

I'm not sad about him tonight. I'm sad about Fred. Crushes are the stupidest things. I'm sad that I have one, that I can't react to him as a normal Prof. I can't deny that I have a crush on him. I just wish I could find the antidote and turn it back into normal admiration. Oh well, it's getting a little better. I'm just hypersensitive around him. Any time he's short with me, I think it's because he knows I have a crush on him and wants to discourage it. The problem with crushes is they take away your ability to see yourself clearly, so I can't tell if I look like I have a crush on him or if I act really curt or what.

I wonder why I'm in therapy if I write out in this book just about everything I tell her. Susan never says much, just reflects what I'm saying. I really don't know that I need her anymore.

2/5/88

I've done it. I've completely readjusted to this new situation. I'm back, involved in life, while at the same time, I believe I'm about as ready as I'll ever be for that transplant call. Not that I can guarantee that I won't freak out when it happens, but I won't lose my shit in public at least.

I don't think I need therapy anymore. I'm calm now—and meditation helps with the tension in my back. And I think I'm no more neurotic than any one else my age. In fact, I feel a lot saner than most.

2/6/88

I just had my first date in two months. Mom and Dad went out tonight, so I called Devin (earlier this week) and invited him to dinner. We had steak Diane, potatoes Anna, salad, and apple pie. Then, at his suggestion, we watched *The Bridge on the River Kwai*, which was good.

It was a wonderful evening. He's a nice guy, I think. And so interesting—we talked and talked—he was here for five hours. We talked about life, the universe, families, and death. His mother was a Communist; he was raised by his grandparents, and he never knew his father. (Why do I always unconsciously go for men without fathers?)

It ended well too. I started worrying towards the end of the movie about The Good-Night Kiss. But I wasn't ready for it, so I figured if he kissed me, that was okay, but I wasn't ready to kiss him. But when it came down to the moment, he put his arms around me and hugged me.

I'm really pleased. Because in a lot of ways, this dinner was the first time we've talked. I feel I know him well—or a lot better at least now. But I feel like tonight we became friends. It'll take another date or two before I want to go beyond that.

In so many ways, though, he's a lot like J.B. He's a worker—that's an important difference, but in other ways he's similar. He's very bright, but socially insecure. I get the feeling he doesn't dance—he seems way too self-conscious. It's so frustrating—he answers some of my needs so well, but others he just doesn't touch. He's intellectually stimulating—he's great to talk to. But although he's a devout follower of the humanities, I don't feel any poetry in his soul. He feels hard: hard work, hard thought, hard partying. Hardness is essential—I don't know if I could marry an easygoing guy like Andy. But I could marry a Fred: he's artistic, but he has a hardness in his standards and his work.

I've probably found my father, but is that really what I'm looking for?

2/7/88

I've been thinking about Devin all day and he has a good aftertaste. Mom and I talked about him and she definitely approves. She says he's serious and whatever he may lack, that will make up for it.

I hope he calls me up. He makes me kind of nervous. Partly, I think, because I'm not sure if I want a relationship with him. Part of poetry is romance—I hope he has some of that. Last night was certainly not romantic—and that was a relief. But if we do go for more than friends, I want a few sparks.

Maybe I should wear the fuchsia heels to Boliou.

2/8/88

Had dinner with Fred and S. tonight. It was great—because of S. Every time she went out of the room, I realized I had nothing to say to Fred. Still, it was a wonderful evening. The conversation never lagged for too long and the food was good. I interjected some lasting humor into their lives by relating Devin's misconception because S. didn't change her name—"Yeah, I met Fred H. and his live-in girlfriend." S. was horrified. Fred thought it was hilarious.

I achieved one of my two goals for the evening, they being 1) to learn to talk to Fred and 2) to find some fault to fight the prof crush. I suppose it's a shame it wasn't #1, but #2 is so important that it really doesn't matter. The fault is this: (besides the fact that I can't talk to him and he has *atrocious* table manners) he is so *damn* paternal with S. He is possibly 5–10 years her senior and my, does he act it.[30] He left for the basketball game, kissed her on the head, and said, "Bye, pal." Fred, she's your wife, not your dog.

Ha ha ha—Fred's not perfect!

God, I'm *so* mature.

2/10/88

Braunlin called Mom and Dad at the cabin today. The insurance came through. She'll call me tomorrow and we'll arrange when I'll come to get the beeper.

If there were anyone in the world more anxious to get this news, it would be me, but I don't need to deal with that here. I can't believe how hard this has hit me. I guess I'd put it all aside. Someday I'm going to graduate. Someday I'll get a job. Someday, I'll get married. Someday, I'll get a heart transplant. Now it's smack-in-the-face real again. Sort of. I'm just tired and terrified, like I was most of December and early January.

I also feel this inexplicable depression. I think it's linked to the tiredness—the kind of thing I could shake off if I

---

30 Fred was thirty-four and his wife, Sandra Spadaccini, was twenty-eight.

could get up and do something, but I'm too tired to do that. By now, however, I know that I'm not really all that exhausted—just scared shitless.

2/12/88

Got my beeper today. It works—yay!! I just got back from a campus party so I'm feeling back to normal. Pretty tired, but mellow. The biggest issue on my mind is not the impending reality of the T-word, but that Devin wasn't at the party. I'm bummin'. I wore my mini and everything. But I met some of Gretchen's friends and they were fun. I'm still a wallflower, but I reached out every so often with relative success, so I feel okay.

ORGAN TRANSPLANTS MAKE sense to most of the American public. We replace the furnaces in our houses and undertake major mechanical repairs in our cars. Why not simply replace a failing organ?

Private medical insurance companies began offering heart-transplant coverage in 1978 on a case-by-case basis. By the mid-1980s, most private payers in the US routinely covered heart transplants. Ordinarily, private insurers follow Medicare's lead on whether and when to accept new procedures as standard, rather than experimental, therapy. But this decision was troublesome for Medicare.

Medicare studied the issues surrounding heart transplants for several years. Medicare's earlier decision to cover kidney dialysis for any American who needed it proved to be remarkably costly. Could the program afford heart transplants? Might that money be better spent on prevention of heart disease? Who should receive new hearts given the shortage of donor organs? Was the quality of life after a heart transplant good enough?

In 1986, Medicare came to a decision—it would cover heart transplants, but with many restrictions. Heart recipients had to be no older than their midfifties and meet all the selection criteria of qualified transplant centers. Of course this excluded the majority of people on Medicare, who were over sixty-five.

Over time, Medicare relaxed many of its limitations including the age cutoff. But the biggest limitation remains: there are not nearly enough donor hearts for the people who need them.

2/19/88

Tonight was the Jr. Opening. It was like a big party, and all these people I knew kept showing up and liking my work. Mrs. Lloyd[31] pronounced my still life the best piece in the whole show. I wore my long black tube skirt and Alison Kettering[32] told me I was too sexy for words. I saw some guys eyeing me as well. Everybody loved my Cat "Sybil" and wanted to know how I had gotten the color on "Sleeping Nude." The whole thing was such an ego trip. It's the artistic equivalent of a curtain call.

---

31 Sue Lloyd, wife of Tim Lloyd, the art professor who led the Junior Seminar that year

32 Art history professor at Carleton

Sybil

Sleeping Nude

2/20/88

I went to *Oh! What a Lovely War* tonight. It was good, but depressing. I feel we're on the brink of economic crisis, which could lead to international trouble, and awful as the trench warfare was, we'll be lucky if we can get away with casualties that low.

I saw Devin at the play—he's stage manager. I did a very good job of trying to ignore him, but he was standing there when I went to get my tickets, so I had to talk to him. It was nice; we talked about inane things like Visa bills. Last time we talked about car accidents. Small talk while courting is simply hilarious. Someone should make a book of all the stupid conversations people have while desperately trying to keep other people from walking away.

He was looking good, though.

2/21/88

It's odd. I'm much happier this year than I was last year. Everybody thinks it's amazing that I seem to be thriving under this pressure. It's not that hard though. It's nothing new. I've always known I'd probably have to have surgery again—I just didn't think it'd be for another ten years or so.

Some people at school feel so fortunate that they don't have any purpose. "WASP-ing out" is Gretchen's term for it: white, wealthy people getting neurotic about their lack of reasons to be neurotic. My surgeries seemed so much in my past that I was starting to WASP out a little. Growing up is stressful—but everybody does it, so no big deal. Then I get hit with this, which takes me out of school and gives me the time to grow up and reflect, while quite effectively removing me from the untroubled and guilt-ridden white middle class. I have achieved, in one trip to a doctor's office, sincerity. No one can doubt my angst, as an artist or as a person. I am instantly an authority on matters that take normal, sincere and thoughtful people at least ten more years to consider in their grasp. Some of this is merited—most people really haven't begun to accept their mortality until their thirties—if then. But how much of it is just confidence? I haven't really learned anything new. I've just thought about old things again.

2/25/88

I shouldn't have written so boldly about accepting my mortality last time; I couldn't turn out the light and when I did there were more monsters than ever.

So I'm back to not thinking about it. Can anybody really think about it? Maybe during the daylight, when darkness is some distant part of the past and future and whatever may be lying in wait for you, it won't get you right now.

This term (or non-term) has been so relaxing. I've completely reordered my priorities. Unfortunately, no matter how clearly I may see my friends, my art, my school, and my career, my 1040 is still due by April 15. I hope not to escape one of the two certainties in life for the other.

Our outside examiner[33] talked today about the time we had in our lives to figure out what we wanted to do. "Unless you die young," she said, "You have 60–70 years . . ." I thought about saying something, like how that makes it all the more important to do what you love when you have the chance and not wait, but that didn't seem to be exactly her point. Her point was that we shouldn't feel trapped.

Still it was odd to hear. I took it like a reminder. Not that it was a cruel thing to say, just that it's something on my mind.

Kevin M. was over for dinner. He looks a little like the boy in *Mask*, but he's kind of cute too. He's pretentious in a lonely way: he has few friends and he offered his phone number in case I needed someone to talk to. I worry that we might not have anything more in common than physical difficulties, but I'd like to talk to him again before I say for sure.

2/27/88

Three weeks ago, Devin was here for dinner. Two weeks ago, I called him again. Last week, I ran into him at the play. This week, I ignored him.

---

33 Invited by the art faculty to judge the Junior Show

I went to Boliou to work on my oil self-portrait. I decided at the end of the day that I look rather like I've been stunned by a large log to the back of my head, but Gretchen *loves* it. Hers is *amazing*. It really looks like her, though right now the background makes it seem pretty flat. She thinks mine's more expressive—I'm fooling with color more. Lately I've been really loose with my painting: just throwing on patches of color where I feel like it. This is my first work with thicker paint and it's a lot of fun. I'm using pastels, so I'm not having too much trouble with overbearing colors taking over the painting.

Oil self-portrait

I'm going to audit Fred's figure drawing next term and
Dad's History 62, Elizabethan England (with Gretchen).
Wonder if I'll do all the work? Certainly should prove
interesting. I think I'll change my name to Bramowitz
in Dad's class, though.

2/28/88

I've been reading one of the diaries of Anaïs Nin. So
far I've found them to be mental masturbation, which
most adolescents can do for themselves, thank you
very much. I hope that, should someone, for whatever
reason, someday, feel compelled to publish my diaries,
they'll have the good sense to edit them down first.

Her diaries are hard to get through, but I enjoy the artistic feeling I get from her work. She goes off on these
lengthy descriptions of Henry Miller and her other
friends *forever*, but while it's driving me crazy, I get the
overwhelming desire to watercolor them as though I
were sitting there with them.

I've started sketching with watercolors now. I am quite
pleased with myself to finally be drawn to do this regularly. I always felt guilty about my laziness as an artist
that I wasn't sketching madly every day of my life.

I like sketching in watercolor—they are small, unim-
portant things, so I'm not under pressure when I do
them. But watercolor is so difficult, because once the

white is covered up, it's gone. Thus, when I go to do an oil, it seems so easy.

2/29/88
Leap Year Day. Wow.

Traci[34] came by tonight. She said she'd cut J.B.'s hair a little while ago. He said he still can't deal with seeing me. He's not quite over me but he'd never try to get back together, or something like that. I can't tell if she disapproves of my actions or not . . .

I dreamt I got the Transplant Call last night. I totally lost my shit in the dream, but I feel good now. I feel like I'm beginning to process this through my subconscious.

---

34 Jen's sophomore-year roommate

The Living at Home Blues

3/2/88

The Grand Crit[35] was last night. It went well, I guess. They said I had a very strong body of work, and seemed to feel that my participation benefited the whole show. They had to, of course, spend part of the time being impressed that I was doing any work at all.

I saw Devin today. I was in Sayles, looking through the record sale selection, when he walked up to the box next to me. I said, "Hello, Devin," and he turned as if he had had no idea I was there at all and said, "Oh! Hi, Jen." I guess he went to the same ignoring school as I.

He has 60 pages due in the next two weeks, and then he's going home for Spring Break. But before I left he said that, since he was really busy, he didn't know if he'd see me much, but to have my folks drop a note

---

35 Art faculty and other art majors in the same year commented on each art student's work .

with Visiting Hours on it in his box when I got the transplant call.

3/3/88

Tricia and Susie both got back today. We went to the Ideal Café for dinner. The Ideal was pretty gross, but it was good to see them again. Susie says Tricia told her about The Others. It seems Tricia gets carried away with it. It's like gaming with her—other lives and stories to spice up hers.

3/4/88

Well, Gretchen was right: Beth won the Junior Show. I'm trying really hard not to care, but it's like not making an audition. I feel rejected. I could have told you she'd win, simply because Andy won last year. They're both so far out in their own worlds, there's no way they wouldn't win.

Now that I have something to pin it on, I can rest. Brother.

While I was meditating this afternoon, I had a sexual fantasy that was set at the cabin. I wanted to write it down—start a diary of fantasies, but I stopped. I know maybe it's silly to worry about what people will think of you after you're dead, but God, what if someone found it before the names involved had been forgotten and long since gone from my life? Two months ago it would have included Fred! Bad enough that he should possibly find out I had a crush on him (though he probably knows), but to have graphic details?!

3/6/88

I've been so tired the last 2 days. I wonder if I'm going down another notch. My chest aches like my heart's trying to enlarge beyond its capacity. It's already forced my left rib out so it stands higher than my right when I lie down. If I still feel like this tomorrow, I'll call Dr. Braunlin.

I made bread today. It worked. First time in ten years. First new jar of yeast in ten years too—maybe they're related?

Hearing country music on the radio makes me think of the cabin. Go to the cabin. Dance. Have sex. Walk a block. I hope I don't have to wait 'til August (or later!).

3/8/88

I just went to *Moonstruck* again with Mom. It was so wonderful. Mom *loved* it. There's nothing better than getting something right for Mom. She reacts *completely* to whatever you give her: a book, a dinner, a song, a movie. If it's wrong, you'll hear about it all night. But if it's right, you'll hear its (and your) praises sung to the skies. That movie is good enough to make you happy on its own, but taking Mom to it . . . !

3/7/88

I had a pretty full day today—and I'm not wrecked. It started with a pap smear at 9:00 a.m. You know it's been too long when you start looking forward to pap smears. Seriously: I had that pleasant, semi-satiated feeling you get from having an object larger than your finger inside you for 15 minutes afterwards. Oh dear.

Then I went to Sayles and saw a friend who is leaving for Australia in a week (yay!!). He tried to get me to feel sorry for him ("all those visas and passports . . .") so I offered to trade my beeper for his plane ticket but he declined.

After that I went to Boliou where someone finally managed to break a sculpture of mine. So I was standing there, trying to fix it when Devin got out of his art history class. He tried to comfort me by putting his arm around me and telling me about what a sorry state Grecian temples were in. Then Scott G. came up to ask me to submit a black and white proof of "Sleeping Nude" to *Manuscript*.[36] Hoo Hoo! They're soliciting *me* for submissions now. Just one step closer to the limelight and success of being Big in the Art World.

At 1:00 p.m., I got my haircut. (Oh wow.)

After that, I went to Joe's[37] studio with the rest of the painting class. He has a beautiful studio, but I got tired

---

36 Carleton's literary magazine

37 Joe Byrne, a landscape painter and Carleton art professor

and went home early. Got home and took a bath to get ready for the formal dinner with Tim at Laura Baker. Tim was so handsome in his new dress shoes and he sat through the entire dinner *and* half-hour show by the Knightingales[38] without a peep. People were being led out every 10-15 minutes, but not Tim. We were so proud of him. And everyone was dressed up and happy. Tim knows just about everybody there and pointed them out and what they were wearing through the whole dinner.

The Knightingales finally have some spunk. I wish I had a good enough voice to join them. Maybe when I get my lungs behind me.

Then I came home and finished sewing my skirt. Whew! (It's actually more of a loincloth than a skirt. Should be worn *with* tights underneath.)

3/10/88

I saw a friend today for the first time since last fall, and we had a *long* talk about Relationships, Co-Dependency, Therapists, and Reincarnation. He didn't seem to really believe in Reincarnation, but he said something that made me resonate with truth. He suggested that there is no such thing as entropy; that energy from a scientifically measurable source has been going into creating new souls and some day, when there are enough souls, they'll come together and recreate that energy. Or change into some new form.

---

38 A female a cappella singing group from Carleton

3/14/88

Just got back from dinner with Gretchen. I saw another woman leaving Devin's room. But I'm happy. I thought I was miserable because I was in love, but I realize now I was just lonely. I can live without Devin, just so long as I have friends.

Gretchen's so cool. Somehow she just makes me feel good. I hope I do the same for her.

I said goodbye to Traci tonight. She's leaving tomorrow morning for LA, next week for Australia. She just finished my sweater—it's so beautiful! I wish I could make things like that.

Dad's supposed to leave for Atlanta on Thursday, but he might not now, because we're both starting to seriously worry that Mom's going to flip. She said today she wanted a prescription for tranquilizers.

3/15/88

Tonight Ed and Toni[39] came over to celebrate a joint anniversary dinner with Mom and Dad. I fixed broiled salmon, wild rice pilaf, spinach salad, and, for dessert, "Poires Helene." Also Gretchen came over this morning and we made french bread.

---

39 Ed Sostek, English and theater arts professor at Carleton, and his wife Toni, Jen's dance instructor

Everything worked.

It was wonderful! Toni and Ed brought wine and champagne (no, maybe we had the wine) and I was *so* drunk, but still, *everything* tasted GREAT! I think it was the best dinner I've ever made. Everything went together, and everything tasted good.

3/17/88

I felt really tired today. I couldn't eat and when I finally did, I felt sick. I went to bed at 3:30 p.m. but didn't sleep. I've had a bit of a backache on and off and sometimes I feel queasy. I guess it all sounds like nervousness. When I start thinking about other things, I feel okay. I got a call from the U today about insurance and maybe that's scared me. Sometimes, I almost can't stand to lie in the bathtub and listen to my heart beat so big and strangely.

3/18/88

I still feel dreadful. Maybe I have the flu. I called Braunlin, who sent me to Mark.[40] He thinks maybe it's a cold, but I'm supposed to call him tomorrow.

Gretchen came down this afternoon. We were going to go to a movie, but we ended up going to the doctor and out to eat. She had her Roxy Music *Avalon* tape in the car, which I *had* to listen to—it made me think of last spring

---

40 Mark Mellstrom, Jen's family doctor

term. It made me cry. I want so badly to be back at Carleton for spring term, to seduce someone to *Avalon* and to graduate and sit in my apartment in ten years with a cup of tea and think back on all the crazy things I did while listening to that tape. I want to get better. I hope this is just a cold. If I have to wait six months in bed, I'll wait six months in bed. Yes, I'll deal with whatever I have to deal with. Just so I can get through it. Just so I can go back to school and take someone out for romantic walks in the arb.[41] I want to live to make love again.

3/20/88

Just saw *The Rose* with Mom and Dad on the VCR. It was wonderful. If you can say that about a movie where the heroine dies on stage at the end. Bette Midler really communicated (what a trite, stupid word) the feeling of the strung-out, on-the-edge artist. Living the life that you cry with nostalgia over ten years later—if you get out of it alive. I touched on it last term at Boliou every night 'til 4:00 a.m., though my drugs were no stronger than caffeine. Just burning yourself out on your art and letting the rest of your life go to pot. Living that intensely is fun, at 4:00 in the morning, while you're on stage, while you're in bed with a guy and there's no one else in the world. But when the sun comes up and you have a migraine or a hangover or an empty bed, it seems so hollow. Even the pain, in retrospect, is romantic. But only in retrospect. Why is living sensibly and happy so boring?

---

41 The Carleton arboretum, an 880-acre conservation area bordering the campus

I wonder if I'll ever be able to abuse myself in that tiny little barely offensive way again?

3/21/88

Rereading what I wrote about *The Rose*, it's obvious that I neglected the main point of the movie last night. She was living in her ART, something that is in itself a possibly pleasurable existence, but she was driven there out of desperation. She was truly miserable and bouncing from sex to drugs to rock and roll with no life in between. What I wrote about yesterday was a tangent of a small facet of that movie. If you could recover from a life like that, I doubt you could seriously, ten years later, weep with nostalgia for it.

I got a postcard today from that cute guy who looks like a cross between Harrison Ford and Ernie on *Sesame Street*. He saw the article about me in the *Voice*[42] and wanted to say he was "pulling" for me. He gave me his address, so I wrote him a card: *"Yoga Master, get $75.00 an hour modeling for local art classes."*

I saw Beth at Sayles today. She was on break from Shop, so we sat down and talked for ten minutes. We're meeting for lunch tomorrow. Hey—maybe I'll finally get to be friends with her. We had a nice talk today.

---

42 The quarterly alumni magazine, *The Carleton Voice*, had published an article about Jen needing a heart transplant.

Mom, Dad, and I watched *Mondo Beyondo's Performance Art Showcase* (Bette Midler), and I now have to take back all the nasty things I said about performance art. There is good performance art. It consists, generally, of various mixtures of dance and commercial art. Or a marriage of plays and music videos. It has little or nothing to do with studio, but whatever it does or doesn't have, Bette found some really good stuff for this show. Bill Irwin was break dancing on it with Bette's husband—they spent 3 minutes in the men's room making farting noises and decorating each other with food. There was some poor boy experiencing sensory overload on an airplane, which sounded like a bad reading of a Laurie Anderson song, but once he got going it was tolerable—even funny. And Bette: "Ciao bambini! Ciao for now, you badda things!"

3/22/88

I just watched *Mondo Beyondo* again with Toni and Ed Sostek.[43] Ed said all the pieces were takeoffs, which makes some sense, as they were almost all humorous. Toni really liked the "LaLaLa Human Steps" piece with two male (we believe) dancers, one of whom is in drag. Whatever their sexes, they were both *amazing* dancers!

Then Toni took me into the kitchen, fed me sorbet, and told me stories. I love Toni. She was telling me of her public humiliation the other day when she flipped off a

---

43 Some of her parents' friends, including the Sosteks, had become Jen's friends too.

faculty wife—the first time she's ever flipped anyone off. I can't believe it's her first time, but she swears that's true.

I got a letter from Joel today! Of course, it was addressed to three other people as well, but it was a 3-page letter nonetheless. He said a lot of trite things about my situation but he also wanted to tell me that he thought I was a really talented artist. He said he always thought so, but was prompted to say it now because the situation was "so immediate." Which I thought is a nice way of expressing the "Don't die, Jen!" sentiment I imagine most of my friends probably feel once in a while.

Dad's painting my room and has moved my dresser and mirror out so that the mirror directly reflects the bed. I think tomorrow, if I have any good brushes around, I'm going to try again at that nude self-portrait (in acrylics this time). If my folks are gone for long enough tomorrow. I think Dad says he's not painting tomorrow. All I need is his drop cloth.

3/23/88

I started it. Gretchen says she still respects me, but she seemed to have reservations. Actually, you can barely tell I'm naked—color patches everywhere! AAGH! It looks like a Matisse nightmare.

I had a busy day today. Gretchen came down and took me to the Cities. We ate lunch at a Vietnamese restaurant and went shopping at Value Village.[44] I got a black swim-suit/leotard, a *cute* pair of black pants, a black tank top, a teal belt, a 25-cent copy of a Salinger novel, and a pair of 3″ Italian black spike heels—all for $17.50! Ooh! What a day. Gretchen thinks even less of the heels than she does of the nude self-portrait. Then we went to Oarfolk and I bought *Hot Rocks*.[45] I have $2 left of the $30.00 I made off of that Cat Print I sold (my first sale!).

So what is my hangup with my sexuality? I'm wearing miniskirts every day, I keep buying these *ridiculous* shoes, I'm painting myself naked. Is it all because I'm not getting laid? Is it normal? I want to be a respected member of the community, not a "slut." I'm pretty sure I still respect myself—can I be so drawn to something I shouldn't do? I am an attractive and sexually active young woman and proud of it. Is it wrong to want to call attention to this? Is it only jealousy that causes people to scorn obvious sexuality? I guess the only thing I can do is what feels right to me. If I can still respect myself in spike heels and a mini then everyone else will too. If Bette Midler and Cher can do it, so can I.

---

44 A thrift store

45 A Rolling Stones compilation of songs from 1964–1971

The Living At Home Blues

Got me a place off-campus
It's really, really nice.
When they asked me to move on in
Well I didn't even think twice.
The cooking is really great there
The best you ever had.
But the people with which I'm livin'
They're my own Mom and Dad.

Chorus:
I got a single
But my parents sleep down the hall.
I got a single, yeah
But it don't do me no good at all.

I saw a fine young man
A walkin' down the street.
I went right over to him
And whispered something sweet.
I said "Hey Hey good-lookin'
"Why don'tcha come by my place."
But when I told him where I lived
Well you shoulda seen his face.

(Chorus)

Well I'm savin' up my money
'Cause I don't pay no rent.
Gonna rent me a nice motel room
They won't know a-where I went.

(Chorus)

So listen to me people
When the money's gettin' tight.
You can shack up with your parents
But you'd better be home at night.
They'll be watchin' where you're goin'
And when you're comin' home.
And if you're sleepin' near your parents
Well, you're sleepin' there alone.

(Chorus)

—*Jennifer Bonner*

3/24/88

I had tea with a friend this morning at the Ideal and we discussed the sexy clothes conflict. She pointed out that there was a touch of camp to my sexy outfits, which makes it more palatable. We also agreed that saying women shouldn't be sexy is just as restrictive as saying they should.

I have this thing for ugly buildings, dirty houses, and frumpy interiors. I did a watercolor of the Ideal this morning, because it's so real. No glitz, no shine, just real stuff that's falling apart.

3/25/88

I finished the nude self-portrait today. It's more about purple and yellow than it is about me, but I *love* it. I think it's the best piece I've ever done. Dad doesn't understand, because it doesn't look exactly like me. Mom said she thought it was "cheap." Cheap?! She doesn't like German Expressionism, so it's not really up her alley. But I was thinking more of Matisse than Kirchner when I did it, and she would have none of that. She doesn't think it has anything at all to do with Matisse. Maybe if I had made the stripe green instead of purple? She thought it was "dime-store"—not even a courteous "bold!" (Once you get hooked on Artspeak, outright criticism is hard to take.) But I don't really care what words she uses, I just can't believe she doesn't like it. Dad I can understand: it's about color and he's color-blind.

But Mom is a color fanatic. How can she complain that it is too "heavy-handed"? It's expressive! It's gestural! It's got life! I don't consider myself to be a pastel person. I don't particularly like pastels. And there's a lot of white in the picture—I just put strong contrast in as well, for the composition. I'll do a self-portrait in Easter eggs for her—maybe that will go over better.

How can my mom, the queen of color, not like German Expressionism? How could my parents let me down like this? I thought they had taste. I really do like it. It can't be that bad, can it? No. No, I like it far too much for it to be bad.

3/26/88

I just finished reading my old diary from 5th–9th grade. It really gave me pause. I sat there, laughing at it, but when I reread last night's entry, I realized that there is a similarity between this diary I hold in my lap and that one from ten years ago.

There's something so nice about time, so forgiving. I may hate something I wrote yesterday, but let ten years pass and it becomes "endearing." I could barely keep a diary before 5th grade, because every day I would read what I had written the night before and cringe with shame. Now it's my high school diaries that I can't bear: all the letters from "The Others," I mean. At least the I LOVE SCOTT TO DEATHs were my own pure, honest,

5th-grade sentiments. They weren't doctored up and put through some psychic lens—I am not cutting the whole idea. I do believe in souls. But I respect them, and imagine their sole purpose of existence is not to satisfy the romantic yearnings of lonely high school girls. I don't need stories of past lives to decorate this one.

But someday, in five or ten more years, I'll look back on these high school books with the same forgiving nostalgia I have now for 6th grade.

I sure swore a lot though.

3/27/88

The students are back. I made baklava this morning, and Maggi is going to come eat some. She's so sweet. We're going to meet in Sayles every Friday at 1:00 this term and have tea.

I had crazy dreams last night. I was in the operating room with a woman who was my only doctor. She was prepping me, and even cutting my chest open, though it seemed to be happening to another body. I wasn't on any drugs, so when she gave me the ether, I was very scared. It's always so scary, because that's your last conscious moment, and you might not wake up again. But you're on a river, and you can't stop and you can't go back. I kept trying to relax and think about how happy I was going to be when it was all over. I tried to say the

Lord's Prayer. But I was still so scared. I still am. I'd like to say I could do it drug-free, but that opening morphine always helped so much before. That's the hardest part to think about now: the prep-time. I don't really know why I'm so scared. I'm not afraid to die. But I just love my life so much.

3/28/88

This evening, I brought S. and Fred some baklava. We talked for a while, but I wasn't sure if the big pauses in the conversation were natural, or hints to leave, so after half an hour, I started to go. Fred said "But didn't you just get here?" So I stayed for another hour and a half. We talked a lot about the Jr. Show prize money. Fred wanted to know if they should just give the money back. He said he felt like he was betraying people by voting for one and not others. It was hard though. We talked about divisiveness. I don't know if we reached a conclusion, but it was nice to discuss my feelings with him. He says there was an art prize in his school and he didn't get it. That fact is oddly cheering.

3/29/88

First day of Dad's history class. Halfway into it, Dad broke down and announced the presence of his daughter, as I was distracting the hell out of him. The lecture went more smoothly after that. I've spent most of the day in the 16th century going from reading to reading.

God—I'm glad I'm not taking any other classes.

I had more weird dreams last night. Another recurring theme: lesbianism. Why? I am in these dreams, quite passive about it, though, as I told a woman in another dream, "Sure, but I might break up with you for a guy." I wish I knew what this meant.

I saw Devin today. He came and sat by me in Sayles, while I was reading *The Lisle Letters* and talking to Andy. We had a great talk for 30–45 minutes about Art, Life, Language, and Other Things. I love what he brings out in me. I feel so completely challenged and yet capable when talking to him. I do like him. I don't know that I love him or just his after-image.

3/30/88

My dreams were a little mellower last night, so I felt calmer today. I did dream I went back to seeing my therapist Susan. I wonder if I should. I don't want to. Maybe if I get so I really can't sleep. I just like being able to do this alone.

Saw Devin again today. *Quelle Semaine.* He came over to see how far I'd come in *The Lisle Letters*. We talked for about 15 minutes about Harlequin romances, "National Hospital Stays on $3.00 a Day," and food. He declined my offer of baklava because of the calories. I'm sorry, but where baklava is concerned, we waive calorie concerns.

Sue S.[46] met him and talked with us. She thought he was blowing me off. But Dad was eating lunch next to us, and he thinks Devin likes me.

This is all completely ridiculous. It doesn't matter if Sue's right or if Dad's just saying that. So long as I think he might like me, I'm happy. False reassurances, please!

3/31/88

There was a full moon tonight. Sarah and I went out for coffee, and after I took her home, I just walked outside and sat under one of our trees and watched the moon. It was so dark and peaceful, I felt like I might think of something important, something that I need to help me deal with this impending surgery, this chance of death. The neighbor's pretty dog found me, however, and insisted on accompanying me on my vigil. He was distracting, but I don't think I would have found any answers even if I had remained there alone. I just sat and watched the moon behind the black lacy tree branches. Moonlight seems to give me strength when I look at it. I wonder why. It's odd: the night feels so much blacker this year. When I think back on last year, and my heartbreak, the night becomes at once more purple. Sorrow is a warmer color than death.

I really don't know if I'm ready. I was imagining the beeper going off on a date a few weeks ago, and I took

46 Jen's roommate fall term of 1987

it farther than I ever had because I wasn't just getting in the car and driving off into the sunset—I was at the hospital. So there I was, reassuring everyone that things would be all right, which got me so alarmed and scared that I could barely get to sleep. So now all I can think about is the prep time. Will I be iced up enough? I guess maybe I will. At a certain point you just stop thinking that there is even the remotest possibility of death. All the reassuring, I guess, kept me nervous. But now, when I think I have put away my fear, or at least my thoughts of death, I have crazy dreams and know that I must really be scared.

I feel like I've thought about death and life as much as I can, but it keeps coming back to me. Partly I think it's because everyone around me expects me to be thinking about it all the time. That must be what they mean when they say, "She's so brave"—why haven't I fallen apart from thinking about death? I don't know. We all gotta go sometime. Numbers and odds don't mean all that much—I could still get hit by a drunk driver on the way to the hospital. If I lay up nights thinking about that, they'd think I was crazy.

Right Now I'm Stuck

4/1/88

Obsession

My body wants only one thing now,
your skin against its lips.

Night after night it stares in the dark

aching, inconsolable,
its throat a cage of tears.

And see where it haunts the parapet

begging for deliverance,
threatening to jump?

Well let it. People don't die from this.

—Judith Hemschemeyer

That poem was hanging up in Boliou. I liked it because it looked like something I could have written.

4/2/88

I had dinner with Sarah. She's lusting after Devin from my descriptions of him. She's not in competition though. I think it's just sympathy lust.

We had a great dinner. All of a sudden, things are good again. She seems a lot mellower and I know I am. I think we must have just both been too stressed out to deal with each other last term. I'm so glad we're friends again.

4/3/88

Sarah and I may be on again, but Gretchen and I seem to be off. I suppose it's only natural, since things were perfect for so long, that there be some sort of rebound. But I hope this doesn't stay. I wouldn't want to lose her friendship. Tonight we didn't seem to have much to say to each other, but last term we had so much—it can't all have gone away.

Well it's bedtime now—I can escape into the world of fantasy.

I want spring to come
I want to lie in the sun
I want to wear my sarong

I want to watercolor again
I want to talk with him
Just talk
All the time
That would make me very happy
(So long as there was still room for more)

4/4/88

Well, it got up to 72 degrees today. I sat in the sun and did a watercolor . . . I think I'm going to have a party on the deck when the weather gets warmer. A Beeper-Tempting Celebration, if you will.

4/6/88

I just got back from *Mona Lisa* with Sarah. I guess there was a hero. It was all about prostitution and that world and it made you think. I, theoretically, consider that prostitution should be legalized. But when you're forced to *see* what goes on, it's really hard to stick with that.

4/7/88

Spring is sprung. The grass is riz! I wonder where the cute guys is?

It got up to 78 degrees today. So Sue S. and I went sunbathing. Spring is so hard. It makes me restless. I feel like I have to be out all the time.

4/8/88

Just got back from the Rueb[47] with Sue S. We got dressed up in our black minis, black tights, high heels, and contacts. We were a little over-dressed for the Rueb, but it wasn't too big a deal. We had fun. I'm still dizzy, but I managed to drive home.

I was down today. Thinking about school and all the classes I'd be taking if I were having a normal term: Printmaking, Mixed-Media (with Raymond Saunders[48], who wants to road trip to Chicago over midterm and then FLY to San Francisco!) and Physics 20. God. I just can't think about it. It's so depressing. I'll take Printmaking with Sue H. next year. I'll have two more spring terms at Carleton to road trip to Chi-town, etc. It's okay. I can still have fun. Sigh.

But I meditated this afternoon, and while I was doing that, it came to me that I have to spend more time at Boliou. Mom met Raymond Saunders today and says he's wonderful. She told him all about me and he really wants to meet me and for me to join the class. I'm going to talk to Dad about doing the 5-page paper to cover everything I've learned, since I'm not doing the final paper. I'm leaving the Sayles Scene and going back to being a Boliou Bunny. Yay!

---

47 The Rueb 'N' Stein, a bar and restaurant in downtown Northfield
48 Visiting faculty in the art department at Carleton

4/9/88

Went to Boliou today and started a painting. It's bad, but it was fun just to work. I'm trying to do that one about the night sky last spring and I'm starting to wonder if maybe my canvas isn't just too small. It's mainly colored crosshatch marks. It looks like one of Mom's color projects. But maybe I can get it to work.

I went to visit Tim today. He was sitting in the little space between his bed and his bookshelf listening to tapes. He was happy to see me and hugged and tickled me. We played about ten games of Uno. He always seems resigned when I see him there. He did a little at home too, I guess. He doesn't say anything, but you know something's going on inside. I wish he could talk more. I always feel like I'm patronizing him when I talk to him, saying stupid little things to try to draw him out. Mostly, I feel I'm talking for my own amusement—he's quite content to sit with me in near perfect silence, broken only by his stopped-up copy of *Sweet Baby James*. I wish he could tell me why he fucks his tapes up like that—what does the rhythmic destruction of a tape by pressing the "Record" button over and over again do for him? He obviously enjoys it. Maybe I should buy him a rap tape.

It's so easy to slip into a sci-fi/fantasy notion that maybe Tim is part of a group of scientists from another planet, and he can't communicate with us, but he's sending complex messages across the solar system or maybe to the future. Or, more realistically, what if he possesses a totally different kind of intelligence that we don't have the power to tap or comprehend? Maybe in a thousand years, people like Tim will be highly sought after to do some job that we couldn't even imagine now, like the Navigators in *Dune,* who were constantly doped out on "The Spice" because it increased their powers. To us now, they'd just be a bunch of derelict drug addicts. Is it just because he's my brother that I think all this? I swear the light's not dull in his eyes—just diffracted.

Bob, Tim, and Jen

4/10/88

I feel like shit today. I'm terribly tired when I go to do anything, but I know I won't get to sleep for hours.[49] I feel restless and tense, which could be dissipated by a long walk if I could fucking take one.

I weighed 110 today. I promised myself if I got under that, I'd go back to Susan.[50] I don't want to. But I haven't made any effort to help myself. What would I say to Susan if I went back? It's just me talking, which is why I always feel I could just as well do it alone.

I'd tell her how fucking depressed I am about classes. That just sticks in me. I'm so disappointed that I can't go to Chicago and San Francisco with Raymond Saunders. But I'm so used to making do with shit like this that I can't even let myself work up a good cry about it. I wonder if that might help? I just rush in to think about the good side—two more spring terms. Graduating with Sue H. Maybe she and I will road trip to California our senior year. Hell—maybe she won't come back to Carleton next year, but I need a good fantasy and this is one. I'm well aware that the fun I'm missing this spring isn't the last fun in the world. I'm just oscillating between disappointment over the immediate fun and anticipation for the future. 'Cause right now I'm stuck.

---

49 Wakefulness at night can be a sign of worsening heart failure.

50 Jen's weight was a source of constant concern. If she lost weight, she wasn't eating enough; if she gained weight it was possibly a sign of fluid retention from heart failure.

I went to figure drawing today and did a painting. At the halfway break, I cleaned up, because I was getting tired. There was a girl in the studio with a Joni Mitchell tape—*Clouds*—but she had left. After I finished cleaning up, she came back in and put on *Blue*. Then the model came in and lay down in a really beautiful pose. But I was tired, and I had already cleaned up, so I left in a funk. I didn't want to go home either, so I sat under a tree and read.

Nothing I can do today can cheer me up, but that's okay with me. I like being depressed once in a while. It's a break. Otherwise, happiness gets to feeling brittle. I just don't like the tension. It keeps me awake.

I still don't understand why Mom doesn't like my self-portrait.

4/11/88

I taped *Avalon* today. I took it in the car and drove around tonight. I pretended I was walking in the arb. It's sexual music, but it makes me happy to hear it when I'm alone too. It makes me feel sexual. It makes me feel positive. It makes me see what is beautiful in the spring.

4/12/88

I got a crackpot letter today from some Carleton alumna who thinks my heart problem is from "bad feelings."

She was a Spirit version of a Christian Scientist and was worried about the "vibrations" of my donor heart not synching with the "vibrations" of my body. She even wanted me to send her money, so that she could send me some sort of technique, for dealing with my current heart, or for getting my new heart to match up with the rest of my body. I can feel sorry for this woman who feels so powerless in her own life that she has to reach out to strangers to offer "help" that they don't need or want. It's insulting at first to have someone like that assume that they could have power over you, but she seems weaker after I think about it. She can only see a superficial weakness in my life. She can't comprehend that suffering equals strength. She sees my situation only as a foothold to get power for herself.

I was at Raymond Saunders's mixed-media class this afternoon when I read the letter. I told myself this morning I didn't need to go back into therapy. But the letter stressed me out so much that the world tipped again. It hasn't happened in a while, but joy of joys, I found out I'm not the only one. Both Mom and Sarah say they have felt similar things. Mom says she lives like this. God! How can she stay sane? My short-term memory goes all to hell. Images and thoughts from dreams and forgotten memories pop into my head. I can't finish a sentence. It's like a migraine with no pain. Just a total time-out from life.

I am definitely going back to Susan.

4/14/88

Sarah and I have been having a lot of really good talks lately. Unfortunately she's decided to take this term off. She's going home Monday. At least I'll have time to write her. And the inclination.

She told me tonight that Gretchen felt smothered by me at the end of last term and the beginning of this term. Gretchen told her in confidence, but Sarah felt I deserved to know, and I agree. In fact, I'm not hurt about it, except that I wish Gretchen would have told me herself. It's hard to say, I know, but Sarah and I agree that Gretchen was probably suppressing part of her personality to be with me—or anybody. That she goes in cycles of pushing herself to please someone and then burning out on them. It's kind of odd. I was so happy with her because I didn't suppress any of myself to be with her, but I didn't look to see if the reason why things were *so* comfortable was because she was suppressing *her* personality to be with me.

Oh well, we'll work it out.

4/15/88

I talked to Gretchen a little today. It was rough though. I feel hurt from what Sarah said. And I felt really awkward because I kept feeling like I was tagging along and being annoying. So I sat in the Cave[51] with her and

---

51 A student-run nightclub on campus

didn't speak my mind. I can't get mad at Gretchen for not being honest with me, if I can't be honest with her . . .

I don't like being depressed any more. I'd like to move on now. I'd like good things to happen in my life.

Maybe I'll just curl up into a little ball and hide from everybody. Gretchen and I have nothing to say anymore. Sarah's leaving. I don't need money. I don't need health. I don't need job security. I don't need balanced meals. But I need friends. Sue S. still likes me. And Jessica. And Maggi. So there.

4/16/88

I figured out today what it is I like about Sue S. She's the only friend I have who actually likes herself. She likes her body. She's proud of her accomplishments.

We went to the Rueb tonight and then to the Co-op dance. It was hilarious! We went 'cause it was Pat's debut with a campus band and I promised I'd be there, but we stayed 'til midnight. We just sat and watched people.

4/17/88

Evan[52] just called. Actually, he called in the middle of Sarah's goodbye party (she leaves tomorrow—waaah!), so I called him back after it was over. We talked for over

---

52 J.B.'s high school friend who met Jen when she visited J.B.'s home town

an hour. It was weird. He makes me feel young. I'm not old enough for that to be good, either. He's still very immature. We're friends but we have that added dimension to remember and joke about. Romance allows for faults—you can have had a crush on anybody and it's forgiven because—hey—it was a crush. He's fun to talk to and the electricity lasts a while. When we saw each other last fall, the sparks flew. At the same time I saw just *how* annoying he would be to go out with. I think I might write him, but I don't know if I'll ever see him again. He does everything he should, and hates it. He doesn't have the guts to break out of his mold, so he calls me up every few months and says racy things to make himself feel like he's got some excitement in his life.

I can't believe Sarah's leaving tomorrow. I'll be so sad without her. She took me to *The Unbearable Lightness of Being* today. It was an artsy movie about a bunch of young, attractive, sexy people in Prague in the '60s. It had many sex scenes, but after a while, you got used to them, and they didn't seem at all offensive. They were all so artistic and passionate.

4/18/88

I saw Susan today. I almost started crying when I told her about Sarah leaving. I was sad today, but I'm getting over it. Gretchen and I talked some and it was a little less awkward. We have a dependency situation built up though, which should be discussed.

I saw Andy when I was leaving Sayles. He wanted food, so I talked him into driving to Tom Thumb. He bought bread and apples and then he bought me two Cadbury eggs. Then I drove him to Boliou. It was weird! He was being *so* friendly. I couldn't tell if he was flirting with me or not—he would stand close to me, but he never did anything overt, like putting his arm around me. He was just being friendly. And he's so cute. And he's Andy. Oh God. He kind of makes me feel like a kid. It's not a good, solid, intellectual electricity. It's a goofy sort of thing. Nothing to articulate. I couldn't even say what I want from him.

I'm happy again. I talked to Jay[53] this afternoon. Now there's a good intellectual attraction—unfortunately, no electricity. He's just *so nice*. I really really like him. Every time I see him I want to talk to him. I want to hang out with him. I adore his voice on the radio.

4/19/88

Showed some of my stuff to Ray Saunders today. He really criticized it. Looking at one piece—the abstraction I was trying to work out about the spring sky from last year—he said outright, "I hate that." I agreed. It didn't work. It was empty. I didn't want to sound like I was just agreeing with him, but he was right and I was glad to have him be honest and not talk about the color interactions and all that bullshit. He's hard to talk to, but he's honest and that

---

53 A history major in Jen's class

makes up for it. I'm really supposed to do what I want, not just some empty gestures after some vague idea that I think might be what he's looking for. He makes you search yourself. He makes you think. It's wonderful!

4/20/88

I'm so tired! I just got back from a comedy/hypnotism show where a guy hypnotized one of my friends to run up on stage and pretend he was a famous dancer from LA. I laughed so hard watching him strut his stuff that I was really afraid I might hurt myself.

4/21/88

Went to the Walker Art Center in Minneapolis with Ray and his students today. We sat in the private collection room listening to a lamp post with a degree in art and a heart for business talk to us about the pulse of art in Minnesota as we looked at new, uncatalogued art. This sent me off into a dream world about the future of my life in the art world. I hate going to private rooms and looking at collections. I'm glad some people like to do it, but I like art on walls . . . my life's work going to various drawers across the country isn't really what I had in mind.

4/23/88

Quel jour. I just got back from a birthday party where I danced—yes, danced—with Devin for maybe half an hour. He was kind of doing the I'm-not-interested dance—looking away a lot. And I was wearing my black mini and everything! Then he said he should go home and didn't take the ride I offered. Oh well.

Before that, I was at Ann Marie's, talking to Alex.[54] It was good. He seems to have matured some. He's still vaguely cute, but, he has a girlfriend—yay! No worries there.

I spent this afternoon in McDonald's having a heart-to-heart with Bryce. He modeled for me for the BDAG[55] poster. So I bought him a hamburger. And we talked for an hour and a half. He's nice. We talked about life and then me a bit and then he starts telling me his life story. It was nice that we were talking and he was opening up and such, but in the middle of it, a friend's cartoon about dealing with the male ego—"If you don't mind, I'd like to go on about myself at great length now"—flashed through my head.

4/24/88

Oh wow—eight-year anniversary of the First Mayo Surgery and we didn't even notice.

I talked to Susie and Sarah K. tonight. It was so good to

---

54 Ann Marie attended the Summer Writing Program with Alex and Jen.

55 Black Dramatic Arts Group at Carleton. Jen continued to work part-time for the Carleton publications office.

talk to Sarah. We analyzed everybody and just talked about people, relationships, and life.

I also talked to Alex and Jay Barry (Prof). What I really want to know is if Alex's lost it yet, because I just can't see it. His girlfriend graduated and he went with a different girl last year and he is a wild college boy of the '80s now, but still, I can't see it. Maybe his new girlfriend's a real take-charge kind of gal. I can tell by looking at him that he still kisses the same way.

4/25/88

Dad said last night that I'd probably wait 'til I was about 23 before finding another "right" relationship, because now I'm looking for an adult, and all the guys here are looking for freshwomen or sophomores. This doesn't really bum me out, though. In some senses, it felt exciting—two more years of freedom! I guess I still have enough negative memories of J.B. to make me tense about relationships.

But 2 more years before getting laid again—Oh God!

4/26/88

I had egg rolls with friends tonight. I hung out and did a watercolor before dinner. It was fun having some place besides home to go.

I just started writing about where I'd like to be. It's basically a description of me living alone in a studio apartment, doing art all the time. It's very poorly written, but it's something to think about. I think that maybe if I write about what I'd like to do, artistically and otherwise, it'll help me realize it and make it real. Ray's taking off for a few weeks (including the Chicago, SanFr Bash—waah!) so I've got to just do work on my own.

4/28/88

Louise and Michael[56] were just here for dinner with their daughters. It was really nice. Louise and I talked a little. I feel a kindred spirit in her. I feel as though we look at our art the same way. When she gets praised, she gets shy and tries to bear it out. As opposed to Michael, who can never get enough. Their daughters were the hit of the evening, as far as I was concerned, though. They are both so beautiful. And so nice. They fit together like pieces of a puzzle. Dad says they must be each other's world. We had a wonderful time playing with them while Michael and Louise went for a walk. They ran around the house, screaming and giggling. Then the three of us sat in the TV room and made playdough animals. I think I will have kids.

Sue S. and I lay out today. I didn't get too tan, though. She started to burn, so we went in before I could get toasted. Sue wasn't feeling too good, as she was still recovering

---

56 Louise Erdrich and Michael Dorris had lived in Northfield for a year in the mid-1980s.

from her typhoid shot yesterday. Then we went to Dairy Queen and had hot fudge sundaes right before dinner.

Sue's leaving tomorrow for a Geo field trip. The Art Cabal leaves next week. Midterm break's this weekend. I'm still haunted by images of travel, but I'll survive not going anywhere this year.

4/29/88

A Good Spring Friday! Wasted the whole day out in the sun with friends. I got up at 8:oo a.m. to go print Cats[57] with Fred. We had a conversation! Maybe the prof crush really is dead and gone, because I felt a lot easier talking to him. Yay!!

Talked to Matt—he wants to NUDE MODEL NEXT YEAR! OH MY GOD!!!! FIGURE DRAWING *EVERY* NIGHT! I was just looking at him in History and thinking that he had really cool muscles and bones and that I'd oh so like to draw him. But you can't just say "Hey, baby, you should be in sketchbooks," so I just thought of it as a crazy dream. Oh say it could be true! Oh!

What was that I said about no sexual feelings for models? Okay, maybe not *during* the drawing, but *after*. Let's, uh, review these sketches, huh Matt?

---

57 Prints of "Sybil"

4/30/88

Gretchen and I should talk. I spent a lot of time around her today and I kept getting the feeling she thought I was just hanging on her. Even if she doesn't think that, we should talk so that I won't feel that way any more. I went to the Cave tonight and she was there. I was really tired, so I was thinking about going home anyway, but if it'd been anybody else, I know I would have stayed. Pat was playing and I gave him the drawing I did for the Fish logo. It was his idea: a guitar that, in 3 steps, turns into a fish, but I really got it well and I was proud of it. He liked it lots. I should get a new T-shirt out of this.

I had the craziest dreams last night. Oh my God. My hormones were really raging.

A Way To Respond To The Beauty of It All

5/1/88

May is here. The best month of the year. Months always go by so fast. I have to be careful of my tendency to try to slow the march of time in the spring. In some ways, that's why I like winter. It's much more relaxing. You're not out constantly trying to make good use of the days. You just sit back, knowing that spring is on the way.

I wrote Traci, talked to Riccardo, and worked on the BDAG poster. So I've felt pretty introspective. I don't know what I'll have left to say to Susan tomorrow. Riccardo's going up with me, because I still owe him lunch from this winter.

Maybe I should appropriate a corner of the drawing room at Boliou. I could have a studio. I couldn't paint in the nude, but I could paint at night more. That's my new excuse—I can't work because I can't stay up late. Well, I only have to be up on Tuesday and Thursday mornings, so I should just rearrange my schedule. I just finished working on the BDAG poster, so I won't be sleeping for a while. Sigh.

5/2/88

I turned out to have quite a bit to say to Susan today. We talked about dreams, the beeper, and sex. She's seen *Wild Thing*, so she knew what I was talking about.[58] She says I am a "wild thing" and am having trouble dealing with my restrictions.

5/3/88

Gretchen and I went to the Big Steer[59] tonight. We talked!! It was really nice. She wanted to spend time with me tonight. We managed to get on the subject of us. Now I'm afraid she might think I don't want to spend as much time with her—but no. I told her how much I cared about her. And I told her how much she helped me last term. It was good. We were honest—or at least, I was. I think we can be mellow friends now.

---

58 *Wild Thing* was a 1987 movie about a child who witnesses a crime.

59 A travel plaza restaurant on the freeway interchange outside Northfield

5/5/88

I'm lonely. I think that's why girls chase boys. I'm just lonely. I have lots of friends, but they're all scattered around. I want a roommate, or friends on a dorm floor, or a boyfriend, or a place where I could go to see people always. Sometimes Sayles works. But not at night, usually. And what I want is someone to talk with, not just prattle.

I sat outside tonight with Gretchen and her Friday crowd while they made fun of everyone they could think of. I felt kind of sick afterwards. Maybe that's why Gretchen never invites me to join them on Fridays. They seem like the real "Carleton elite" to me. They're either friends with or cooler than every big name on campus. They just strike me as so ragingly insecure. I have decided to quit not saying hi to people because they're not "cool" enough, or whatever. I really don't give a shit if the Friday people want to talk about me. I take my value from myself, and if you don't have self-validation what do you have? I have no desire to go through life looking at the world from a close-minded, petty, defensive point of view.

Matt's girlfriend's name is Julie. Sigh.

I tried to do art again tonight. I need some new canvases. I just can't seem to do anything. I want to paint Matt. God—ever since he said that about modeling, I've been fantasizing about drawing him. I want to go all over his body. I want to use every medium I have. I want to explore the texture, the color, the shape. I want to do to Matt's body what male artists have been doing to the female body for centuries. I want to explore all the sensual possibilities of two-dimensional art. I want to do paintings that will make people question my relationship to the model. I don't ever have to touch a model, but he should be someone who I could fall in love with.

5/6/88

The Print Sale started today. They've sold about ten so far, four of which have been mine! I'm so thrilled. Talk about external validation. Internal validation may be the main thing, but it's impossible to live without a little from the outside too. Maybe I can make it as an artist!

I have to stop looking at the No-Devin-No-Matt situation as a No-Boy situation. Bryce certainly likes me as a person. Nat and I are going out Monday, though Sarah K. assures me I have nothing to fear. Edwin and I are going to buy each other flowers next Friday because we haven't gotten any all term. And, of course, two of my Ex-Boyfriends are making noises in the Get-Back-Together direction. None of these things makes for serious possibilities but I am not manless. I hung out at Happy Hour today and Jay is acting less shy.

As Sue S. says, it takes a while to get back into circulation. Things are beginning to warm up—they'll get hot soon.

5/7/88

$150. I sold about $150 worth of Prints at the Sale. The last time I was up there, I had done over 1/3 of the prints sold. I'm so happy I can barely think about it. Modesty clamps down right away when I mention it to anybody. But here I don't have to worry. People like my stuff! I'm good! I sell! I may have a future in the Art World! People like my stuff enough to actually plunk down enormous amounts of money for them! I could be an artist and not starve to death.

5/8/88

I had a good day today. My horoscope said (oh God— she's back to the horoscopes!) that expanding my social circles would cure my loneliness. Well, it did. I taped my Buckwheat Zydeco record this morning and was so excited to drive around and listen to it that I went out to Farm House.[60] This guy Dan was really interested in the tape, so I brought it in. While we were listening, I was looking at his record collection. He has some great stuff! He's going to lend me a Professor Longhair album in exchange for Buckwheat and S. African Zulu Jive. And we're going to do a radio show next year!

It started to rain while I was there, so I offered Joseph[61] a ride when he said he wanted to go to Hattie's.[62] We both

---

60 An off campus student house
61 Another Carleton friend
62 A coffee shop in downtown Northfield

got totally drenched running from the car to the building where we found two cups of cappuccino—the most amazing substance on earth, elixir of the Gods. Joseph and I had a great time. He's fun to talk to. And so cute. He has a girlfriend, but he still flirts.

Tonight I went to Parish House to borrow a list of Country Music Quotes. I took them to the library, copied them, did my closed reserve reading, and brought them back. I hung out at Parish House for a while, and went to Study Break.[63] I hadn't been to a Study Break in a long time. But Study Break itself is a pretty boring occasion. And then, the local Republican Contingent brought up the Handicap Access issue. The same people who were just bitching about how the college wasn't spending enough on sports started bitching about how $250,000 was a lot of money to spend on a handful of people. "Let's be realistic here." I was so mad. Actually, I kept calm while I was there. And I argued back. But hindsight always sees things more clearly and I kept (keep) thinking of all the things I should have said.

5/9/88
The day started out all gray and with half a headache. I kind of stumbled around, running errands. I went to Susan, came back, went to Farm House. Dinner was good, but rushed. The concert was *great*, but I was

---

63 Students in dorms and campus houses met in the lounge for a study break around 11 p.m.

furious at Nat on the way to and from. He doesn't like to hold the steering wheel. He figures it's not important to drive straight so long as you're between the lines. This would be bad enough in *his* car, but *mine*? The opening act was pretty good and then Steven Wright[64] came on—worth every penny of $20.00—and he reminded me of where I first heard him and of the good times with J.B. I wanted to talk to J.B. and tell him all the jokes and make nice. (Not make up, mind you, just make nice.) But I didn't.

I dropped Nat at Boliou and went to Sayles. Bryce was there so I went over and talked to him while he played pinball. Then we walked to the PO when Devin came in. I waited until it seemed like the right moment and then, sure I would be rejected, suggested we all go to the Steer. They were in the car in a flash (especially after I said I had money).

We had the greatest time! When we got our plates of eggs and grease I said, "Well, I don't have to worry about my arteries. I'm getting 'em all replaced." Bryce laughed and said, "Jen, I love you."

We were there for 3½ hours. Occasionally they would wax literary and drop names I never had been exposed to, but most of the time we joked or discussed ideas. I was kind of sleepy, so sometimes I felt a little dumb. And I'm an Art Major. I don't know, I always wonder if

---

64 A comedian, actor, writer, and film producer

it's a little residual sexism. Am I socialized to acquiesce? Are they socialized to pay me less attention because of my gender? Well, I felt pretty equal, so whatever it was, it wasn't too bad.

5/10/88

I just got back from a lecture by E.P. Thompson on "The Sale of Wives in the 18th and 19th Century." It was really interesting. I found out who Thomas Hardy was (*Mayor of Casterbridge*). Bryce and Devin were talking about him last night. And I learned about Relativism—a term for historical analysis which could also well describe my position on Art. It allows different points of view, while still maintaining the individual's perspective and set of standards. That's it! That's what I spent ten weeks looking for last term. All we did was the first part—undefining Art. But if Art is everything, Art is nothing. And to leave it there is to do what Alan Bloom believes divergence from the Great Books will do—cause widespread decay of standards. As my father maintains, Bloom is wrong, artists cling to their individual integrity. A defensible theory may be respected and tolerated, but we are not required to agree.

I wish I'd had that to say when Devin and Bryce found out what Ray's doors[65] went for and wanted to "get in on the racket."

---

65 Raymond Saunders created mixed-media art on wood and doors.

5/11/88

I finally made it for figure drawing. It was really good even though it was a female figure. I did 2 paintings, which weren't bad. They made me so tired, though.

Then I came home to finish my African Film Series Poster. I only had two days on this one, so I don't hate it. I won't get to sleep for a few more hours though.

I was happy today. I hung out with Kris. I bought new shoes: cute little black flats. I wore my contacts. I don't know why I feel so happy sometimes. I drove around the arb with Buckwheat Zydeco blaring at 5:00 in the afternoon and racked my brain for a way to respond to the beauty of it all.

5/12/88

Three-month beeper anniversary. Whee. Three more to go for average.

Kris and I went out for dinner. Then we went to the Senior Art Opening. It was *really* good—a lot more consistent than last year. Everyone seemed to have put a lot of work in. Dan's was the most sellable. I really liked it, but I felt it was completely unchallenging. It seemed so attractive that it made me nervous. I wanted to find a reason not to like it.

Nat's piece was a triptych. He had 2 other pieces but they

were hardly noticeable next to the triptych, so although I know he put a lot of time into it, he seemed under-represented. The triptych was a monumental collage of magazine photos, pictures, drawings and some objects. The inside was very finished and impressive, very well combined, but the outside seemed just pasted together. He had a very nice representation of the globe, but the magazine pictures pasted around—some from *Penthouse*—just floated there. They didn't seem to be fitted in at all. The *Penthouse* pictures were especially shocking—I just can't imagine Nat looking at those things, much less buying a magazine like that, even for art. Collage needs a lot of work to remove it from the realm of grade-school art, and while he made it on the inside, the outside was disappointing.

Andy's stuff was also rather disappointing. I liked it while I saw him working on it. But it all looked the same on the wall. I think he overworked it. He just kept going over all these paintings until they all seemed to be at the same temperature. Also, I think I'm just not on his wavelength. I've never really been able to get into his stuff.

Kevin, on the other hand, I can identify with. He did a series of portraits which were pretty good. In some ways they seemed as pat as Dan's, but because they were faces, they had more of a message. He did a lot of work, I think. I'm not in love with his style, though. He's so tight and controlled, and I can feel that come through in his work. His paintings have a preponderance of solar yellow, fuchsia, and lime green, which I find hard to bear.

5/14/88

Yesterday: parents left for cabin, Taj Mahal concert, got home late, didn't write. Today: spring concert, retro '60s minidress and love beads, much fun and some dancing, barbecue, many strangers, general enthusiasm.

5/15/88

I was a wreck all day today. *No* energy. Tim came for dinner, but had to play Uno with Gretchen because I had to nap. Gretchen also brought Dan and I just wanted to be alone and veg out.

The beeper went off today while Kris and I were home.[66] I knew in my brain if it were real, they would have called the home phone, but still, we had to call to make sure. It was so terrifying to actually make that call, the one I've been thinking about for 5 months. The one I've been planning, wondering, Will I lose it? Will I be stoic? Will I be "brave"? Will I be excited? Will I cry? Will I flinch? Will I be strong? Will I be weak? And the answer is "Yes." All of the above. I tried so hard to be calm and brave and I was terrified. There it was, in all three dimensions— that afternoon, me, heart surgery, hospital, operation.

---

66 Kris and Gretchen were staying at the Bonner house while Jen's parents were away. Jen arranged for friends to stay with her in case she got the transplant call.

I knew it was probably a false beep, so I couldn't get excited, couldn't get my hopes up. Calm, resolute, only paused once as I dialed the phone. But after it was over, I went upstairs and cried.

And no one understands. They all think it was "Oh, just the battery going dead. No big deal." They don't understand that for five minutes, I was on the road to surgery. They don't understand what that means. Gretchen said, "So, do you really not want to have it?" I don't know anymore; doesn't the imminence of an operation, which you have a 12% chance of not surviving, give you a good enough reason to freak out? Odds don't mean anything to me anymore. Do people think, since I've been waiting for months, that I'm ready?

Oh, I know the answer already. People don't think.

5/16/88

Thank God for Susan. Not even my *parents* gave me the response I expected. But if you're paying somebody $80 an hour, they tend to be extremely sympathetic. I was a pile of tenseness on the way up there. I don't really know why and even though it felt like a good session, I was still tense on the way home.

Not tense now, though. Real drunk! Fun! Kris's birthday today, so I made her a "Love Delegation" card which she loved. Then we went out to dinner with Gretchen.

5/17/88

I showed more of my stuff to Ray today and he pronounced it to be what it was: sketches. He comes down
hard against accidental occurrences in your work, which
is refreshing because you can't half-ass anything and
get away with it. And I never feel personally attacked by
what he says, it's just good criticism.

5/22/88

I didn't see any boys today. I painted. Which means that
I saw myself for the first time in ages. It was so fun. Just
to go to Boliou, play tapes, and paint. And not hardly
even think of boys. Gotta do that more often!

I smell like paint and completing a painting has created
all the right chemicals in my brain. My brain feels sati-
ated in just the same way my belly does after sex.

5/23/88

The night is purple-blue and soft, like cotton. It's so
dark, almost black, but bleeds out to clear white light,
with blue on the edges. I played Joni Mitchell and drove
around looking for the soft, peaceful places that make
me want to paint them, even though I could never do
it well enough not to look trite. The corner by Hard-
ee's and the R.R. tracks. The curving road between the
Rock Shop[67] and the 4th St. bridge. The reflection of the

---

67 A downtown Northfield shop that sold rocks, polished stones, and minerals

street lamps in the Cannon River and the surrounding stone terraces as seen from the 2nd St. bridge. The road by Tisdales[68] in the afternoon sun and in moonlight. Why do country scenes just seem so hopelessly overdone? Maybe I can do the Rock Shop Corner on a big canvas.

5/24/88

The best conversations are when things come spilling out like a stream and you keep thinking of new things to say and sidetracking so that it winds along leaving more unsaid than said. It has that feeling of richness from all those left-out things. Things that you could go back to some time in the future. If I could paint that . . .

5/25/88

J.B. came and talked to me today. His hair is long and curling and so is his beard. It was too long even for me. He is so gorgeous with a neat-trimmed beard. Still, he made my heart skip over once when he appeared. I must have loved him. We chatted for a while, and we're going to go to the Happy Chef[69] sometime. He's annoying to talk to, though. He patronizes me. He tries to put me in a box to fit into his world. Mom says we all do that to some extent, but I think he oversteps his bounds.

---

68 A Carleton faculty family

69 An upper-midwest restaurant chain that served breakfast all day

5/28/88

I painted today. I got an idea for my comps: Carving a life out of Styrofoam. We saw the movie *Diner* tonight about male bonding taking place in this wonderful, dirty, traditional '50s diner. Then we went to the Happy Chef. The Happy Chef is too plastic to have the inherent integrity of a diner like the Ideal. But the Happy Chef is cheaper and has better food and is open 24 hours. So we go there. So we make it our place. So it must change from a sterile-perfect-plastic world to a real, solid, maybe even dirty world. The organic must reclaim the formica. This happened in high school at McDonald's. Real human beings must take these plastic places and wrest them from the world of TV commercials, bright white smiles, and clean fingernails. That's why the smoking section of Perkins always looks better to me—it's dirty. Smoke has already started to discolor the Happy Chef's smoking section too. We've got to start spilling coffee on the carpet on our side. But even without doing that, I just want to paint the Happy Chef, the McDonalds, the McStops from the real person's perspective, from the grungy traveler's perspective. The Big Steer is not a chain, so it has integrity. The Happy Chef has bright green carpet and plastic souvenirs. It will take work.

5/30/88

I sketched at Happy Chef and Big Steer today. Dad calls this my "Diner Series."

Tim in the Bath

Sleeping Nude

Oil Self-Portrait

HEY BABY—
Wanna Make Love
in the Warm Rain
and order Some Daquiris
What? You're trying to
Quit DAQUIRIS ?!.

Card sent to Kurt

"It wasn't really that red—but it was beautiful" written on back of frame

Another card for Kurt

Highway 3

One of Jen's posters for the Carleton publications office

"A thousand points of light" costume

Jen's Elvis

Safety Valves

6/2/88

Tomorrow's my last appointment with Susan until after her baby comes. Wednesday's appointment was great. I didn't have any specific event to tell her about, so we focused on the tension and I just cried and cried and cried. I still can't believe I'm going in for surgery. Actually, since Wednesday, it's a little better, but I know it will get hard again. When I first came to Susan, I wanted to find the thing that made me tense, get it out and be rid of it. But now I know that tension, like anything else in the world, is cyclical—it comes and goes. There is no shut-off mechanism, only safety valves.

I'm listening to Suzanne Vega, the record that used to be my second skin, like *Blue* is now. It evokes those beautiful warm red and deep blue pictures from 5th Watson[70] last year, when I'd play it in the room to fall asleep. It is the hardest thing in my life to deal with

---

70 Jen's sophomore-year dorm floor

happy memories that I can no longer relive and happy times now that I know will soon be memories. Maybe as an artist, I can paint these memories and have them as tangible pieces. But I fight against the urge to keep scrapbooks. I am just happy to have the mental pictures. They don't take up any space, and they don't collect dust. I like memories as artifact if they're combined with some useful function, like a song that others can listen to or a painting that people can look at. But wilted prom corsages? Ick.

6/3/88

I have a migraine and feel all bubbly.

Tomorrow's the big Sangria fest. I sent out 45 invitations, inviting people to come burn down Bob Bonner's house.[71] Mom was looking askance at this.

Had my last appointment with Susan today. I didn't want to get intense so soon after Wednesday, so I just rambled around and didn't say anything. She's going to send me a note when her baby is born, though. That's nice.

---

71 Jen created several invitations for the party. One read "Let's all go to Jen Bonner's house for a ~~Wild Orgy~~ Nice Party. We can all ~~burn Bob Bonner's house down~~! play musical chairs and Go Fish. Please bring ~~alcohol~~, food or whatever your Mom will let you. ~~Sangria~~ Strawberry Kool-aid will be served. ABSOLUTELY NO sin, decadence, or debauchery will take place."

6/4/88

The party was a raging success. At 10:30 p.m. we hit the Boliou fountain and I got to see Matt naked along with many others. A bunch of them streaked 3rd Hue[72] and then we all came back here for Kahlua and coffee. Several people are still downstairs, but I'm so tired. I'm going to try to sleep despite the noise.

6/5/88

Well, I'm still alive and am feeling okay despite the hits[73] I took out on the back porch. I can never really enjoy that—I always feel too worried that I'll hurt myself. I was coughing a lot after the fountain last night, so my lungs were a little sore tonight.

We're having a great weekend.[74] Kris fixed batter-fried chicken for dinner and we (Gretchen and Sarah K. as well) ate until we were nearly sick.

I've just been re-reading my diary from the Senior Art Show and the main thing I get is that I should paint more. I also thought I'd better add that I have since gone back and looked at Andy's paintings and I really like them. They're just hard to appreciate in an opening crowd that is more suited to art commercials or rock videos.

---

72 The third floor of Goodhue, a dorm

73 Presumably of marijuana

74 In part to give Jen independence at home, her parents spent several weekends that summer at the family cabin. Once again, friends stayed with her at the Bonner house.

6/6/88

Dad's 50 today. All his family's been calling.

I felt terrible this morning. I vowed I'd never smoke again. I couldn't breathe at all. I know it was tension, but still, it's not worth it.

Spent the day studying with Gretchen, Kris and Sarah K. And talking. And eating. I've gotten stressed out about my History final because I have a lot I could study and I didn't start soon enough to get through it. Oh well. I'll do okay, I think. I don't imagine I'd do worse than a B, and while Dad would love me to earn an A, a B will be livable.

I saw J.B. in Sayles and then he called later to say that I looked nervous when I talked to him. Now—do I need this? I broke up with him to get *away* from shit like this. Why can't he relate to me as I am? I just want to relate to him as a person, so I am never prepared to deal with his shit. I answer his question and then later think how I should have rebuffed the asking. I like talking to him. He's intellectually satisfying. But if he's going to be more trouble than he's worth—forget it. I always feel when I'm talking to him that I'm in a spider's web and these barely discernable strings are going around, pulling me further and further in. But I am not going out with him, so this is just a once-in-a-while irritation, not something that actually affects the way I live.

Jay dropped by this evening—I don't know if it was to
see Kris or me or both, but I was glad. I've got his address. I hope he'll write back.

6/7/88

Bryce and I had lunch with Gretchen and talked for
hours about Philosophy. He makes me feel really
self-conscious about talking a lot. I spent today feeling
like a dumb girl. Sometimes I just feel like my personality's so weak.

Why is it so hard to be myself? Why do I find it easy to
start saying what people want me to say, and hiding the
things they don't?

Kris took us all inner tubing down the Cannon tonight.
Unfortunately, the river does not follow the road and it
took us three hours to get to where Kris had driven to
find us (after getting out and hitchhiking back). Kris felt
awful—I was very cold and tired and she, of course, felt
completely responsible. But it all came out all right. I'm
really going to miss her.

6/8/88

I'm starting to look forward to summer. I can't wait to
get to Boliou and start working.

I dreamt about Kurt[75] last night. I was noticing the hair on his arms and there was such a strong feeling with it that I thought about it all day. Then I saw him tonight at Treats.[76] He cooks there now. He gave me a big hug and I noticed how big he's gotten. Oh Kurt. We should have gone out in high school. Maybe now. Maybe a summer fling? This could be a great bit of fun.

6/11/88

Graduation was so sad. Kris was almost crying all day. I don't want to be so sad when I graduate. At least I will have had an extra year, so I won't feel it's over too soon. I definitely want to get right out of town. No staying around getting nostalgic—I want to get out and get plugged in and get excited.

But I'm glad I get five years here.

6/12/88

Four months with my beeper. Is it about time yet?

I spent today painting at Boliou, listening to the Rolling Stones. This could be a great summer.

Kris would scream. They're playing Buddy Holly on

---

75 Jen's friend from the forensics team, three years behind her in high school

76 Breakfast at Treats, a downtown Northfield restaurant in the historic Stuart Hotel building

K102. I'm going up to see her and Gretchen tomorrow. Yay! Kris is so great. I've been trying to be low-key about her because I don't want to do the Gretchen-Crush-Burnout thing again. I'm not convinced she's God's gift to me or anything. But she is so much fun. She's not pretty and she talks on and on forever. Actually, once you get to know her, you think she's cute. But she doesn't project herself as attractive. Guys get to know her and fall in love with her as a friend. She is responsibility and practicality embodied. She is herself through and through and a hell of a lot of fun. She is decent, nice, and loving throughout every fiber of her being, one of the calmest and most guilt-free persons I have ever met.

6/14/88

Spent last night in the Cities at Kris's apartment. She invited me to live with her this fall, if I have my new heart. Except I wouldn't be able to take classes at Carleton and I'd be removed from the community. It would be fun to live with Kris and paint all day. (I'd have to get SSI[77] to stay alive.) But it could be really lonely.

Sue S., Gretchen, and Sarah will all be gone next fall. Who will be here to miss? Just the new friends I would make in their places.

---

77 Supplemental Security Income program through Social Security for disabled children and adults. In 1988 the maximum monthly SSI payment for an individual was $354. Jen applied for SSI after she turned twenty-one, but she had not yet been approved.

I had the weirdest dream the night before last. I was at Carleton in Parish House, but there was some sort of concentration camp/scientist type of power there, killing us to study our brains. I had been sentenced to be executed at some point and was dealing with it very straightforwardly. There was something about intestines and other minor organs showing up in the food and they turned out to belong to a guy who was sentenced to die, but was currently still alive. Then this guy seemed to be me because I was dealing with accepting the pain and the fact that I would have to try to live without these organs. Then I was resentenced and that was fine because I figured I wouldn't have to endure any more torture. A guy was in the parking lot crying because he was sentenced for the same time I was. I hugged him, but didn't cry. The idea of the dream seemed disgusting and awful but the point—the overriding feeling I got from it was the way I was dealing with the idea of death. I got this feeling of calm and strength from it. I don't think anybody'd have any trouble understanding where a dream like this might come from.

6/15/88

Naomi[78] and her husband Jeff are staying here for a few days on their way to Canada. It's nice to be able to have people stay without overloading the house like when Tim was here.

---

78 A childhood friend

I gave Dad the album I found for him yesterday, the original Band album. He was so excited. I taped it today, along with Joni Mitchell's *Mingus*, the Rolling Stones' *Made in the Shade*, and the soundtrack from *The Blues Brothers*.

6/16/88

Naomi and Jeff have been really fun. I've only seen Naomi once since I was 8, but our families were so close when we were little that we're like sisters. Naomi talks an awful lot, but she's so convinced that the entire world's in love with her that she's sunshine incarnate. And Jeff comes up nice every which way you turn him. Dad asked Naomi to give me some pointers on how to catch a guy like him.

6/17/88

I went to Sue's shower[79] tonight and we watched *Top Gun*, *The Princess Bride*, and *Dirty Dancing*. *Top Gun* (for the 6th time) was really interesting: Tom Cruise was a headstrong asshole, a ladies' man, gorgeous, unstable, etc. Not that the movie is in any way an accurate portrayal of life, but one thing it has to have is correct male/ female vibrations. Kelly McGillis is intelligent, quick, cutting, and beautiful. And if she had made the first move, she would have scared him off. *He* saw *her first*. A

---

79 Jen had three close friends named Sue. She had known this Sue since grade school. Sue S. was her Carleton roommate fall term of 1987, and Sue H. was a fellow art major at Carleton.

guy as unsteady as he has to feel in control. If she does all the work, he feels inadequate.

Sue's wedding shower was fun. I hope I get that many teddies when I get married.

6/18/88

Kris and Sarah were just down. It was nice to see them, but I'm glad I didn't go up to the Cities with them. I'm very tired.

I'm getting sick of the Diner series. Dad said Joe Byrne wants to talk to me, that he likes what I'm doing. That's nice to hear. I don't go to the Happy Chef any more, so it's harder to visualize. I brought my fuchsia pumps over to paint because I love them so much. I'm thinking of a large self-portrait with all those little things I love to look at: those shoes, my rolled-up jeans, my smock or maybe a different outfit and other things—fruit? Coffee cups? Naked men?

Maybe I should step back into my larger fascination with decay and organic repossession of human-made matter: houses, sidewalks, buildings, etc. That's why I like diners—I like taking restaurants out of their packaging and making them real. I've said this all before, but I have to keep reworking it so it will be logical and coherent by the time I have to write it out for my comps proposal.[80]

---

80 A comprehensive project or exam was required of Carleton seniors.

6/19/88

Went driving around tonight, looking for new things to paint. The air has new asphalt in it and it's saturated with heat. The whole thing just screams "West! Drive! Travel! Car!" to me. Every summer this happens. But now, since I can't even go to the cabin, it's worse. So tomorrow, I'll go sketch by the Super America on Highway 3. If I don't put the Cities in on the Highway Mile sign, it could be anywhere in America.

I feel clipped. So trapped. I'm going to explode. I just can't stand it! Oh GOD! I just want to *do* something— won't this goddamned call just come? Just let me fight. Just let me go. Let me do it—let me act! I'm seizing up inside at the terror that it might not come this summer. Summer's full of promise. So full of car accidents. If it doesn't come this summer, when will it come?

It will come. It will. Somewhere out there right now, eating, sleeping, drinking, buying a motorcycle, going on a date, swimming, being careful, acting reckless, is a 110- or 120-pound boy or girl whose heart sometime soon will be in me instead of in him or her. Somewhere right now, there is one person whose heart has my name on it. So I shouldn't be impatient. If he or she is so generous as to give me his or her heart, I shouldn't begrudge him or her every last day of his or her life.

I wonder who this person is.

I can't fantasize about a crush anymore. There always comes a point in a fantasy when I feel it's gone too far. Maybe I'm afraid to take it further because I don't want to start preferring it to reality. It's so removed from the realm of possibility. That always makes me nervous. I don't like the idea of setting up an entire alternative reality for myself. I like my life. The only things I'd change are my heart and my sex life. And they'll come in time.

God, it's so hot. I'd better not have any good fantasies tonight. I think I'm going to have to sleep with the door open.

6/20/88

I did a watercolor of the highway by McDonald's and the Super America at dusk tonight. The bugs weren't too bad, but I was a little afraid that some teenage boys might stop—or worse yet, overgrown boys, but none did.

I moved my studio into Nat's old space at Boliou tonight. I didn't want to before, but now I love it. It's my own little room, so it feels even more like my private space. And I have a table and cupboards and chairs. Oh—it's just great! Now all I have to do is finish this dragon that I was commissioned to do, so I can get back to painting highways and coffee mugs and my fuchsia pumps.

6/21/88

Just broke up with J.B. as a friend. I was happy about the idea of being friends with him. I actually started crying. He hugged me and his arm smelled so familiar—it stirred up memories I thought didn't mean anything anymore. Oh brother. But I like him. He's still intelligent, nice, and funny: my three big attractions in a guy.

Poop.

And we had a nice evening. I always wish there were some way to tell him what's wrong, so he could fix it all and we could get back together.

It's 85 degrees out. At 2:19 a.m. They say it might not break through August. They're talking about 1934. Dust bowl.

Why does it make me feel less attractive to know that J.B. thinks I'm beautiful? He's so insecure, anybody who is *really* beautiful is "out of his league." He could be quite a prize if he had a little confidence. God dammit. If only he had some confidence. And I could go back . . .

He's already retreating from the world. Holing up in his own single muddle. Of course, I'm doing that in different areas. I'd like to go out and take the world of boys by storm, but I no longer want to take the rest of it by the ears and turn it upside down. I just want to hide away and paint.

6/22/88

I have to call Gretchen. She wants to know when I want to come to their lake. I want to stay put in Northfield instead of chasing around after her and Kris. But it'd be fun to see Gretchen again.

I just got back from a video party at Rick and John R.'s apartment downtown.[81] It was fun. Except *Blade Runner* was the most sexist movie I've seen in a long time. Rick's a sweetie. Ever since sophomore year I've wondered about him.

Kurt called tonight. We're going to go to *Big* on Monday. J.B. says that it has one of the best sex scenes he's seen in a while. What am I getting myself into? What if . . . oh, I'm just getting neurotic. Kurt and I are friends and we can have a good time without anything extra. If something else decides to happen, we'll deal with that when the time comes.

He just turned 18. He celebrated by gaming 'til 4 in the morning. Oh God—he games. Well, he's a freshman. And this is a fling at most. Flings are allowed all the faults they want, so long as they're a good time.

I xeroxed the last story in Toni Cade Bambara's short story collection *The Johnson Girls* for Sarah. It's about these women talking about men and they reminded me of conversations Sarah and I have had. "Gotta get

---

81 Carleton students who were staying in Northfield for the summer

me a Blue Plate Special 'cause life's a bitch ala carte."

6/23/88

I'm so tired. I was out with Susie and Tricia at McDonald's throwing napkins when someone pulled a chair out from under my brain. So I have to write fast and do some sleeping soon.

I didn't paint much today, but I felt good in my brain because I wrote Sarah a four-page letter that flowed out really well and made me happy. Mom says I should xerox it, but there's just one part I really like, outside of the letter context, so I'll just copy it down here:

> *You are a passionate poetic soul who knows that you deserve love in your life. Everyone else lacks either the passion to understand my affection for being in love, requited or no, or the self-confidence to think that being in love is not just taking your ego out and wiping up the pavement with it—a thing to be avoided by the sane at all costs.*
>
> *Isn't it about time I got myself a healthy man instead of picking up these table scraps like I wasn't worth anything first rate? But what I chase is that spark, the intelligence, the raging and awesome power of a smart boy's mind.*

6/24/88

It's hot again tonight. Mom and Dad are sleeping downstairs. I can enjoy heat when it's natural, when it's just part of living in Minnesota in the summer, but this is the greenhouse effect, the result of our fucking up the atmosphere for 100 years. That turns it from an elemental challenge to the wages of sin, a sign of shame, the punishment upon all the earth for us overstepping our bounds and our role in the ecosystem. It's a sign of things to come. It's not just a chance bad year; it's something we have brought upon ourselves and it will only get worse.

Aside from ecological guilt, the summer is wonderful. My life has never before had so many of the right colors in it. I don't know why. This spring I would drive around at night and listen to Joni Mitchell and look at the deep blue of the night against the warm street lights and wonder how I could put it down somehow. Now I drive home from Boliou, listening to *Court and Spark* and thinking of red, and dark night sky, and black cast-iron railings, and somehow, in the heat, caught in the humidity, reflected in the streetlights, it's there. It's a start, at Boliou, where I am putting down some of them—the afternoon heat, baked asphalt, dead yellow grass, the traveling highway that I want to take but can't. That calms me. If I put one down, I can reach out and touch the other one. Maybe by the end of summer I'll have all of these down.

But I feel like I am starting to live how I want to live. I have my room, I have my food, I have friends around. And I have my studio. I know that's it. I knew I wanted one, but I never thought it would bring *this much* happiness to my life.

And Mom thinks I should be a writer. What do I write? Letters and journals. Essays. Articles? There are very few people who spark me, like Sarah, to write well.

6/25/88

I am up at Gretchen's cabin on Lake Minnetonka, listening to the roar of motorboats at 1:15 in the morning. It is exactly the same sound I heard in John R. and Rick's apartment above Division St. last night at about the same time. I have been trying so hard to find some way to share in Gretchen's joy over speedboats, but I cannot. I just *cannot*. They are everything that is bad about cars, stripped of the one aspect that makes cars worthwhile— usefulness. They are noisy, dangerous, expensive, hazardous to the environment, and a waste of fossil fuels. They embody everything to be loathed. What do you do in a motorboat? Kill fish? Scare birds? Pollute and destroy aquatic vegetation? Wake the neighbors? This is not a cabin on a lake—this is a cabin on a freeway!

We came out here after driving through low-income districts in St. Paul. Then, as we drove the boat through the channels under the highways, we saw groups of people on the embankments, fishing. They were all black. The people in the boats were all white. The people on the bank didn't look up at us. We didn't wave at them. To be surrounded by all these obnoxiously wasteful wealthy people trying to show off in front of each other and then running up against people who were outside of that system, people who might think of $15,000 as a year's wages, not a new boat, that just made me feel all the worse.

Not that I'm such a wonderfully moral person. I just don't particularly like speedboating. I love my car. And I don't need to drive as much as I do. I chop down trees for my paper and poison rivers with my turpentine. I enjoy two houses while millions can't afford one.[82]

6/27/88

It's 2:55 a.m., I just got back from my date with Kurt. We went to the movie and then back to his house for daiquiris. I thought, "Daiquiris, hmmm," but he took me home and I hugged him tonight. It was the right thing at this point. We've been friends for four years, so it's a little sudden to start a mad, passionate, physical relationship on the first date. But he said he'd call me.

I feel like a kid with him. I feel like I'm back in high school. It's annoying. I guess I'm just not sure what there

---

82 Jen is counting the Bonner cabin in Minnesota's Ottertail County that Bob and an assortment of friends built when she was in high school. At first, Barbara was incredulous that Bob wanted to complicate their lives with this project. Jen told them, "That's the first normal thing this family has ever done."

is to talk about with a recent high school graduate. But we had a good talk. I really do like him. Maybe I can just keep hold of myself around him and not feel like that anymore. Then maybe we could have fun.

Fun, as he says, is the bottom line.

He is a sensible boy.

6/28/88

I've been thinking about Kurt all day and thinking all goofy. Oh dear. It's a bad sign. It's just that when I'm with him, I feel like I'm showing off to my old high school self. I feel like I'm constantly under comparison. If I can just relax and be myself around him.

He did use the three worst words in the English language: "I'll call you." But maybe he's nice enough to actually mean it.

I drove around tonight and listened to *Avalon* to see if I could imagine myself with Kurt and that song. Kurt fit okay.

Went to the Happy Chef with Lisa tonight. She's kind of daunting—would never have become friends with her if she hadn't been Kris's roommate. She's so cute and popular—she scares the shy part of me. I catch myself thinking, "Oh, she won't like me. She'll think I'm a nerd." I just try hard to be myself around her and forget that. I'd like to make friends who aren't basket cases. If I can't get over the idea that I'm not cool enough or cute enough or flashy enough to be somebody's friend, I'll never meet any people who don't have some big weakness that makes me feel that they're my equal.

6/29/88

I spent the day in the Cities today. Mom had her therapist appointment at 9:30 a.m., then we had lunch at Perkins and talked and talked until our conversation ran clear and cold, all the rusty small talk washed away. That was enough to wear me out, but then I had an appointment at the U. I had a long heart echo with a very cute tech. Finally, I saw Braunlin, who always looks like she's been up all night worrying just about you. She said, "You've been waiting a long time," and other things to make me feel that I have every reason to expect that it will come at any minute.

I left with my thumbs tucked into my fists. I'd forgotten. I was so afraid that the transplant wouldn't come this summer that I just put it out of my head. Now I'm not prepared. I'm all scared again. I came home and took a bath. Then, lying on the bed, listening to the radio, I heard "Shining Star." It doesn't dissolve me like it used to, but I cried some. I cried to think that all the hospital terror that it recalled was up ahead somewhere, waiting to jump out at me from around a corner. And then it will be all down around my ears, all over again. All those forgotten things. Those little smells, the hidden pains, the doped-out memories I don't have of pain and things I really felt. The feel of wind on my face and hands as I covered my eyes and pretended I wasn't swinging past the yawning abyss of death.

All again. Where are my shields? Where is my armor? They're too heavy to haul around long, but I have to know where they are for when the trumpet goes. I'll be up there, sitting in a room. I'll be rock solid. I'll be ice cold. I'll be squeezed dry. Bright-eyed and practical. Quiet intermittently on the way up, squeezing the last of my feelings into the emergency storage boxes. No problem then. All my adrenaline a running current, keeping the lids shut on those boxes. No fear then—brave, charged through with electric wire.

I will be fine. I can do it. I am the Queen of the Hill. I am the toughest kid on this block. Nobody can push me down.

But oh—now how do I sleep?

I have to write again. It's bedtime and I need my unwinding writing. The last entry was at Happy Chef, writing to release the fear building up inside. It woke me up. Now I need a few sentences about mundane things to tie up the day and go off to sleep.

Okay, okay, so I have a crush on Kurt. And I want him to call me right soon. But I just saw him Monday. For a non-doped-up-on-love person, that should last a week or so . . . maybe I'll call him. I could stop in at one of his places of employment and just say hi. I'm actually kind of filled up schedule-wise, so maybe it will naturally wait 'til next week. I always get this silly pressured feeling that I've got to get hooked up soon so as not to miss out on any fun.

Baloney. Go to sleep. These things take time.

6/30/88

Tomorrow's July. Summer's really here. I'm afraid I'll get sick of *Court and Spark* soon. I love the fresh early days of anything: summer, school, a relationship. But they move on. I'm not sick of Joni yet.

I had a two-hour conversation on the phone tonight with Sue H. She is *really* bright. I connect with her in Art, but she's also fascinated with math and writing and music and life. I'm so excited. She's coming for lunch tomorrow. The sort of person I've been combing the earth for. And the girl I practically idolized freshman year. Now she's seeking me out. I don't want to go all to pieces now, but we just kept talking and talking on the phone tonight. I don't idolize her anymore. But she's a genius and she loves life. And she's here this summer and graduating class of '90 now, just like I am.

I went to Dunvegan's bookstore today to order *Sex Tips for Girls*. Ostensibly, I could say I did it because I didn't want to order it from Mom, but we all know it was to see Kurt. He's so cute. I love his hair; just a little too long but just exactly curly enough. And how he looks young but manly somehow. His face is boyish, but his shoulders are older, or is it just in the back of his eyes somewhere? I do have to get him to stop calling me Jenny, though. I think I'll take him to Happy Chef with Kris and me this weekend. They have the same color eyes.

While I was in Dunvegan's, I read one of the Sylvia cartoon books—cartoons about a fiftyish writer who is a feminist and mother, keeps cats, and takes baths all the time. Think maybe I should buy one for Mom. Except that I can't buy her a book from any place besides the Carleton bookstore if it can be found there, which it can. So I didn't buy the book but I told Mom to go read them when she was at work.[83] They're hilarious! I am once again inspired to cartoon. A fortyish to sixtyish feminist writer who lives in the Midwest and gardens all the time? Mother? Grandmother? College professor? I think I'm on to something. She would definitely be a list maker. If I do go into cartooning, I think I've found my direction. Thank you, Nicole Hollander!

---

83 Barbara managed the fiction section at the Carleton bookstore.

The Toughest Kid on The Block

"Oh those Friday night blues, they get in your shoes."
Country music is hilarious. Actually I had a very nice
Friday night. I called in sick to Sue and Stuart's rehearsal
and groom's dinner in hopes of preserving my strength
for tomorrow. Then I went to Boliou to paint a wedding
card for them. I'm wimping out in the present department and giving them a check and a card. But maybe
the card will be worth $5,000 someday. That woke me
all up, so I went by Kurt's house and talked to him for
an hour and a half. It helps to see him to tone down my
fantasies. I wasn't sitting there lusting after him. We just
talked and talked and before I knew it, it was 10:30 p.m.
And he said he'd call me and we'd watch a movie. I'd say
he means it—perhaps he'll redeem those three accursed
words in my eyes. He smiled big when he answered the
door. I have absolutely no idea whether he *likes* me or
not, but it's reassuring to know he likes me as a person.
I think I could go without a fling this summer, so long

as I could hang out with him. I'm just looking for some company.

Sue H. and I had a good time today. I gave her some of my little tubes of paint so she could get started. She has the most beautiful brown eyes. I always forget that when I don't see her. I like to talk to her and she's invited me to stop by her place, but I'm kind of afraid. She seems scattered—would she be able to deal with me if she wasn't in "Jen" mode? Then again, she's so mellow, she'd probably say, "Hey Jennifer, come on in!" and slap aside whatever she was in the middle of and give me a beer. I'd just like to get to know her past acquaintance-friend. Right now I feel like there's nothing really there, we just run into each other every so often. But that may change.

7/2/88

I feel like absolute hell. What was once a mere sore throat yesterday rose to my sinuses and is now in the process of annexing my lungs. My nose is raw. My chest feels thick. My body aches just slightly. This is July—what the hell?

But I made it to the wedding. I skipped the reception, but I'm really, really glad I went to the ceremony. It was beautiful. And I felt the weight of tradition, and the comforting web of community. Sue and Stuart's families and all of Webster[84] and all the friends I went to grade school with were there. I got tears in my eyes

---

84 A township near Northfield

watching Stuart watch Sue come down the aisle. I hope it works for them. It's easy to talk about weddings and marriages and divorces and everything, but those moments in the church seem so powerful, so holy. Someone Mom was talking to said that the trouble with Western religions is they separate out the holy and the spiritual from everyday life. I agree. If those few moments in the church could be extended somehow, maybe there would be fewer divorces. But maybe that's just a pat answer to a problem that will exist as long as we're human and another useless rule to apply to the patternless and changing music of life.

7/3/88

I'm taking my temperature while listening to Marie Osmond. Gag. Even country music has its low points, though it's generally all so similar that the low spots don't stand out as glaringly as they do in rock or pop. It's all silly, cheesy, and trite, so how do you tell the good from the bad? The truly awful is the best of all.

Well, I don't seem to have a fever, though I feel awful. I just meditated for the first time in four months, which was good, but not enough. I probably should go to bed, but I feel too bad to sleep. And Kurt is coming by at 11:00 p.m. Stupid? Company late at night while I have a cold? Well . . . we're just watching movies, so if they're not too funny (like the movie we just saw: *The Producers*) it's fine. And I haven't eaten dinner yet. And I can't sleep.

Oh, silly girl. Silly, silly girl.

Oop—now my temperature is 99.2. If I leave it in another five minutes, will it go up to 99.8? I can never figure
out how to take my temp.

No, it topped out at 99.4. Well, that's not good, but it's
not horrible, I guess. Taking horrible as anything over
100. But I am inviting company over? How awful—Kris
may have to live with this,[85] but poor Kurt shouldn't
have to be exposed. Well, I warned him on the phone
and I'll warn him again when he gets here.

I'm feeling a little better, but I think I'll stay upstairs
until he gets here. Save my conversation energy for company.

Kris and I are having a nice time, although I ask her to
move her coffee cups and not to put her feet up on the
counters, etc. But it pisses me off when she does those
things, so what to do? I like her because we can get into
good conversations. She has a tendency to repeat herself
on certain subjects, but there are always new subjects.
And she's thoroughly amiable, so even if I do annoy her
with house rules, I know she'll forgive me. And she is
screamingly intelligent, so I know I'll forgive her for being tiresome on occasion.

---

85 Kris was staying with Jen.

7/4/88

I still feel like absolute hell. I have been wondering whether this is related to the heart failure. I told Kris, it's like seeing a German movie twice: first you just follow along the action, the second time you start picking up on some of the lines. I wonder if this is the pneumonia. I've been on amoxicillin for days and it hasn't done a thing.

Kurt stayed until 4:00 a.m. last night. And he came back again today. I wonder if he might rather like Kris. She seems to have this appeal for younger men.

Well, she's invited me to bring him up to the Cities, so we shall see.

I'll call Braunlin tomorrow. Wonder if I'll be writing from the hospital next entry.

7/5/88

Nope, I'm still here. And although I still ache, am coughing up green phlegm and am blowing my nose a lot, the fog has lifted. I feel that untraceable spark of energy that marks the turning point in an illness. And my nose is blowing now with purpose—that wonderful feeling when you blow something out and the space is not immediately refilled with more. The wonderful feeling of being able to breathe with your mouth closed.

I did call Braunlin today, who told me to check in with Mellstrom, who told me that what I have is an infection, not related to the heart failure. So I got a new antibiotic, which I don't believe I've ever had before. I don't ever remember seeing a bottle with a picture of a hoagie on it saying "Take with FOOD." Kris felt obliged to reassure me about this new pill, saying she had had it many times and that it was a routine drug. I already have quite a stockpile of defense mechanisms, one of which is to play the role of the thrice-decorated-for-bravery, stiff-upper-lipped veteran—I don't want to be treated like a pansy, dammit! We seem to have a clash of defense mechanisms here.

7/6/88

This stupid pill is making me want to throw up. But aside from that, I'm feeling a lot better.

I went out to Sayles and Boliou just to get myself tired tonight. I slept all day, so I knew I wouldn't now. But it worked—I'm a wreck. I played Joni and drove to my painting spot on Highway 3 by the Happy Chef and the Super America, where I'm doing the picture. So it felt like summer again, though the change has come between beginning and middle. I knew July was about time for it, but it took the sickness. That broke the continuity. Now Traci's back. That'll probably change things too. Oh, Traci. She was by tonight and she can still make me feel small and silly, though probably it's just empathy. I don't know. She's very different. She's so very neurotic. Of the two, I think I prefer Gretchen. But then, they're both better than Kris the same time as they are worse. I wish Sarah were back. I'd like to know where she fits in. I think she wins, but maybe that's just 'cause she's away and I can make her how I want. Sue H. left me a note. Sue S. still hasn't sent me her address. It was good to talk to Traci.

All my friends . . . my crazy, mixed-up, brilliant, wonderful friends.

7/7/88

Sitting here now, after sleeping all day and going out to Dunvegan's tonight to get my book from Kurt, I feel well again. I'm still coughing a bit and hoarse, but I switched antibiotics again so my stomach is better along with the rest of me.

Oh, I hope I didn't annoy Kurt. I went there at about 8:30 p.m. and stayed until—oh God—10:00. We just kept on talking. I wonder what he thinks about me. I wonder if he even considers the possibility of me having a crush on him. He said he'd call me and maybe we'd do videos and daiquiris Sunday or Monday night.

I feel weird going for someone so young. I feel like I'm shrinking myself down for him. Well, he's a fun friend anyway. It doesn't have to be any more and we won't let it be anything that's not fun.

I'm just afraid that he's not ready for a fling. At that age I was all-or-nothing and he might very well feel that way too. I wouldn't want to corrupt him.

7/8/88

I'm so tense. I'm sitting here in a ruffled, floral patterned room with rosemaling[86] in a town that I have never been able to think of as having real beds. I'm at Rick's house in Rochester, out of range of my beeper. And it's home closet to all those creeping memories I can't quite recall and don't know if I want to.

There is nothing to be tense about. Mom and Dad have his number. If we get the call, they'll know where to find me.

I almost ripped my fingernails off on the way down. Even though the only time I've come to Rochester at night has been in an ambulance and we took a different route and I couldn't see anyway. Night driving is a little nerve-wracking unless you feel all loose, wild, and hell-bent for fun, which I can't now. Tied up on my leash. And it is Rochester. I was nearly sweating as we got to the 2nd St. exit and then, almost immediately, began to calm down as soon as we'd passed it. Night time in Rochester. I kept trying to think, "Hometown. This is Rick's hometown. We're coming *home*," but all I could see was St. Mary's. Hospitals. Surgeries. The times I've

---

86 Decorative Norwegian folk art

stared at death in this town. I don't want to go back. I don't want to stare at it again. It is hard, because the transplant won't be in this town. The old paths won't help. But I have only sunny memories of the U. And I know that some of the dark of Rochester will have to be there too. But I can't juxtapose the images because the memories here are too precise, like smells. You can't divide them up and apply them to other things.

7/10/88

It's 3:46 a.m. Yes, I had my date with Kurt tonight, though he doesn't consider it so. Oh well. We watched *The Big Easy*—which had the *hottest* sex scene—and we made two batches of daiquiris and talked about sex.

Perfect! Perfect date! And yet . . . ! AARGH. He gave me a wonderful hug good night. Mmm . . . Jen, stop drooling on the page . . . well, it never seemed right to do anything. Oh God, I told him about everything—everything! Every sordid detail of my life that could possibly be amusing, I told him. The talent show progressive, the game of "I Never." Oh, I can't even remember what else.

He's so sweet. He's nice. He's decent. He's a lot more mature than many guys my age. But he doesn't consider this dating. He's still taking these things very slowly— something I'm all in favor of, but . . .

But what do I want more than what we have? Just a kiss.

We get together and have a great time. All that's missing is physical contact. I don't even think I'd want to expand his horizons too much. Just kiss him.

7/11/88

I had a *wonderful* day at Boliou today. I'm working on the still life of my fuchsia pumps and the Old Milwaukee bottle that was called "For My Roommate Sue." It's losing that flavor now, though. It's steeped with me and doesn't remind me of Sue S. any more. I guess I'll have to paint her something else. Something crisper. Something raggedier. Maybe in oil would be better. Well, I have all the time in the world.

I thought up a good postcard for Devin.

Hey Devin—

Almost broke the coffee pot again tonight and thought of you. Hope your summer's going well. I just broke my Rolling Stones tape (Hot Rocks) from overuse. You know, you have the best musical taste of anyone I've met at Carleton. Take care—Jen

But I sent one to Kurt instead:

Hey baby! Wanna make love in the warm rain and order some daiquiris? What? You're trying to quit daiquiris?

Cynthia Heimel[87] says that when one is obsessed, one "composes and re-composes fascinating postcards." Sigh. Kurt knows Devin. He knows the (or one of the) high school girls he was going out with. He says he saw Devin in Dunvegan's flirting shamelessly.

Card sent to Kurt

7/12/88

It's almost suppertime. I'm recording a Band tape for Dad. Mom is grocery shopping. I have to write now because I'm losing my appetite again. Losing is the wrong word to use, though. I don't feel empty. I have the rising feeling of tension inside me. My nerves are tensed up into wires again. I had a nectarine with milk and sugar for breakfast. I had two open-face cheese, tomato, and ham sandwiches for lunch. That's not so bad. Except I

87 Feminist humorist and author of *Sex Tips For Girls*

didn't have lunch until 3:30 p.m. And the thought of carbohydrates slams my stomach shut. That's the sign that I'm tense—I am indifferent to doughnuts.

"The Weight" has come on now. The song is a Religious Experience. I don't really know why. It's the blues way of singing. It's those notes at the beginning on the guitar, banjo, or whatever. It's the piano thumpin' baseline. It's their harmony in singing. And then they go on—five verses? It's enough. It actually lasts as long as you want it to.

It's happy and it's sad. It's real life, like the Stones' "Can't Always Get What You Want." It's a true song.

And if I try, I can still see Dad drinking beer with his running buddies when I hear them. Dad, beer, sweat, Prairie and Wood.[88] Summer as a kid—hot and dusty in Old Green[89] on a gravel road.

So here I sit, nervous. Why nervous? I just get going all happy and it comes. Lots of friends and Kurt around, but I feel like I'm forgetting something. If I balanced my checkbook would I be happy?

Surgery? I didn't want to bring it up, so maybe that's the problem. Ugh. What else is there to say? Why am I always

---

88 A summer program created by Carleton students to teach grade-school kids about natural history

89 A 1968 American Motors Rebel station wagon

sick? I tell people I have pneumonia and they look at me like, "Of course, the Illness Girl." I didn't used to be the illness girl. For seven whole years I was lucky. (Funny, I don't remember fixing any mirrors.) I always feel like inside I am strong. Nothing beats me. But most people don't get into so many fights. Am I really weak on the outside? I've always hated being fragile. But I always have been.

Only half a year more—but no. After the transplant I'll be immunosuppressed. I'll be more fragile than ever. AAUGH! No, no. I can lift weights. I'll get tough. And I'll stop all colds so fast, I'll always be healthy. I'll be Healthiness Queen.

If I could run and run and go dancing all night, I wouldn't feel weak, no matter how many pills I had to take.

7/12/88 (second entry, later in the evening)
Heaven is 70 degrees at bedtime.

I came the closest I may ever come to making love to Roxy Music's *Avalon* tonight. I was out taking pictures to maybe paint from. I started at the Old Rock Shop Corner, then by Hardees, then Super America with the sun setting on it. I put in *Avalon* and went out on my old country road by Tisdales and Highway 19. There I started taking photos of the grass. Oh God! It was like painting when you get caught up.

I saw a beautiful ditch in the sunset, but didn't stop, so I went back later at 65 mph to catch it. But I missed the magic. Shot it and drove away like I'd just been spurned by Devin or something. Then I saw a better one. Purple clouds, orange light, blue sky, light green grass, yellow-gold grass, blue asphalt, all in bands on top of each other. And all the grass different shades, long and soft and waving. That's when *Avalon* came on, while I was out shooting up the roll. It was better than sex. I was so happy driving back. Relaxed, the way you are afterwards. The word "bliss," I think, is used to describe that feeling. My heart was singing and sighing at the same time.

Oh, it's hard to go down the country roads looking for beauty—you see so much, you almost hurt.

I hope those pictures come out. Pictures are usually flat and lifeless. Oh well. Maybe my memories can turn them into paintings.

Finished the Dragon for Doreen and made $26.00. And Mom says SSI said they'd pay me retroactively for the time they're wasting. My checking balance is under $3.00—my finances go up and down fast.

"It wasn't really that red—but it was beautiful" written on back of frame

7/13/88

This is for last night, because I left my diary downstairs and couldn't write. It was 4:00 a.m. when I went to bed. Kurt came over for movies. I think he's getting the idea. The way he was talking after we hugged goodnight. I don't know. Just something about our hug and the slight sort of intimacy afterwards. Maybe next week he'll kiss me. It would be nice if he made the first move. Then I wouldn't feel like such a cradle robber.

Last night, though, was weird. We talked about a lot of things, not all satisfactory. Why does rape always come up? I remember talking about it with J.B. They all have different reasons for not doing it. J.B. didn't want to get kicked in the balls, Kurt doesn't want to be disowned. I never understand these conversations. I just want to look at these guys and say, "Who are you kidding? You are far too nice to ever do anything like that. Why are we talking about this?" But I guess they're nervous. I guess every guy knows he has the potential to do it and it's scary.

We talked about me. And the transplant. And the doctor who told me that "80% of transplant patients live a year after surgery and the percentage goes down only a little each year after that." We talked about death and fear and life and happiness. But he didn't say anything about his dad.[90] I wonder if I should have brought it up. But I felt it was something he would have mentioned if he'd wanted to, so I should just wait. There was a point where he looked like he was about to say something. But he didn't.

He seemed younger last night. It made me nervous. I wondered if he was too young to go out with. Probably. But see, if he kisses me, then he wants to too, so it's not so bad. I'm starting to wonder if I like him enough to start it myself. He's sweet and nice and so cute. And very mature—for his age.

---

90 Who died when Kurt was ten

7/14/88

Mom thinks Kurt is a hunk. A cute, smart, sweet hunk. So, he's a little young? I've just been talking to Rick and John R. about the traumas of love. Rick is a happy person, except when it comes to love. Then he's as forlorn a romantic as they come. But at least I don't have to worry about whether he likes me or not—if he likes me, he'll wine and dine me. He's beautiful. His face—like an Italian sculpture. I kind of wish he did like me. The only doubt I have is that Rick's so nice, he has no mystery left. Somehow, Kurt is cute, sweet, nice, *and* mysterious. You know he's got a libido hidden away somewhere. Rick, I think, does too, but it doesn't exude any air of power about him. He doesn't have that confidence that you need to impress others with your sexuality. Even though I've talked and talked with Kurt, he still acts like he has a secret. Maybe that's what Cynthia Heimel meant about never talking about how good you are in bed. Preserve the mystery.

Anyway, after talking to them about the hopelessness of it all, the strength of my feelings for Kurt was renewed. He is happy and is maybe even getting the message about this thing between us. Maybe. Oh, I hope.

But even if nothing happens, I still feel good about him. I don't have that "all-pervading sense of doom" like I do with Devin (which signals obsession). I'm forgetting Devin. He's not happy. Not by a long shot. I am, from this point onward, never chasing anyone who is not happy. If Devin showed up with wine and roses, I would (and only because of the residual crush) go out with him, but I'd keep my eyes open.

7/15/88

I dropped in on Rich and Maggi.[91] I haven't seen them all summer and I was feeling restless, so I just showed up. They invited me in, gave me cookies and coffee, and we talked and talked. The oppression politics get on me a bit—they've got the good Carleton combinations of liberal guilt and yuppie possessions. But they're pretty thoughtful. I don't know how much of it is just a hostility release mechanism, but I imagine that's the part that annoys me. I consider myself a good liberal, though perhaps a bit apathetic. The cure for my apathy, however, does not lie in anxious pissing and moaning about liberal causes. If I have money, I'm glad to contribute it. If there's a petition, I'm happy to sign it. I should kick my ass and get involved in more things, or at least read about things so I know what's out there to do. But as far as daily conversation goes, I consider politics outrageously dull.

We talked a lot about art too, and I enjoy talking to Rich about art. He's down to earth. A lot of art people leave the English language behind, or they're so into a different scene that you have no common ground. But Rich and I actually had some things to say.

---

91 Carleton students

7/16/88

I saw Sue S. today. I may see her once again before she leaves for Nepal. It was nice, but sad. It was just enough to remind me of how much I'll miss her. There's something about her that's so comfortable. She reminds me of me. We like so many of the same things—we can just sit back and be. We'll agree on how we want things done when we're ready to do something. She's not witty and articulate and snappy like most of my other friends. But she's the only one with whom I feel the merging of ourselves; the only one I would ever care to lie on a bed with and kiss her hair. I really don't think I have any homosexual tendencies in me, but touching Sue has gotten past that hollow I'm-just-touching-a-person-because-it's-the-thing-to-do feel. I can't just touch people I don't know extremely well. But I know Sue. What is between us is calm, unspoken. Her touch has none of the thrill of a lover. It is through and through a friend's.

Dear Sue. Confused sometimes, but happy. She is my calm, happy friend.

7/17/88

Eight years ago today I had my last big operation. I got out of the car tonight, like I have so many times this winter, spring and summer, and looked out across the street. Each time it's like I'm looking through an invisible fence. How many more nights will I look through that fence? How much longer? How can it be that the transplant could come any day? How can it be that I could stare through that fence for the rest of the summer or never again? Maybe tonight? Maybe next winter? Time always seems continuous in retrospect. It fools us into thinking that it is continuous in the future too. Fools us into thinking that we can predict the future. Like the time I went crying into Mom and Dad's room because I thought I was going to die before fall because I couldn't visualize going off to college.

Now I search for foreshadowing in my life—a sure sign of doing too well in English class. I'm so goddamned scared of the transplant, but I wish it would just come so I could bite the bullet and get it over with. So I could have the energy to put behind my passions again. So I could GET LAID!

I'm tired of sitting around thinking about it. Addressing my anxieties. Trying to conjure up the face of death so I can give it a steely look in the eye. I'm tired of chasing my fears with a magnifying glass, tired of playing encounter group with myself. I don't want to know what the fuck is hiding in the dark. I just want to have the energy to kick whatever it is in the teeth and go back to bed.

I am having a fine summer though. If I weren't horny all the time, I could forget about this waiting more often.

7/18/88

I feel like myself sitting here in the cool air that's outside right now. It's rare in this summer heat—so stimulating—like cold water. I feel like it's a fall morning up north and I'm in a red plaid flannel shirt smelling wood smoke. That feeling clears my foggy brain. Even now it's shifting, but for a second, I was on top, right there, reading last night's entry, thinking about Kurt, basking in the cool air and my long-sleeved night shirt.

Kurt brought it on—thinking about him. A pattern is emerging: I see him, think "no," think "it's never the right moment," think "maybe this just isn't right." Then he leaves, and, desperate for someone to dream about, I start thinking about him. He's a good jumping-off point.

Tonight I don't think he's "getting the idea." Though we spent a large portion of the evening engaged in tickle fights, there never seemed anything more on his mind. He is oh-so-friendly, but that may really and truly be all there is. Oh, maybe, maybe, maybe. But maybe it would be wrong. I can be very honest with him, but I never feel like quite myself. Though at this point, I feel it's mainly because I'm trying to hide the fact that I might be interested in more. So I think—maybe I should talk to him? But no! I don't want to *talk* about it. I want it to just happen, that's so much more fun.

Sample conversation:

"Kurt, I've had a crush on you since high school."
(pause)
"Oh really?"
(blush, look at floor)
"Yeah, and so, I was wondering if maybe you'd make my dreams come true and give me a kiss. Just one, that's all I ask."
"Are you serious?"
"Uh huh."
"Well, okay. Let me finish my daiquiri."

Hmmm—maybe it would work. Maybe I should try it. I brought up the "Jenny—I just want to bite your toe" event from high school, but to no avail. Oh, it would probably never be the right moment to bring it up. And if I did, and if he kissed me, he'd probably follow it with,

"So there's your kiss. Happy?" or something even less romantic.

7/19/88

Sue H. wanted to know what happened last night, and when I fessed up the tickle fighting, it did sound a little suspect. Tickle fighting is *always* a bad sign. (Or a good sign, maybe we should say.) But there I go again, doctoring it up after the fact.

I had dinner with Maggi and Rich tonight. It was so

good! They're sweet. Sue H. came by and watched *The Man with Two Brains* with us (bleah! cheesy!). Two women I completely worshipped freshman year, and they think I'm cool! Maggi doesn't believe I thought she was cool freshman year—I told her kind of joking and she said, "Oh yeah." It's still weird that these girls a) like me and b) don't know how cool they are. They do have egos though. They do and they don't. I don't know anybody who is *completely* secure.

Wonder when this damn beeper's going to go off. Kurt said "It must be hard waiting" again, like he did last time when we talked about it. I didn't take it this time; I had nothing new to say. But sometimes I think, "What if I die from the surgery?" Then every extra day I have to wait is another day of life. So I can't get too impatient. And I can't shut my life away until post-op.

But I would like to have sex again. Lift weights and learn how to run in high heels. Paint enough stuff to have a decent postmortem retrospective. If I could choose my poison, I'd like to keel over on my feet after printing for five days straight—either from exhaustion or passing out into a pan of turpentine after staying up 'til 5:00 a.m. too many nights in a row. Fucking to death would be fun, for you, but your partner? No—uncool. I'd prefer work-related caffeine poisoning. None of this heart shit. I'd rather die as I lived. It would seem more fitting. It would make sense. If I die from this surgery it would be like being nipped in the bud. "Oh Lord, don't let that cold wind blow 'til I'm too old to die young." (Country song on the radio right now.)

7/20/88

Country music may be cheesy, but adults sing it. It's real people trying to make comfort out of real lives. Pop music is preteens trying to make a perfect world out of nothing and styrofoam.

Growing up is the process of seeing through all the myths adults feed us as children. Why do they do that? Are kids really unable to deal with truth or does feeding them the straight truth take all the fun and point out of growing up?

Happiness. That's the big bug-a-boo, myth, star player, leading role on everybody's mind. Every movie I watch seems to center around it. When I was young and uncomplicated, I decided that that was the meaning of life: happiness. And I'll stick to it. It's a hard enough question to require a simple answer. You can't think too long about it. But I'm tired of theorizing about it. Seems like everybody's for or against it. I don't know how you can be against it, but so many people are. Misery is inherent in humanity but everybody still fights over their claim to it. The rich insist that they're just as miserable as the poor. Whites cry that they're as victimized as blacks. Men scream that they're just as stereotyped as women. Who fucking cares! We're all miserable! Everybody has a different situation and a different capacity for misery. People are happy if they feel they have some sort of power over their lives—maybe. I don't know. People are happy if they realize that everybody is miserable and they might as well play the cards as they lie.

I just watched another Mickey Rourke movie about a brilliant alcoholic poet bum. I love movies about people living lives I can't imagine and couldn't stand and they're happy anyway. This rich magazine publisher "discovered" him and fell in love with the romantic genius that she knew lurked underneath his unwashed hair and unshaven beard. She was the child of the Carleton English department: beautiful, innocent, self-righteous, loquacious, and dumb. Mickey Rourke went back to his alcoholic girlfriend and spent the $500 she gave him for his story on "all my frennnds" at the bar the next night.

It was an interesting dramatization of the old starving, crazed, bohemian artist myth. A man who wrote out of his drunken despair with only the occasional thought of postmortem discovery. No romance, no fame, no beauty, no love. Just bottles and bars and backroom brawls. He was happy, but not in the lusty way we want to imagine. But living life as he chose.

7/21/88

Kris and Gretchen are reentering my life. Kris today, Gretchen tomorrow. We (Kris and I) had dinner with

Fred and S. tonight. It was much easier than my previous dinner with them. Fred and Kris talked about music all night and Kris led the conversation everywhere it went. Then we went to the Rueb and ran into Bryce. I did not want to deal with Bryce. The event at the Rueb was a history discussion with Dad, Rick, John R., and Susie. Bryce did not belong. Neither did Kris or I really. I was there to listen and Kris was an unfortunate accident of circumstance who ended up transforming the discussion into a tirade against a professor instead of a discussion of history. Bryce was quickly bored and left. I resolved right away not to try to make him feel welcome at the expense of my pleasure and pride. I think perhaps he has an idea now of my waning feelings for him. I just don't want to deal with one more personality bulldozer in my life.

We stopped in to see Kurt at Dunvegan's today. He was adorable, as always. We ran into J.B outside and J.B. tried, as always, to leave his personal agony in a heap, much like a dead bird from a cat, in front of my feet.

7/23/88
I'm so tired. I just got back from videos at Traci's. J.B. was there. I watched him during the movie. He is still cute. His body—he may be pudgy, but he is strong. And he has such a cute ass. And he wants to get back together so bad. It's like a vacuum cleaner. No, a flame to a moth. A black hole? So attractive in one way, but once I get inside, so bad.

What a shame. It's odd, because if I had just met him, we might get together. And it might not be so bad, because we would dig a whole new space for ourselves that would fit our new selves. But getting back together means risking falling into the abandoned mine shafts of our old relationship. AAAAAAaaaahhh! Co-Dependency! Guilt! Dishonesty! Lord Knows What Else!

7/24/88

Joni's on the radio!! My new semi-oldies station is playing "Help Me" from *Court and Spark*.

I'm writing early tonight, because I have a date with Kurt and I know I'll be too exhausted at 3:00 a.m. to write. I'm really tired now. I've been doing stuff all week.

Pat called this afternoon. It was wonderful to talk to him. I like to have a conversation once every month or two with him. If it's infrequent enough, he really focuses on you. If it's all the time, you get sick to death of personal anecdotes about people you've never met. But Pat's a sweetheart and he does like me. I can't imagine being in love with him—I can't imagine the feelings I *know* I had for him. It was all in my head. He reminded me of someone I liked in my imagination. I wonder how often this happens?

I wonder if this is happening with Kurt? I got off the phone with him this afternoon, once again reminded of the real Kurt, as opposed to the guy I think about at night. Kurt is swell, but he's only going to get better. Maybe we won't go out at all now but in 5 years we'll get married. Three years age difference matters now but later, no one will give a fig.

My heart feels big and shaky. It makes me tremble inside. Ugh. Maybe I'll come home at 2:00 tonight.

4:00 a.m.

Kurt's so lovely. So nice. So utterly nifty. I seem to like him better at his house than at mine. Maybe I'm just sick of my house. Maybe he's slightly more comfortable at his.

How can this be? How can I have energy? He's one of those magic people who can give me energy. It was a wonderful hug goodnight. Very long. And he put his forehead against mine afterwards because I was falling asleep against him. He even said I could collapse on his couch if I wanted, but I knew I was too tired to do that! I'm going to need to sleep long and hard this morning.

4:15. a.m. I'm finally sleepy.

7/25/88

Kurt took the girl he works with at Treat's cliff jumping tonight. I am *horrendously* jealous. Ooo—what if she has designs on him? She's older than I am! WHAT IF

SHE KISSES HIM?! Oh Kurt! No! No! No! Think of me, Kurt. Our friendship is stronger. Isn't it? Kurt, give me one more chance. Don't give your heart away.

Don't be interested, What's-Your-Face, girl that Kurt works with. Don't be forward enough to actually *kiss* him. For God's sake—he's far too young for you. Kurt, prove me right and be shocked by her if she tries to kiss you.

He tells me he's not dating her either. I refer to her only as What's-Her-Face, so he knows I'm jealous, but he thinks I'm joking. Hahaha, I laugh ruefully.

7/26/88

I am utterly exhausted. I just got back from the Twins game with Rick, Kris, and a nice art history major. I feel tired to the point of pain. I'm too enthusiastic for my physical capacity. Baseball's really fun live, though. It has a rhythm. I would love it if I could just let myself go and get into it. I had to stop cheering after the second inning. Rick is the perfect person to go with—he keeps you completely involved and informed.

I bought Kurt some more rum today. He's going to come by at 4:00 or 5:00 p.m. to pick up his rum and say good-bye.

Kurt isn't going to lose his heart in North Carolina. If it's not right to kiss him tomorrow, don't push it.

7/27/88

It wasn't. When I'm with him, I still act like a kid. Only now it's because I'm in love with him. I hate being in love and feeling like I have to be able to fit inside somebody. That's not what love's about, but it's how I always react. It's not right of me to get involved with him if it's in a way that will make me hate him later.

Kurt's leaving is a blessing to me. Time to pull back into myself and find out who I am before I push further into a relationship. This is long past a fling—I want to give this every benefit I can.

If I painted him, what would I paint? He is dark brown, but with light blue eyes. They are calm and small in his face. His glasses stand in front of them. I think they're too thick and dark, but they're almost right. I wish they didn't block his eyes so much. He is growing a soft beard that I am falling in love with as much as the rest of him. His features seem somewhat thick, but he has a magnificent jaw line underneath them, which his beard accentuates.

He was at my house today, and once again, seemed younger. In his house, he has purpose. In my house, I am still trying to follow him around. I do not have purpose. I have surrendered myself to him, hoping that he will love me for it. But if he loves me for that, I will quickly hate him. I must get my purpose back. Then we will not have to be so confused.

I watched *Apocalypse Now* and *The Mission* with Rick and John R. tonight. Both wonderful, disturbing movies involving lots of pointless bloodshed based on real situations—Vietnam and the conquering of South America. It's hard to accept things like that, but it seems that is what humanity is all about. The struggle of people trying to occupy themselves while they live out the lives they don't even understand why they have.

7/28/88

Kurt's gone. I'll fantasize about him so much, he'll be all blown out of proportion by the time I see him next.

How can I tell Kurt I love him? I always imagine it, but it always feels different when I'm with him. Honest discussion? Clever line? Heavy, blunt object?

7/29/88

I need to get back to work. Traci's coming over to make batik tomorrow. That counts as art. I'll go buy lots of dye and go crazy. And I shouldn't feel so bad about my output. One intense painting over a summer isn't so bad. If I can finish the big one of the highway, I'll have put a lot of work into it. And I've done other things. Hell, it's more than I've ever done in a summer before.

7/30/88

Sue H. and I are going to get married. She's staying here this weekend while Mom and Dad are at the cabin. I can barely write. It's 12:30 a.m.—we've been talking intensely for 3½ hours and I've been up since early this morning. I guess I'm tired because I batiked this afternoon. Whew! My hands still ache.

Sue H. is wonderful. God, I almost feel sexually attracted to her. She's comfortable like Sue S., but intelligent and articulate too. Sue S. is intelligent, but she doesn't rush to think about things like Sue H. We just had the best talk in the world. I feel like I'm going to pass out. We really connected. I mean purely. Like a beam of light. I hope I can sleep.

7/31/88

It hit 105 degrees today. Forty degrees Celsius. What a summer. I'm not as sure as I was earlier that it's all the greenhouse effect. The entire decade of the '30s was like this and worse. Minnesota gets the greatest extremes of temperature in the world.

I said some important things to Sue H. last night. Some things I'd been thinking about for a while. Like how external everything is to you—being handicapped, female (colored—I imagine). How you're still yourself inside, while all these things happen to you and you adjust. But when you're too tired to be yourself, like at the Twins game, like late at night, laughing with too many friends, like in bed when I want a good fantasy to lull me to sleep, *that's* a handicap. That and nothing else. Physical obstacles you overcome. Catastrophic events you deal with. But your personality—that is you, that is your center. No one should have to lose that.

"I Can't Get No Satisfaction" is on. Kurt wrote that down as my theme song in high school. Good Lord. What's my *real* theme song? "Leg"? (This is my diary—I don't have to be modest here.) "Wild Thing"? "Help Me, I Think I'm Falling In Love Again"? Who cares? Did I mention that I think I'm in love with him?

Sue and I watched *9 ½ Weeks* last night. Mmmm! Gorgeous movie! Diary of a sick, sick relationship and an evil man—but oh, did they have good sex! And so beautiful. It was—the whole movie—like an especially good MTV video. If Kurt likes watching movies with good sex scenes, I'll have to show him this one. Ooh boy! Wonder what he'll say about it?

Maybe the phone will ring tonight and I can get fixed up and start truly appreciating my hormones again. Oh please . . .

Another card for Kurt

Awash in Adoration

8/1/88

Kurt gets home a week from tomorrow, I think. Sue H. and I are still having a ball. I almost told Sue today how much I idolized her in freshman year. I don't think it would go over right yet. We're working so hard to get each other to like the other—it would just sound like more butter. Also, I don't think she'd believe me. She's insecure—she's asked me to marry her about a million times. I hope it's just part of the initial nerves. Right now, we're quite happy, but kind of tense. I have to remind myself that I don't have to do anything extra to express my affection for her—I like her enough—it will come out. I keep wondering if I should touch her while we're watching a movie. Then again, I should be careful—she was touching me somewhere tonight, on the leg, I think, and I got a little horny. She says she likes to flirt with women and I wonder if she's flirting with me. If I had to pick any woman to "mash" with (her term), it'd be Sue H. Maybe I am bi. Maybe everyone's bi and it's just a matter of conditioning and mellowness. That makes some sense for me—life without penises would be a sad life indeed. Well, being bi means you don't have to give them up to fool around with women.

Still, I could never see lesbianism as more than a wild, drunken, one-night stand with an otherwise friend.

8/2/88

I feel restless, frozen in time. It's finally raining, but muggy and sticky. Mom got back tonight with Grandma, Grandpa, Dave, Diane, and Toby.[92] I was supposed to cook dinner for them, but Sue H. and I went to the Cities and didn't get back until 7:30. My excuse was the tornado warning that had us in the mall basement for half an hour, but we know what excuses are worth. I just wasn't thinking. And I didn't remember how much I'd missed them, how much I loved them all. God, it's been so long since I've seen them. I shut it out of my heart because I couldn't go up north with them. So I blew them off. I could have hauled ass to get back home, but Sue H. and I were having a good time and I thought they were staying the night.

Now I'm so tired, I'm mixing my memories with old dreams and I can't remember which is which. I just want to curl up and cry. I miss the family. I always loved going

---

92 Bob's parents, brother and his wife, and their son joined the Bonners at their cabin to celebrate Bob's fiftieth birthday.

to Powell. I always loved having everybody around. I did my best to shut all that out so I wouldn't miss going to the cabin this year, because I knew I couldn't go. If I had gotten back just a half hour later, I would have missed them all together. Mom would have been mad and I wouldn't have cared.

I keep trying to focus on the benefits of this surgery: the time off from school, the extra classes I can take, etc. I do my best to shut out the negatives. I mean, I had myself convinced, utterly and completely convinced, that I was having just as much fun, if not more, with Sue H. here this weekend than I would have had with all of them. I mean, I really do like Sue, and we did have a blast, and this weekend was probably a major building block in our friendship. *But*, I love my family. I feel so isolated from them. We *never* see them. Our very lifestyle is a denial of the importance of family—we're so solitary and cut off out here in the People's Republic of Minnesota. But there's a basic love and bond—almost as basic and invisible as the fear of death—the love of family. Both quantities I cannot measure. I can only feel around the edges as I surprise myself by crying endlessly over some unexpected event or thing.

8/3/88

I wrote them all apologies today, and have put my conscience to rest on the matter.

I'm starting to feel energy again. I wonder if the cycle is turning again. I wonder if I can think about Kurt tonight. It's *so* annoying to be so tired that I can't even work up a good fantasy. They're usually the best soporific.

Ann, Mike, Kate, and Robin were here tonight.[93] Kate no longer goes by Katie and it seems awkward to me. Maybe it's just because she's only 13. The "ie" is so inoffensive, so easy to say. I know "Jen" is more awkward than "Kate." I signed the cards to the family "Jennifer" and generally expect them to call me Jenny. You can't change your name to your family.

I see Susan again in two weeks. What the hell. I can feel the tensions growing again. I told Sue H. that in a perfect world, therapy would be covered by insurance as part of the transplant experience.

I just finished a comic book *The Watchman* that dealt with this idea of a perfect world. I hated that comic book. But I couldn't put it down. It was violent, sexist and far too black and white for my tastes. But catchy. Like advertising, I suppose. Impressive, mind catching graphics—but overall I hate the style. Maybe it was because the women's breasts were larger than their heads . . .

---

93 Bob's sister and her family

8/4/88

August is the tail end of summer, tagging along behind June and July, and crushed under the impending weight of September, school, and fall. It just seems odd, when re-reading a diary entry, to find it from August. September a little too—because they're from the beginning of the school year. Like Sue H. and I were talking this afternoon, about the beginning of life being like the beginning of a strange movie; you can never remember the first few scenes by the end because you were so busy taking in new information with nothing to associate it with. Just so, the beginning of the school year. So, having a record in a diary, it is amusing and unreal to go back and read sentiments you barely remember feeling.

Sue H. and Mom and I went to the "Sculpture Inside and Outside" exhibit at the Walker today. I have never seen that much good sculpture all together in one place—never that much good *art* all in one place. It was exhausting. Especially because it was sculpture: you get assailed in all your senses. It was wonderful: a large ocean buoy covered with dice; a tiered circle of flowers, stones, and moss; an installment of wrapped, organic, dark—almost moving—reclaimed garbage; a harpooned piano. Oh! So much stuff. So much *good* stuff. It's a feeling. How to explain what good art is? It's not a verbal communication, so it's hard to write it down.

One piece was a metal shell of a face with a six-foot mesh extending behind it, and intricately connected, tiny objects suspended in the mesh. It was marvelous though, because it was so similar to what I've thought about people and their lives and their minds. He got the essential in his piece: the little bits suspended inside, and the area extending beyond the physical form. When I hear of massive disasters, I pause and imagine that many people with all their lives and promises and ideas. All their memories and images. Everyone has seen life differently. Everyone has different visions of beauty inside. This vision gets deadened in most people. I wonder if children's creative urges could be sustained. And could our society handle the results? There's an awful lot of bad art in the world as it is. Or, if our natural creative responses were nurtured, would we all create good art?

8/5/88

If we all created good art, we'd have to change its function in society. Competition for gallery space is bad enough now.

Been thinking about Kurt again. Too much, really. I'm back to my urge to put him above me. He's too young to put above me. I do not have to become the Incredible Shrinking Woman or put him on a pedestal. Good grief!

Sue H. blew off going to a movie with me tonight because she was talking with her boyfriend. I was a little annoyed. I feel like I'm past acquaintanceship with her, but still, it's not easy. She is a swirling bank of clouds that I couldn't see into to save my soul.

I just finished *The Bean Trees*, a good book about a tough woman from Kentucky. She grew up with just her mother, who was tough as nails and acted "as though I'd plugged in the Moon and hung up the stars besides. Like I was that good." I decided that I'm going to do that for my kids. I think Mom wanted to do that with me, but wasn't sure either of us was quite up to that. Or perhaps that was just normal insecurity. I know she did her best for me not to feel ashamed of anything. And she always treated me like I knew what I was doing—asking my opinions on colors and things, until I figured I might as well sit down and figure out what they were. Just a little while ago, she asked me how I was so sure of myself (after giving that to me herself). You see, nothing matters in this life—there is no quantitative judge—it's all *attitude*. Nobody knows the truth. Just some people have the guts to stand up and have their say.

8/6/88

Damn. I can't sleep again. 1:42 a.m. "Can't Always Get What You Want" is on the radio. Maybe that's my theme song. It is a spiritual. No, "The Weight" is a spiritual. But this is like a spiritual. It has the truth in it.

I have knots in my stomach, my hands, my jaws, my

eyebrows. I haven't eaten in two days—not real meals anyway. I'm going back to Susan in two weeks. But in two weeks, I will have my surgery. I know because the quote in my calendar for that week is "Even cowards can endure hardship, only the brave can endure suspense" (Mignon McLaughlin). That was put there for me. That will be my lucky week. I know it. I've had a feeling about these empty August weeks.

Oh God, if it comes tonight, I think I'll explode. I want to weep. I want to run out under the moon in a field. See red, green, and maybe gold woven under a deep blue night, like an Indian tapestry. Like what maybe I should do with the *Love Medicine* print.

How can I stand it, thinking the call could come any minute? I am living it—have lived it for six months next week. Oh shit. This is going to be the most wonderfully forgettable year of my life. I'll look back on this suspense, shudder, and thank God I don't have to live with it any more. Why does the tension have to rise in me like some tide responding to some far-off, irregular moon? As soon as I forget, there it goes. It's the maintenance of my armor, I know. I know. But it's so heavy. Couldn't I put it down? Could I slip it off and go swimming, just for a little minute? Go for a roll behind a bush?

If I were talking to Susan, what would I say? I don't want to say anything. All the words are locked inside. I want to go to sleep, but I know I won't. It's 2:05 a.m. now.

Devin. Fan. Dress. Ring. Telephone. Kurt. Postcard. Beach. Sand. Sea. Glass. Water. Sink. Dishes. Fishes. Crackers. Salt. White. Castle. Stone. Alex. Door. Dachshund. Sausage. Grease. Hashbrowns. Happy Chef. Smile. Teeth. Grin. Win. Pin. Fin. Fish.

That relaxed me. God only knows why. Don't know if it means I'll sleep. Something about the image of an orange fish swimming in the dark green/light blue ocean made all the tension flood out of my heart and arms. Maybe I have to learn how to be comfortable with all that deep water. I can float, after all. I can sort of swim. I think of the ocean like death—huge, terrifying, uncontrollable. But an ocean is life too. It can buoy you up, support you, move you along, even feed you. Life is an ocean. Learn to move comfortably with the water.

8/8/88

The Chinese consider today very lucky, but as it is now technically the 9th, not so for me. But next week is my week. Let's see how far we can carry the power of positive thinking.

I still haven't gotten my postcard from Kurt, but I have certainly been cleaning up on the mail otherwise. Today I got a two-page letter from Jay and a postcard from Matt.

I finished my letter to Pat today and, while writing,

realized that I wasn't sure I was completely ready for the plunge with Kurt. I could have seen it with Devin. (Or the Devin-esque character I created in my brain.) But do I really want to commit my near future to an 18-year-old St. Olaf freshman? Kurt is very mature. But he can still act his age. He's safe, sensible, smart. He is sexy, but for some reason, lately I've been thinking about Dangerous Men again. Maybe it's September coming.

8/9/88

Kurt's back. I just talked to him on the phone. Yes, awash in adoration. Is that what I said? Well, that's what I am. He sounded enthused about the party on Saturday.

Rick and John R. came to dinner with Rich and Maggi and me tonight.[94] Such a proud hostess am I. Rich and Maggi are so sweet. It's nice to have an opportunity to get to know them as real friends.

Yet another silver lining in this giant cloud . . .

Being so convinced that the transplant will come next week is freaking me out. The last minute, just as they put the mask over your face, it's so terrifying. You are surrendering all control of your very life. You feel like you do when you sign something long and complicated that someone else has just paraphrased for you. "Wait—are you sure this is right? Isn't there something I should . . ."

---

94 Rich and Maggi were staying with Jen.

But you convince yourself that everything's all right and try to calmly breathe in.

8/10/88

Tonight, I went to a movie with Kurt and saw two falling stars. Kurt said "Make a wish!" and both times I wished for my surgery to come soon. I didn't know what to wish about Kurt.

8/11/88

I feel like I might as well not have gotten up today. I got up at 11:00 a.m. and promptly got a migraine while cleaning up the house. So I spent most of the afternoon napping on the couch. I finished two strings of love beads, though. So I got *something* accomplished.

Mom and Dad got back from the cabin at about 2:30 p.m. They were happy. They want to go up again on Sunday, so Maggi and Rich might come back. I hope it won't be too much of a good thing. Maybe Rick and John R. could stay, but I don't think they would be as cute and adorable as Rich and Maggi. Or as good cooks and housekeepers. They were the best babysitters I've had, though Sue was good too. With Maggi and Richard, somehow, I feel less like I have to bend myself to accommodate them.

8/12/88

Six months. I have an inner feeling that it will come next week—the 18th.

Today was a full day—it made up for yesterday. I put a pocket in the blue and orange paisley dress for tomorrow, which inspired Mom to go to her old trunk and see what else she might have in there for me. We found a silk robe, Dad's Nehru jacket, and three classy, fancy party dresses. I can't wait for the mid-winter ball.

I hope I can dance then.

I'm so glad to be free of J.B. When I'm not horny, it is nice not being with anyone. Love clouds your thinking so much. Close proximity to another person pulls your mind in their direction so strongly. I savor this time to get to know myself, to make myself stronger so I can withstand the onslaught of my next relationship. It's only because I get horny that I think I have to pick somebody now. I don't need a lover. I would like one, sure, but I'll have one in time. Meanwhile, I know all these wonderful people and we can share our thoughts. We don't need to share toothbrushes for it to be personal, important, and meaningful.

And I can't get laid now anyway.

Tonight I went to the Rueb and had an important and meaningful discussion with Rick, Chang-tai, Dad, and

John R.[95] Rick wanted to know why he should be a historian instead of a poet. It was a discussion of life, occupation, and social responsibility. I *love* discussions like that. My mind feels alive and I feel like a patch of grass that is expanding itself over a plot of ground.

8/13/88

The party was great. I just got back. Kurt took me and we had a discussion on the way home about love. I told him how I want to go out with someone and maintain our separate identities. He agreed that that sounded great. We weren't sure if it was possible, though.

He reminded me of how he doesn't want a girlfriend freshman year. Oh yeah, I'd forgotten that. Good idea. I guess . . .

Our friendship is feeling more and more wonderful. It's so cozy, so intelligent, so open, so sweet. One of the main reasons I can never kiss him is that when I'm with him, I never feel the need to change anything. When I'm away from him, I'm lonely and my hormones get carried away with me.

Rick was sweet at the party. Toward the end he was flirting with me. He told me my dad was his role model for everything that was good about masculinity. It was hard not to be terribly embarrassed.

---

95 Chang-tai Hung taught history at Carleton

8/14/88

In an insecure, self-absorbed sort of way, I wish someone had taken a picture of me sitting between Kurt and
Rick last night. Yeah, okay, so my ego still wants proof
of my attractiveness.

Rich and Maggi are here again. I'm calm with my parents
gone. They were stressing out about whether they ought
to leave me or not, so much that I almost freaked out and
asked them to stay. I was so tense about the whole thing,
I started thinking maybe Mom was right and it was the
sublimated desire for them to stay. Wrong-o. They're gone
and I'm mellow. I remembered in the back of my head
how I started eating again the last time Rich and Maggi
were here. I'm just too big to live at home. We get along
quite well, but it's by no means the ideal living situation.

I wish Sue H. didn't live up so many stairs. Maybe I
could get my surgery and move in with her.

I love living alone (w/o parents). I feel calm and in control. I can take care of the house alone. Mom gets in my
brain. Their concern and cares and nurturing fill up the
house, so there's no room for me. That's why I don't eat
when they're here. I feel filled up with nurturing.

I feel happy, calm, horny, anxious . . . I wonder if it will
really come this week. That would be wonderful, she
said in abstract, then quailed at the thought. (Is that really a verb?)

LIVING AT HOME was hard for Jen, and not always easy for her parents, because they all valued the notion of her independence. The three of them shared the compact Carleton campus happily enough. Jen appreciated her mother's role at the bookstore and her father's standing as a respected and well-liked professor. But, once she enrolled as a freshman, Bob says Carleton became "her turf." He remembers running into her in a gym stairwell as she was going to dance class and he was leaving after tennis team drills. "What are YOU doing here?" she blurted in surprise. Seeing her father had apparently been far from her mind. When she gave up being a full-time student, she feared losing territory, autonomy, and campus relationships that were precious to her.

Within a few months, a lot had changed in the Bonner household. Jen was disconsolately at home for an indefinite time and Tim was adapting to life at Laura Baker. The Bonners tried not to express their fresh worry about their children. They were advised to give Tim space and time to adapt to new surroundings, but they knew how hard it was for him to be exposed to unfamiliar sounds, sights, and routines. And though Jen hadn't minded parental limits in high school, she clearly didn't want them now. She was quick to say, "Don't tell me what to do!" She needed space and time too, which were not easy to provide in a relatively small house.

The VW Dasher Jen thought of as her car was actually the family station wagon. Fortunately Bob and Barbara could walk to most places in Northfield and they gave her near unlimited use of it. They did what they could so she felt like an adult who was in charge of her life.

Jen grew up surrounded by Carleton faculty and students, and she often had more in common with these older friends than kids her own age. Most of the time she behaved very responsibly, following her medication schedule and maintaining generally healthy habits. Her idea of a fine time was to throw a dinner party where guests could indulge in topical jokes and intelligent conversation.

Barbara remembers coming home to a freshly baked apple pie when Jen was ten or so. At loose ends that afternoon, her daughter had looked up the instructions in *Joy of Cooking*. Barbara says, "We lived a closely constrained life. Cooking became a sensual creative thing, a way for Jenny to express herself."

Now, unlike most Carleton students, Jen had a Northfield venue where she could entertain, most freely when her parents were not around. Her first thought was to cook for friends when she had the house to herself.

Understanding this, the Bonners frequently retreated to their cabin, 230 miles northwest of Northfield. The cabin had a phone, and if the transplant office called, they could be at the U of M hospital within three hours. Bob was always happy to go; completing the cabin construction felt like a respite from the cares of home. He loved the thought that Jen might have a family someday and bring her children there. But Barbara traveled north reluctantly, even though Jen always had friends staying with her. "It's hard to leave when the chick is in danger," Jen's mother says.

The Bonners knew their daughter wanted the occasional chance to be wild. They were not surprised. Growing up, Jen most wanted to be like Toni Sostek, who not only was a talented dancer but also had what Barbara calls a "risqué edge" to her humor.

When they left town in early June, the Bonners knew Jen was having a big party, but they weren't expecting the mess they found on their return. Jen so rarely did anything that wasn't smart and considerate. As they restored order in the house, they wondered how the walnut candlesticks, back in their usual place on the mantle, had gotten so charred.

Considering that Jen and the house survived the night, Bob and Barbara found they weren't particularly upset, as this might be one of her only opportunities to throw a rowdy party.

JEN KNEW HER PARENTS exceptionally well and shared many of their tastes. She still listened to the music they played as she grew up—the Band, Taj Mahal, and Aretha Franklin. Away from the family setting, she interacted with them in their workplaces, and she could see them as others did.

The Carleton Class of 1989 contained a talented group of history majors, including Jen's friends Jay, John R., and Rick. They all took classes from Bob and viewed him as a mentor. Though this made Jen proud, it also embarrassed her a little. In some ways she and Bob interacted like peers, with the shared goal of propagating laughter in the house. They loved many of the same television shows, especially comedies that skewered normal expectations and pomposity. Together they built a personal collection of comic allusions and, between the two of them, it was hard to say who had the better grasp of *The Fall and Rise of Reginald Perrin*, *Soap*, or *The Hitchhiker's Guide to the Galaxy*.

Barbara shared Jen's sense of humor in a different way. She always enjoyed when Jen, as a young girl, laughed boisterously at funny moments, a surprising guffaw erupting from her small form. And Barbara appreciated the wit in Jen's art. She fondly recalls the time when Northfield wanted families to display a drawing of an open hand to show their house was a "safe" house for children. Jenny drew a hand that morphed into a claw, and then into a scathing portrait of a teacher she didn't like. The Bonners did not participate in the earnest safe house campaign after all.

In 1988, when Jen wanted to banter and deflect tension, she went to Bob. When she was in the mood for a searching discussion, she had it with Barbara. "We had real talks when we were side-by-side in the car or the kitchen, not making direct eye contact," Barbara says. "Nothing was off-limits."

8/15/88

Kurt was just here. Maybe at some point I should ask him what he thinks of me. We sure are good friends. Actually, I guess that's probably all he'd say. He's going to Milwaukee on Thursday, so he came by to see me tonight before he left. We had a nice two-hour talk about nothing in particular. Then he tickled me good night. But I'm not going to start up again about how I think he's getting the hint, because I don't think he is. I think I am, though.

8/17/88

I didn't write last night because it was so hot. Maggi and I slept downstairs by the AC. It was wonderful! I got up at 9:45 a.m. and felt so on top of things. Now a cold front has come through and it is actually down to 70 degrees! I could pass out with the excitement.

We are 1½ hours into the 18th. I wonder, wonder, wonder. Hope. Pray. Try not to think about it.

I was at Boliou today for the first time in a while. So happy. I cut out favorite ads from *Vogue* and *Elle* and put them up on a large piece of paper. Now purple, orange/brown, and green dyed deep in leather are in my head. Wonderful colors. I want a brown suede miniskirt and purple tights for fall!

I've decided that the purpose of artists is to show what is beautiful in life. The balance between beauty and despair is always shifting in every individual. If I can paint something that will shift someone's balance toward beauty, I will have contributed to their overall happiness and to what I consider to be the base intent, purpose, and necessity of life. What better service to humanity than to aid in tipping people's souls toward light?

That is why I lately tend to infuse black into my paintings. Or a sense of roughness. Or why I think that way when I get my ideas. I want to ground my beauty in reality, so it will strike people in their hearts and they will feel it to be true. It cannot make you happy if you don't see any relevance in it. If something is real, it will strike that chord deep inside you and you will relax and your heart will feel glad inside. I don't know—in fact, I'm pretty sure I haven't managed that in any of my work this summer, but I'm working toward it in my piece about the highway. My escape from Northfield this summer.

8/18/88

Ten more minutes of the 18th, though I'd call it if it came before sunrise. I have, as expected, not thought about the transplant much more than usual today. I saw Susan again. So I'm starting to feel like I've addressed it and can afford to turn away for a while.

My session with Susan was wonderful. I never feel like the tension all goes away in one appointment, but I felt it pouring out today and I feel happier, just knowing there's a release.

Just got back from the Rueb. Rick didn't have any more intense questions but it was a warming discussion nonetheless.

Why is it that I spend all day thinking of things to write and when I get here, I write two sentences and want to say, "That's it. Done." What were all those things I wanted to write down?

I dreamt the other night that I was sitting on Rick's lap and he was kissing me. I was really psyched about this, except that it was a really sloppy kiss. Yuck! It tasted terrible—all this saliva in my mouth. So I tried to communicate, through a few examples, more preferable forms of kissing.

8/19/88

One of the Chuo[96] students from two years ago showed up on my doorstep today. No letter, no phone call, just showed up. I remembered him right away—he was intense, unfocused, and unpredictable. And very poor English. Today was a series of communication breakdowns. He followed me around for part of the afternoon and then we went to the Rueb at 7:30 p.m. Susie came with us—thank God. I didn't have to go at all, I know. But I did feel sorry for him, here in Northfield for two days with no one at all. Tomorrow he's going to Minneapolis.

I think I finished the painting of Highway 3. I'm happy. I feel I've got it to a good point. I could muck around with it more, but it feels good and mucking more might just wreck it. The only trouble is that it has an autumn feel to it instead of the hot, baked summer feel I wanted. Maybe I should try some smaller watercolors with a summer feel—on site—and then maybe I can change the Highway 3 painting. But it looks good this way. I should just do a different painting about summer.

8/20/88

Evan stood me up today. He called twice this summer to say that he would be in town today and would like to see me. So I hung around all day waiting for him, but he never showed. Or called. I don't know what happened.

---

96 Students from Chuo University in Tokyo spend a three-week summer program at Carleton focusing on conversational English and American culture.

I'm pissed off because my parents wanted to take me to the Cities to see *Babette's Feast* and eat at the Black Forest Inn.

It was an interesting evening anyway. First night I've been alone in months. It was quite depressing—reminded me of how important friends are to the care and feeding of one's esteem.

I did get some work done at Boliou. I finished the Happy Chef painting. It's by no means my best work, but I put in a lot of colors, so it's bright and strong. Maybe a bit too strong. But balanced. I think it works. So what do I do now? I tried starting a self-portrait but couldn't get past the charcoal sketch. Maybe I should bring some sort of costume.

Big, small, finished or no, I have eight works up in my studio right now. That makes me feel a little more productive.

8/21/88

I started a print today. It's an etching of the watercolor I did of the geraniums and morning glories on the front steps. I'm going to monoprint and etch it, though if that doesn't turn out right, I'll have to make color plates. This will be an annoyingly slow process, as I still can't wipe or press[97] myself. But I'm sure someone will be glad

---

97 Printmaking processes

to help. And if I could manage to wipe on my own, I could get Kurt or someone to do the pressing. It was a wonderful feeling to go down to Boliou and smell the smells in there.

Geraniums and morning glories on the front step

I feel slightly sad. Phil Collins is on the radio, reminding me of freshman year. I dreamt last night that it was fall and I was walking outside and was attacked by two men. I was trying to kick the shit out of them with the self-defense tactics I learned in class but I woke up.

I wonder if that's another metaphor for the surgery? It will sneak up on me sometime this fall. But I've given up on premonitions. I'll just live in the shadow and it will come when it comes. As of yet, I'm still in great shape. I can go out as much as I want. I can paint. I can hang out the laundry. I can drive around town. I can stay out late. I can't dance and I can't fuck—so? I'll live. Lord knows there's worse in the world.

What I wrote earlier about not having the energy to be myself is not a handicap new to the world. And it doesn't mean I can't express myself. I just have to change. Oh no! I have to change. That's certainly not what life's all about. No one should have to change. They might accidentally *grow* or something.

I've learned a lot this year about patience and quiet and slow actions and thinking. These are important lessons. I was on my way to an ulcer before I had this heart failure. Maybe most people would prefer an ulcer to a heart transplant—but hey, I needed a new heart anyway, and I've learned some valuable lessons. I think I will have a much happier life because of it.

8/22/88

I started *Tracks* today, Louise Erdrich's latest novel. I forget how much I love her writing between books. This one seems more finished than *The Beet Queen*—very much the second and middle novel. Her writing laps you like waves of warm water, like a big cotton blanket just out of the drier. Even as she writes about tragedy, the rhythm of her words lulls the message into your heart.

There is no avoiding her power. You drink it up and look for more. She can write about anything. Explicit sex scenes are not "dirty"—everything is natural. She writes with open honesty about every part of life and you acknowledge it fully and easily, only remembering afterward that that was supposed to be a touchy subject. Louise does completely what Dostoevsky instructs to all artists: "Caress the Divine Details."[98]

Mom and Dad came to Boliou tonight and liked my stuff. Dad really liked the painting of the Ideal Café. They liked the one of Highway 3 a lot, except the drips. Mom said the sky, the trees, and the buildings were great, the colors were great, but all that work I had done on the road and grass, all the layers, all the dripping I had tried to encourage, the effect I had worked for, she didn't like. They said it looked like I couldn't control the medium. I meet with Joe Byrne tomorrow.

Not that this criticism makes any sense. Or difference. Only if everybody agrees something is wrong would I change my mind. Like the Happy Chef painting that I don't like anyway. But if I like it, critics be damned. The trouble with the Highway 3 painting is that I'm not sure about it. The dripping *doesn't* quite work. The road does also look like a ledge. Perhaps Joe will have words of wisdom.

---

98 After finishing *Tracks*, Jen sent a letter to Louise Erdrich, who had been a Northfield neighbor a few years earlier. Erdrich sent her a two-page handwritten letter in return, which thanked Jen for her response to the book and gave an update on her own family. Commenting on the heart transplant support group, Erdrich complimented Jen on sharing "the hard work of your own understanding."

Highway 3

I saw Kurt tonight. I made him a card from one of my cut-up magazines. Actually, it was six index cards with pictures on them that said: "Multiple Choice Quiz— Which of these four things would *NOT* be illegal were Pat Robertson to become President? a) Raspberry Daiquiris b) Kahlua c) Haagen Dazs ice-cream bars d) movies on the VCR (drawing of a love scene). ANSWER: So when are you coming over to celebrate the end of the Republican Convention with me?"

Yes, it's very silly. I took it over at 9:00 p.m., all nervous because I couldn't just stick it in the door like I did last time. His sister answered the door and called him down with this secret smile on her face. She went back in the kitchen when he came down so he wouldn't see her smiling. He gave me a big hug, and we chatted for maybe ten minutes. But he was doing something upstairs, so with more hugs and a promise to call me tomorrow between 6:00 and 7:00 p.m., he bid me farewell. And left me to ponder the conversation that must surely have been going on in the kitchen as we giggled out in the hall. And to sit here now, enlarging on the memory of his sister's smile.

With many hugs, but without a promise to call me tomorrow, Gretchen bid me farewell today. She leaves for Italy tomorrow. I dreamt frantically about her last night.

8/23/88

Sue H. slept through our lunch date today. Kris has been in town 24 hours and has yet to call. Evan blew me off Saturday. By 7:00 p.m. tonight, after Kurt had failed to call, I was beginning to wonder if I had done something awful or had developed dreadful breath or *something*. I was seriously verging on paranoia, thinking remorsefully how I criticize my friends and how it must have gotten back to them and they all hated me now. But I marshalled my forces and called Sue H., to find her extremely contrite. Kurt called and apologized profusely. And made a date for Thursday.

So I'm back in the thick of things. It was great to see Kevin T. again. He seems to adore me. I expect that I will freak him out, but whatever I say he thinks is a scream. I have determined that I am his lunatic fringe.

8/24/88

Mom feels she is partly responsible for me criticizing my friends, as she does it all the time too. I had thought of that, but realized that to blame it on her would just be an excuse. She does a lot of things that I have chosen not to imitate. There's no reason I can't choose not to do this. I told her about this and she was pleased I had come to that on my own. She gave me a quote from one of her books that said to identify with your friends, not dissect them.

Fall is coming and I am feeling a lot calmer. I am still enjoying life quite fully. I miss having energy, but who am I to claim the big brave soldier role if I sit about and whine because I have to wait for something. That sounds pretty spoiled. I am blessed with the beauty in my life. Loving parents, many friends, good food, my own studio—I have my own studio! Life is beautiful. I will enjoy however much I get and whatever form it comes in.

8/25/88

Kurt just left. Once again, platonically. Sigh. There's no point in trying to rush things. I can read pretty well that he's not up for anything more.

8/26/88

Yesterday Dad and I went to Support Group. Gene was there—he's been waiting over a year now. Ernie's at 10½ months. They heard I was at six months and said "ah—just a rookie." The group leader said it used to be uncommon for people to have to wait three months. It's all the new transplant centers springing up all over.[99] It's criminal! I ought to write a letter to the paper.

I can't see Susan tomorrow. Nobody's going to the Cities. Maybe I should have called a neighbor. Maybe I should drive myself. Maybe I'll go to Support Group again next week. I really wanted to see Susan.

8/28/88

I didn't write last night because I slept with Sue H. in the other room. We've had a great weekend. Last night, she and Julie A. came over and we drank beers and talked. I liked Julie and tried not to be too insecure about whether or not she likes me. Sue H. is good for me. Somehow, with her around, it is easier for me to remember myself. Something about the way she decided she wanted to hang out with me this summer.

I don't think it got up to 70 degrees today. I can't remember what it was like to be so hot. Humans are such here-and-now creatures.

---

99 In 1983, there were twelve heart transplant programs in the United States. Five years later, when Jen was on the list, there were 141 US programs.

8/29/88

It has been such a long day. It's 3:30 a.m. I just got back from the Big Steer. I was woken up at 9:30 this morning by Sarah, calling back. We talked for an hour and a half. It seems like days ago.

It was *so great* to talk to her again! She's not coming back and she hates her job, but it was wonderful to talk to *her*. In a letter it would have been depressing, but on the phone, we could connect personalities. She misses me too! She still loves me. She's still fun to talk to. But she's transferring to Albany State. She says she never wants to live out of New York again. But it was so great to laugh and remember how we're unique in each other's lives. Since she never wants to come back to Minnesota, I said we'd have to do Europe together.

Sue S. is going to Nepal on Thursday. Today I got a letter from Tom, who was the cutest guy on campus. It's exciting to have these friends all over the country and know that they'll be there for letters or to drop in on or whatever for a very long time. Real friends. Maybe I'll live in New York for a while for art. Yay Sarah!

I feel a little sick. I had a lot of beer tonight at a party. A lot of people came through, including Matt, who gave me a big hug and asked if I'd gotten a heart yet. Something about the way he asked made me feel really sad to say no. He was so hopeful. Just remember—flirt—no crush.

The party was fun. People laughed at my jokes.

8/30/88

The summer is coming to an end. I will not see Kurt again until after school starts. We went to *Bull Durham*—great sex scenes—and came home for piña coladas. He left at 1:45.

We had a good talk again. I told him that when he asked me after our first date if I wanted some "decadence" I thought, "Hmm . . . I could have a fling with Kurt. He's graduated. What the hell?" But it didn't happen, and then we became such good friends that it didn't seem right. But I did add that it was kind of difficult to know what to do with the momentum. He said, "Yeah, do you roll with it or slam on the brakes?" I don't know what that means. But he didn't take the opportunity to kiss me or confess any similar feelings, so . . . well, I kind of knew it was like this.

I drove him home and he hugged me goodnight. Then he got out of the car and held up his hand to squeeze mine. He always looks straight at me then too, so I can't really read him. Just serious, clear blue eyes.

8/31/88

I just made Kurt another card. I spent all day today working on job posters, so to do a big collage-mixed media poster for Kurt was a total blast at the end of the day. And it stimulates my creativity. I get out of expected and formal mode and back to images and things that I really like. I should do this more often. The card, which I will send him by campus mail, says "So we've kind of talked about this, right? And we're not having a fling, right? So hey—you wanna get married? (You're trying to quit ceremonies too? Aw shit.)" I wrote him a short, innocuous note on the back and reassured him that we could wait 'til he graduated.

Sue S. woke me up to ask me to go out with her and Binks for dinner. So I got dressed, went downstairs and chatted with Dad. I told him about my extra-heavy period and my high protime[100] because I was still bleeding and was getting a little worried. So the next thing I knew, I was lying on a table in Mark Mellstrom's office, wrapped in a large napkin, visualizing myself calling Sue S. and Kurt from the hospital and canceling all our plans. But Mark assured me I wasn't dying and that my plans were just fine (provided I didn't get into a car accident as they probably wouldn't be able to stop my bleeding).

So then it was off to see Sue S. and gorge ourselves on African finger food. She leaves for Nepal tomorrow. I went back to get Kurt for the movie. I was so glad I was dressed nice (tan shorts, black turtleneck, contacts, and Aborigine earrings) because I had to go in and call

---

100 Prothrombin time, one measurement of how quickly blood clots. Because of her artificial heart valve, Jen was on an anticoagulant and she had this test periodically.

home. So he brought me in and introduced me to his brother, sister-in-law and their kids. Then I went into the kitchen to get the phone and found his mom. He didn't even have to introduce us. She looked up and said "Oh, hello."

She knew who I was, and I, she. And we were united by our mutual love for Kurt! *(Cue violins.)*

She looked nice. Happy, lively, grounded in reality.

The movie was great. We sat behind Edwin and Missy. Ed and I teased each other mercilessly today. I've never had so much fun maintaining that someone was "just a friend." Had I said he was my sex toy, they would have guessed that nothing was happening.

Back To Normal

9/1/88

Kris showed up at my door in tears this morning. She had just taken her boyfriend to the airport. I brought her in, gave her a beer, and fixed us some pancakes.

My cards to Kurt really do help my posters. I was getting sick of trying to come up with the right font for the convo poster, so I pulled out an ink pot and did the chicken-scratch print I always do for Kurt. It looks great! Yay!

9/2/88

I just got back from the Big Steer with Kris. I am so tired, I was driving poorly. I hope I'm just pooped—not getting worse.

I can't sleep. My heart feels all big and flippy-floppy. I feel tense and full of Big Steer coffee and food. Fits right in with the country music I just switched back to.

I can't wait to see Susan on Tuesday. I've tried to stop thinking about the surgery. There's nothing I can do but get impatient. I can't prepare any more until the beeper finally goes off. But again, I'm starting to forget it's real. It's hard to think about it because I get so anxious. Especially times like now when I get tired and scared. I've given up on being horny. I just want to be able to enjoy those thoughts for some time to come. It's so hard to sleep. My brain is hard to distract when I can't wear my body out.

9/3/88

Fall's settling down like a big wool blanket. It's wonderfully cold. I've never been so happy to see fall come.

Oh, but it makes me want to curl up in someone's arms and rub my cheek against his beard.

I do wonder about students returning. Do I want to get involved yet? I was just getting to enjoy being single again.

Kris left today. The summer's really over. I'm sad she's gone, but I'm happy that our friendship is good. Tomorrow I have to work on that stupid poster and write letters. And freshman week starts.

9/4/88

I thought of Kurt's mother while I was working on the etching of the geraniums and morning glories on our front stair rail this afternoon. She makes me think of little blue flowers. So bright and cheerful. That's how I want to look at that age. There's something magic, so blessedly wonderful about brightness and cheerfulness coming from seriousness. I want to marry Kurt! I want to eat Thanksgiving dinner with his family!

I talked to him today. College is okay. His roommate is pretty nice. He says they're treating them like 3-year-olds. I told him Mom and Dad were going to the cabin next weekend, so he's going to come for dinner. By then he will have got my card.

9/5/88

Went out tonight with Susie and Tricia—pizza and the Rueb. Came home and there were 10 freshmen in the living room discussing *Love Medicine*. They all looked like Carleton students. And they *all* looked related to someone I know here.

I spent today at publications. It was fun and exhausting. It was good to work all day.

9/6/88

I got the phone call I was expecting from Kurt tonight.

I knew it would come the minute I put the card in the mail: "Jen, you're a weird chick." We talked for half an hour and our dinner date is on for Saturday. He said he was going to write this down in his calendar. He's never been proposed to before. And he said he'd "think about it—just for you."

Tomorrow's Wednesday. Everybody will be back. What is so romantic about Devin that I am so curious to see him? And everybody else. It's exciting. And here I am, proposing to a St. Olaf student.

9/7/88

Summer is over. Everybody's back. Except all my friends who are on leave, off-campus, or graduated. Which is pretty much all of my friends. I was excited this morning but now I'm just tired. There were people I wanted to see, but nobody close to me. Nobody came back today who would call me up specifically to go to the Rueb and talk. So I'm sad now. Though I did go over and visit Jay and John P.

I saw Devin today. I'm no longer in love with him! I talked to him and he danced around and played with his cap and looked every-which-where. Hell with it. I still feel like I'm just getting to know myself. Like I'm still deciding who I want to be with. I *like* being single. I like flirting. I like hanging out with different guys.

9/8/88

Today I feel more in favor of a relationship. It would solve a lot of problems.

School makes me tired already. I miss the peace from summer. There seems to be so much static: people I don't know, stuff going on that I don't want to do. Just having all those people there, I always feel like there's something going on that I'm missing. That's the side effect of living at home. At the dorm, this didn't bother me. Maybe I don't want to live off campus. But remember—most of it's static: people I don't know, doing things I don't want to do.

Have to remember this frustration for when I finally do graduate, and start missing Carleton. I will miss the special moments, but the day to day routine can be a drag.

9/9/88

I'm pooped. Had a huge dinner party tonight. It was fun but 10 was too many. Jay got really quiet and shy.

I started Chang-tai's class today: Imperial China. Jay's in it with me. I'm so psyched! Chang-tai is such a great lecturer.

9/10/88

Had the big talk with Kurt tonight. Had a great date— dinner, *Moonstruck*, Mississippi Muds, and talk until

3:00 a.m. We talked about a lot of things. And, finally, about dating. He said it had crossed his mind too. But he said he wasn't ready. He said he thought we should wait, but also that he wasn't sure he could love me. He said he likes me, though. He knows I'm disappointed, but it's no more than a ripple in our friendship. My feelings for him are of such a solid flavor—they shine in and out of the friendship, intermingled. I felt awkward talking about it with him, but that's the way we are. We are solid friends. We discuss it all.

I am sad. But inside me I'm a bit excited. Light and free— I'm still single! I don't have to fight that pull to become more like him. I don't have to fight my wrong-headed notions that I have to change. The love and security of a relationship can settle like a weight on your chest.

9/11/88

Slept late today and woke up down. Hard to come off rejection. Sue H. was home. She came over for coffee and girl-talked me out of my funk. I was glad she was free, I needed a good girlfriend to talk to.

What I want is an independent, confident, intelligent, mature man to fall in love with me. I'm sick of all this tentative, tippy-toeing garbage. I want to be swept off my feet.

9/12/88

Seven months. I've stopped thinking about the transplant. Except for every day. Life is back to normal. I know I can handle it. When it comes, it comes. I'll be glad and scared and I'll get through it and it'll be over.

I'm driving myself up to see Susan tomorrow. I haven't driven to the Cities alone in ages.

I was in such a lousy mood today. Just awful. Got up, had a cup of coffee, went to class, got out, got a migraine. Kevin T. was insufferable! I am so sick of him hitting on me! I can't believe he could really be interested in me. He's too fucking TIDY to be interested in anyone! He doesn't know how quickly he'd hate me if we lived together.

9/13/88

Saturday I am going shopping with Sue H. and I cannot believe how excited I am to go buy purple and emerald-green tights, a yellow-brown suede mini, and royal blue and emerald green turtlenecks—or whatever variations on those themes I can find. The thought of wearing all these colors is exciting me to the point of insomnia. Oh no! I have an early class tomorrow.

Susan was trying to see herself in my dreams again. I dreamt I was in a hospital in Faribault[101] and freaking

---

101 A town twelve miles from Northfield

out because it wasn't Mayo or the U. I think I'm nervous about the surgery because I don't know *exactly* how it will be, like I would if it were at Mayo. Susan thought maybe it was my anxiety of not being able to get a ride up to see her and thinking about switching therapists. Good grief!

It was a strong dream, though. About all the pain and ooky things that hospitals involve. Well, at least, as I told Susan, I'm not a kid anymore. I have other things to think about when painful things happen and can understand fully what is happening. Kids feel everything. They have no distance from what's going on.

Kurt called this afternoon. It was good to talk to him after The Discussion, to establish that I still think of him as a friend. I sent him a note by campus mail that said, "I've been thinking about what you said last Saturday . . . I thought you didn't drink coffee." We're going out next week.

9/14/88

Dinner was great. John P. is really nice. Jay got quiet even in a group of five. I'm really tired now and I feel weird because I was just talking to Dad about Chang-tai and sexism and how Chang-tai seems more humble and open about things. But we got down to fine points and I'm too tired to think and I hope I didn't hurt Dad's feelings. I'm enjoying Imperial China more than I did Elizabethan England and I really like Chang-tai as a prof.

9/15/88

Today was one of those gray autumn days that screams out for apple pie. I couldn't resist the "roasted coconut" coffee at the snack bar this afternoon but got away without a migraine. Mom was not so lucky—she's had one all day. So I came home from the library to a cold, empty house. Mom was up in bed; Dad was at the hospital with our neighbor who cracked her skull. He got home at 5:30 p.m. and we pondered dinner until I hit upon stroganoff. We never have it any more because Mom doesn't like that much fat in one place, but Dad and I adore it. So I fixed it up in about a half hour along with an apple pie which made Dad the happiest man in Minnesota.

What am I going to do? I have studied so well how to please a man, but he's not the man I want to marry. When I meet a man who doesn't fall over at the sight of apple pie, I am in a quandary. After dinner I made some miniscule reference to our *Beyond the Fringe*[102] album, which Dad picked up immediately. AAAUGH! I want to marry my Dad! I know how to please him. We like all the same things. We have all sorts of inside jokes. I wonder what he was like at my age. Maybe that's where my idea of the ideal boy is from: a young, lithe, intelligent, all-American type guy.

I wish I were not living at home any more. I can see how a quiet young woman could get sucked into spinsterhood

---

102 A 1960s British comedy revue starring Peter Cook and Dudley Moore

if her mother died and she had to care for her father. Not that I could do it. But like those quirky Anne Tyler novels, there are little things in life that seem comprehensible to me, skewed as the whole picture may be.

9/16/88

I just got back from the All-Watson Annual Heaven-to-Hell progressive party. I violated all of my ethics by driving in this condition. We were too drunk to see any alternative and really didn't realize how drunk we were. Somebody said the sangria was actually wine and vodka. I think it's still hitting me. God, I should never get this drunk. I get so depressed.

9/17/88

Went shopping with Sue H. today. Got *wonderful* things: cranberry tights, a fuchsia turtleneck cut well out of good heavy cloth, and an emerald-green suede mini. We went *all over* looking for a brown suede mini, but there was none to be had. But I am more thrilled by the second with this green one. I wore it to the symphony tonight with Jay and Kristen P. and felt totally hot.

The concert was *amazing*. Music is like sex: I know I loved it. I felt *wonderful* afterwards—but I can't remember any of the details. It's just all a really happy, rich, warm, full-feeling blur.

Dr. Jamieson was fired this week. Found out this morning and called Braunlin. She said she'd call on Monday after their meeting to decide who will do the heart
transplants now. She said if it was Kriett[103] "it would
probably be all right." Well just what the fuck does that
mean? Jamieson was the only one in Minnesota with
experience in transposed hearts. And the best one for
the job in the world.

So, what? I was taking things too easy? Didn't realize
how lucky I was? Not quite nervous enough about this?
Well, what can you do? When they find a heart, they'll
find someone to put it in. It is one of the best two transplant centers in the world. They're not going to half-ass
the job.

The only thing you can count on in life is that it keeps
on going. Got to trust the river of life, because you don't
have any choice in the matter. Might as well lie back and
enjoy this ride for what it gives you.

9/18/88

Despite my comforting and rational words last night, I
slept too late this morning and couldn't breathe when I
woke up. It's been a heavy and humid day and that plus
tension means no air for Jen. My rib muscles just choke
up.

---

103 Jolene Kriett, a U of M cardiothoracic surgeon

But now my song is on: "You Can't Always Get What You Want." I just hope I can get what I need. I've been reading about Taoism all day, the philosophy of acceptance. Wonderful bits and pieces but the philosophy as a whole was a bit too otherworldly for my tastes. I think I should read the chapter again.

Philosophy is annoying. I would never want to be a philosopher. I merely observe the world. It is so large and complex—to attempt to regulate it would be to deny part of its existence. Taoism is good as an observance: as a reminder of the Yin and the Yang. But in the instruction of the natural man it goes too far. In its rejection of education it denies itself—for where would Tao be without teachers and scholars to preserve its ideas and spread its words?

9/19/88

Kurt is the most wonderful person I know. I love him. In a calm and patient way. In a grateful way—glad just to be with him as a friend.

Braunlin called today. I am going back to Mayo. Once again, the world tips. Once again, the acid-bath, biting me one layer deeper.

I just spent two hours with Kurt. He is the only one who knows there are no answers. The only one who knows that a hug is all he can give, and knows how to give it right. So it communicates his calm and not his worry. I told him he was a reservoir of calm, and finally sat long enough for it to make me sleepy. He just held me and we talked. He is in my center now. When I get scared, I think of his arms. It is almost enough to smooth the lumps in my stomach.

9/20/88

It doesn't stop. Today, I got a letter from "Caring Friends" saying not to trust Dr. MacGregor,[104] that he had no experience and that Mayo had only a 50 percent success rate. If I hadn't been with Kurt last night, I think I would have cracked. As it was, my foundation suffered quite a blow. As if waiting wasn't hard already. As if I *wanted* to go to Mayo.

I'm so tired now. I feel like I've been crying all afternoon, but I only shed two tears in Susan's office this morning. I don't have a plan. I don't know where to go. I don't know who to trust. Well, Braunlin, Mellstrom, and Weidman[105] we can trust. But these new programs . . . they have the training, but what about the experience? I swore up and down I wouldn't be anybody's first. I couldn't understand *why* anyone would go to a starting transplant program if there were more experienced ones available. But at Mayo, I can keep my connection

---

104 Christopher MacGregor, a heart transplant surgeon at Mayo. He previously led a successful heart transplant program in England and worked with Jamieson and Norman Shumway at Stanford.

105 William Weidman, Jen's pediatric cardiologist at Mayo

with the U, I can keep my place in line.[106] What the hell? What to do?

9/21/88

Braunlin called this afternoon. Two top, experienced surgeons, Ernesto Molina and Sara Shumway, are staying at the U. Molina has experience with congenital heart defects. Shumway is the daughter of one of the first transplant surgeons from Stanford. She will be in charge of the post-transplant immunosuppressant program. She has *lots* of experience.

We are all so happy. So relieved. We have a place to stand again. I sent Kurt a red rose today. He hasn't called yet.

I wake up and my life doesn't ache. No more "Oh no— this is not my reality . . ." The pain is only comparable to heartbreak—except in heartbreak, at least, there is a little voice in your head saying, "This is not *that* big a deal." No little voice in this situation. But for now, it's over.

9/22/88

How odd: this waiting, which was once the hardest thing in the world, is now "normal." I'm so relieved to be safely back at the U; waiting is the even keel. Everything is relative.

---

106 According to a news report about two weeks later, fifteen people were on the U of M heart transplant list.

Kurt still hasn't called.

I didn't finish my China reading tonight. But I'm *auditing.*

DR. SARA SHUMWAY took after her famous father in looks, quiet demeanor, and chosen field. Soon after completing her extensive cardiothoracic surgery and transplant training, she became the newest attending physician in Stuart Jamieson's department at the University of Minnesota. Norman Shumway's daughter and his protégé Jamieson would work together at the hospital where the heart transplant pioneer got his start. It was a satisfying, almost movie-worthy story line.

But scarcely a month later, on August 2, 1988, the Minneapolis *Star Tribune* reported that the U of M Hospital was investigating Jamieson for two alleged surgical mishaps: ordering heart surgery on a patient who was near death with no chance of survival, and leaving a surgical forceps in another patient's chest. The undisclosed sources also said Jamieson removed the forceps without informing the patient during a subsequent operation to control bleeding.

The next day, the University announced Jamieson would temporarily step down from his leadership role. A day later, the *Star Tribune* published a front-page retraction of its initial story about the Jamieson investigation. The newspaper had relied on sources without firsthand information, committing what the publisher called "a serious lapse of journalistic judgment."

Though none of the allegations against Jamieson were proven, on September 17 the university announced Jamieson would not be reinstated as head of Cardiothoracic Surgery. The dean of the medical school, one of Jamieson's superiors, commented that the decision was made because of Jamieson's "interpersonal leadership problems." Apparently his surgical technique was not in question after all. It was this news story that captured Jen's attention.

Over the previous two years, Jamieson had been in the Twin Cities news regularly, all positive reports about his skill and dedication. His transplant patients were alive and thriving. Jamieson's sudden removal from power at the U of M was a jarring surprise to the public and referring physicians.

Perhaps most shocked were the people on the University of Minnesota heart, heart-lung, or lung transplant lists. What were they to do? John Najarian, Chief of Surgery, sent each a letter saying that he was recruiting an experienced surgeon to fill the vacant leadership position. Jamieson met with patients and referred them to the new heart-lung transplant program at the Mayo Clinic.

Then, many people on the transplant list received the anonymous letter from "Caring Friends," urging them to disregard Jamieson's advice about joining Mayo's transplant program. Who wrote the letters, and how they obtained the addresses of those on the transplant lists, remains a mystery.

Though she had limited information, Jen needed to make a decision. Months earlier, she believed the second-best transplant program in the world was good enough for her. But that was assuming Jamieson would be in charge, which now seemed unlikely. An experienced surgical patient, Jen was wary of new programs or being someone's first case; she recognized the faint endorsement when her cardiologist Elizabeth Braunlin said a different surgeon at the U would "probably be all right." And now she had to accept that, skilled though they were, the surgeons who would hold her life in their hands were fallible human beings with conflicts and failings.

As soon as Jen received straightforward advice to remain with the U of M transplant team, she took it, eager to leave confusion behind and get back to her normal life.

9/23/88

I almost cut class this morning, but got myself out of bed with the promise of wearing my black miniskirt and bright colors. So I dressed way hot today—black mini, tights and boots, green sweater, fuchsia belt, and cranberry sweater.

I wasted most of the day in Sayles and didn't get any flowers and didn't hear from Kurt. But tonight Sue H. and I partied. I went to her place for beer about 8:00 p.m. and then we went to see Julie A. crowned Homecoming Queen at 9:00 p.m. But it was over so we went around trying to find her and ended up at a really fun party—most of the social people and granola people on campus who I know showed up. It felt so good to be dressed up.

9/24/88

Kurt can make me think . . . the way we argue, it's an intellectual pursuit of big answers. Kurt may know there are no answers to the random tragedies of life, but he'd like to know the reasons for everything else. He thinks about everything so much—it all gets sucked up into his perception, his interpretation. He accepts that everyone has a different perception, but still is very intent on defining and communicating his own. Nothing wrong with that. But in a discussion, this generally leads to either agreement or argument, more discussion, and eventual agreement. So it gets, I don't know, exhausting. Or maybe it's that I feel by the end that I've agreed too much or started seeing the world from his point of view more than my own.

The wall across the street isn't there any more. The invisible wall I used to see every time I closed the garage doors at night. I stood outside tonight, under the full moon, singing "Runaround Sue" softly to myself. I felt sadness, fear, peace. But, I thought, maybe it's just life. Maybe it's just being 21¾. Maybe not. This surgery has been very relaxing in some ways—it's given a name and face to the formless terror of life.

9/25/88

I am tired. My heart feels bigger again. Breathing seems harder. I can't suck the air in right. Sometimes I can't get to sleep on my left side because my heart shakes the whole bed. Sometimes my back hurts and I wonder if it's the size of my heart.

But today was a great day. I had dinner and watched the presidential debate with Jay, John P., Bill N., and Dave B. It's such an ego trip to be the only woman in a room full of guys. Dave is a big flirt. I felt witty and attractive. The debate made me think of freshman year and how insecure I used to get around men and politics. How I always used to feel like understanding what was going on was some sort of male secondary sex characteristic. Tonight was hilarious—I was just as quick to comment as anyone else and Jay said he was glad to have another counter to Dave's conservatism. Social acceptance and popularity are still novel and exciting to me. I keep careful track of what I say and how it is received.

And they all loved my chocolate sauce.

9/26/88

I feel like a little old woman. I feel like a bodiless head. I slept through class this morning because I felt hollow. I can't even walk at my normal pace. I'm feeling very hot now—maybe I just have the flu.

I dreamt last night that I had a little, furry, warm, clinging duck burrowing into my chest, hanging onto my shirt. My new heart? Fall has turned into the most terrifying season: so breathtakingly beautiful—driving straight towards the killing cold and death of winter. The ominousness of this feels more than symbolic this year. I am not looking forward to the cold. I remember what season it was the last time I went into heart failure. But it was beautiful out today. I love fall. Spring and summer's beauty is too easy.

But can I love the winter?

9/27/88

Had dinner with John P., John R., and Jay tonight. Can't seem to see enough of them. Jay came running in and threw his arms around me. "I missed you! Don't ever scare me by missing class again!" I was pained to respond that I was skipping class again tomorrow for my doctor's appointment. Wow—it was a real hug.

I haven't done anything lately. Well—I finished the Hayden White poster. But I'm *way* behind in China and I haven't painted in a week. All I've done is hang out with my male friends. I'm such a socialite. I feel so self-conscious about all this. I'm still so *psyched*: this was my true definition of popularity *all* through my childhood. I am beside myself.

9/28/88

I did a lot today. Or at least, I got so little sleep, it felt like a lot. I had an appointment with Braunlin, who has lost 20–30 lbs. since I last saw her and smiled when she walked into the room. She said my color was better than ever. We made an appointment for Dec. 28 and met the new surgeons. Made little difference to me—I trust them and the program and leave the finer details to them.

I think I was in shock on Monday, the day I felt hollow.

One of Jen's posters for the Carleton publications office

But overall, I feel calmer and calmer about the surgery. It's been 7½ months. I'm going to do it. I have to do it. And I can do it.

And it will come eventually.

Wu Wei.[107]

9/29/88

I *am* getting tireder. I have to rest while I'm climbing the stairs and on the way to the library now. Damn winter. It's because I have to wear all these clothes—they weigh me down.

I studied for Imperial China with Jay in the library. Everybody loves Jay. All the girls who walk by know him and wave.

Oh please let me have my heart transplant by winter, so I can go to the winter ball and dance all night. I can't wait to dance again. Imagine—I'll feel young again. I feel so old. I sit and watch. I restrain my impulses. I think instead of acting. I try to be mature about what I can't do. But imagine—to be able to kick loose and do anything! To be young and reckless and frivolous!

I'm so lucky to have that in my future. Most people, old before their time, have no reprieve to look forward to.

---

107 "Not doing," a term in Taoist philosophy

I never want to write in here unless it's new and well-phrased. But I'm lying in bed now and all I can think is how scared I am. I can't breathe. It's not new and I don't know how terribly well I'll phrase it, but I'm scared I'm going to die. I'm scared, even, that I'll get very sick and have to go to the hospital before the transplant. My life is wonderful. I am happy where I am, surrounded by so many friends with all these things I like to do. It almost feels too good. I get this terrified feeling (from taking too many English classes) that it might be some sort of grand send-off. That the reason my life is going so well is because it's about to end. I don't want to die. I'm too young.

9/30/88

I was in a funk today. It was one of those natural down days after a period of happiness. So I didn't really mind. A down day is kind of relaxing. But I am glad that I'm going to see Susan tomorrow. I am depressed about how tired I'm feeling. It's scary. I'm starting to get used to it a little now. I am sick and I am getting worse.

Kurt called tonight. He's good at sounding distant. We're getting together with Sue H. and Rusty next Saturday. It was a fine conversation, he's just so, well, curt. If you're feeling the least bit insecure he can drive you into a panic. He's very Himself. Not free-flowing and open.

Wu Wei

10/1/88

Saw Susan today. I'm getting more mellow about being tireder. I just am.

I drove out to a sunny gravel road this afternoon and did a pastel and a watercolor. It made me feel whole again to do some art. And I keep meaning to put down some of those wonderful fall colors. Finally I did.

Sometimes the irony of my life amazes me. Do you know what I got this summer, my most inactive summer in eight years? Athlete's foot. I ask you—

10/2/88

Sue H. just came by to talk for half an hour. It's nice of her to do that rather than just talk on the phone. It feels more personal. I feel like our relationship has become important. I feel like she likes me for my honesty, my reflectiveness, my seriousness and my calmness. I feel good to be there for her when she needs to see someone and talk. She never depends on anybody.

I was talking earlier with another friend who started talking about her family. Then she apologized and I said, "No problem." She said she felt I wouldn't judge her and I said I didn't mind her going on. It's weird. Everybody at Carleton has a story. Everybody has a past pain—whether, like Kurt,[108] they've dealt with it—or like most everybody else I've met, it's quivering behind their eyes. John P. is so much calmer than some of my friends: his story is easy to see and he has accepted it. He may have had a rough life as a blind boy, but he's not damaged by it.[109]

10/3/88

I spent $20 on love beads today . . . yikes! But I made John P. a string tonight and John R. informed me last week that he had broken his last strand. Maybe someday they'll be $200 collector's items.

I did a fall grass painting today. It was one of those rare and wonderful works from a sketch that starts and finishes on the same day. I didn't feel as post-orgasmic as I did after I finished the last one like this (the Ideal Café) but I'm so happy now. Usually I never feel good about

---

108 During childhood, Kurt lost an older brother, as well as his father.
109 John P. had been blind since birth.

a painting—there's always something nagging at me, something else I could do. Maybe I could do something to the—no, it's fine. The grass is wonderful. I could remember what it looked like well enough to be able to improve on the sketch. Finally, I've done a painting about the grass I've been thinking about all summer.

It might freeze tonight. All summer I wanted this, didn't I?

Jay was so sweet today. I complained to him about something and he looked at me with his big sorrowful eyes and put his hand on my back. Wu wei, man. Wu wei.

10/4/88

Okay, I worked on the painting a little more today. But I still love it.

Dad carried me up the stairs tonight. I didn't want to ask him, I knew he'd look at me with worried eyes and say, "Oh, baby." But Mom yelled at me for trying to protect him and we sat on the couch and cried for a while. I hate crying about it. I think about all the people in the world in wars and hospitals and bad situations in general and think that I have no right to be upset about this. But maybe sadness is everyone's right. Happiness isn't the basic emotion we all must have. Somebody always has it worse—okay, somebody else can be sad too. We can *all* be sad. And tired. And disappointed that life isn't going easier than we'd hoped. And depressed. Depressed looking at the darker side. Acceptance is good, but it is tense and suppressing. I should allow myself to feel sad, depressed, tired. I have joined the masses, who know that life is not easy, but it's okay to wish it were.

So I've gone back to country music. I find the more history I study, the more I like pop culture. Not pop-music teenage pop culture, but the real undercurrents of Americana. Adult pop culture: Elvis, country music, truck stops, fuzzy dice. There's something appealing in pop-cheese-culture, the ancient solace in ritual, tradition, and symbol.

I'm making Kris a Velvet Elvis for Christmas. Actually, it's velour, but I'm having so much fun telling everyone it's Comps research. I may very well end up doing something like that in a series of works on pop culture.

10/5/88

I've been reading about Elvis all day. What a gross, perverted, codependent, sexist, disgusting, depressing person. Abused and abusing. A great puppet, a skulking wreck hiding in worthless luxury under a miraculously lucrative image. Good thing he's dead. He could probably get elected President. It's almost enough to turn me off of the painting. But Kris will love it. Joe Byrne laughed his head off when he saw it.

Sue L.[110] came to lunch today and I confessed to her that I was interested in Jay. She says she'll be my spy. We'll see if he will tell her if he likes me or anybody else. I'm not in love with him, but he is so nice. Going out with him might be fun.

Dad talked today with Braunlin and told her how tired I've been. She told him that if I get really tired I can go into the hospital intensive care unit and be on an IV of dobutamine[111] for a few days, which will recharge my batteries for 6 weeks. Hey! That sounds pretty good. I wonder how risky it is. I wonder how many visitors I can have in ICU. I wonder if it will make my heart beat more or less irregularly.

Great river, let me pass through this transplant before I have to examine any more life-extending measures.

10/6/88

I just got back from Jay and John P.'s. I brought them brownies—another brownie crisis, it was awfully good of them to take them off my hands. John and I spent about two hours talking and then Jay came home. I was afraid he wanted me to go so he could work, but he put "Velvet Elvis" (Weird Al) on for me, so he must have wanted me to stay. I asked him to play me some

---

110 Yet another Carleton friend named Sue

111 Dobutamine stimulates heart muscle receptors and improves cardiac output. It could be given over three days as a temporary treatment for severe heart failure.

Hank Williams and spent another hour listening to Hank yodel and wrestling with John's guide dog Baron. Baron really accepts me—it's great. Baron and Tim both act as barometers—it they like you, it's a pretty good indication of how the other people in the room feel about you. As John says, "Oop—you're part of the family now."

Watching Jay listen to country music makes him seem alive—he comes out of his studious shell. I could never see him at the cabin because there'd be no desk or bookshelf to hide behind. But if there was Hank Williams on the box, he could kick back and have a beer.

10/7/88

Jay cursed me all day. "'Play some Hank Williams for me, Jay,' she said," I heard him telling people as he explained why he had to stay up until 6:00 a.m. to finish his work. He lit up when he saw me in class this morning though.

Kurt called last night. We were finalizing our plans for tomorrow. But I was blue afterwards. Finally I admitted to myself that I was, indeed, bummed out that he didn't want to go out with me. And I miss him. I never see him now. I don't know what the heck I want to do with him, especially as things seem to be going so well with Jay. But I've decided I'm sick of being single. I want to be kissed. That's my goal. I'd like someone to hang out with. I'd like that kind of support that comes with a boyfriend: someone who loves you and wants to be with you more than anyone else.

Mom and Dad left for the cabin tonight and Sue H. is staying here again. I called the Pediatric Cardiologist on call tonight because my chest hurt. I said I didn't particularly want to come in and be tested, but neither did I want to die in my sleep. She was very reassuring, though. She said a weakened heart is more susceptible to adrenaline and other stress-related chemicals. So it's not all New-Ageisms. She also suspects Dr. Shumway bruised the sac around my heart when she was "click-ing" my sternum. I'm sure that's it. The doctor was really nice—she just talked and talked. I love the U—every-one is so friendly. Like to go spend a couple weeks there sometime soon . . .

10/8/88

Pipedream come true: Kurt is sleeping in the guest room. Unfortunately, I am sleeping in my bed. Oh well, I get to have breakfast with him.

He's sleeping without his shirt on. Oh Lord. Remember! I'm too tired to get horny!

Dinner with Sue H. and Rusty was fine. Sue and I weren't quite as wild as I anticipated and, of course, Kurt and I analyzed everything afterwards. But I like doing that.

So heck.

He dressed up tonight. He looked so good. I like him so much. But it's probably for the best that we're sleeping apart. I don't want to pressure him. Give it time to grow.

I wonder if he'll ever like me that way. Heaven would be sleeping three rooms west. And I admitted to Susan this morning that I am tired of being alone and I want a boyfriend.

But I also want to get this surgery over with. I guess I'll have to carry both burdens a little farther. It's just not having to carry one would make the other seem so much lighter.

10/9/88

I just traded pillows with the guest bed—one of them still smells like him.

This morning I got up at 10:00 a.m. and at 11:00 a.m. woke him up with coffee in bed. He slept in his shorts and was lying there with the blanket just up to his tummy. Oh my. He has a lovely, hairy chest. (And the start of a goody trail.) And nice shoulders. And a beautiful back. He drank his coffee without his glasses on—he was thoroughly gorgeous! (He asked me later if I thought he looked different without his glasses on. I said I wasn't sure—he was a little cuter, but maybe that's because he didn't have any clothes on.) We sat there and talked until about noon, when Sue H. called. Then he got dressed and we went downstairs for a leisurely breakfast. It was wonderful. Except that it was utterly platonic.

I dropped him off at St. Olaf and got stung by a bee while driving home with my elbow out the window. It was a drag until I remembered the last time I got stung: just before I went into the hospital for my last surgery. It's a sign! Maybe I'll have the transplant this week.

Wai-han and Chang-tai had their baby last night—an 8-lb. baby boy! I brought Wai-han a card and a Sybil print in the hospital. On the card, I copied the Chinese song Chang-tai taught us in class. She could read it!

10/10/88

Was it just last week I was afraid to ask Dad to carry me upstairs? I'm so tired. I can't breathe very well— I'm going to try to sleep on five pillows tonight. Maybe I'll feel better in the morning. Maybe I'll go to the hospital.

I'm back inside myself. The burden of loneliness is still a drag, but I'm so tired, I've stopped trying to carry either of these burdens anywhere. I'm just going to sit on the side of the road and stare at them for a while. I'm too tired to do anything. If someone would come and sit with me, fine. But I can wait . . .

Wu Wei. I have to learn the Chinese characters for this.

Mom and Dad got back today, but we're not fighting. Maybe it's because I'm so tired. I told them about Kurt staying after all the wine coolers and they thought that sounded very "civilized." Kurt won't know what to make of that either.

10/11/88

Had dinner with Jay and John P. tonight. John had called me up this afternoon while I was feeling tired and sorry for myself. So it really helped get me out of my pity party. I'm still tired, but I feel more cheerful. Jay fixed good, mild burritos and I brought chocolate chip pound cake and they played Hank Williams, Jimmy Rodgers, and Roy Orbison.

I dreamt last night about roads again. Always roads. Is it the Tao? Is it because I always drive to ease my mind? Is it because they symbolize the freedom I don't have— moving on in life from this place I'm stuck in? I identify with my car so much. In my dreams I swing along the highway—my car carries me, I feel my body swing back and forth. The sun is on the pavement, the sky is blue. So far, it's always summer.

10/12/88

May died today.[112] I called up J.B. to tell him about May on the 11-month anniversary of the last time we made love.

And today was Robin K.'s memorial service.[113] It seems that this fall is one big memorial service.

The unspeakable fear that I can't let out except in here is that there'll be another service in a few months and it will be for me. And of course, my parents think this too. But none of us say it.

I'm going into the hospital tomorrow. Dr. Braunlin told Dad today that I was high priority now.[114] We know she wants to bump me as high as possible to get a heart for me soon, but I heard the fear in his voice when he told me. Now that I'm going into the hospital, other people will worry about me, so I can concentrate on being cheerful and getting through it. It's like a deal I have with the doctors: they take care of me and I keep my parents convinced that I'm fine. It's such a relief to be going to the hospital. It's an action. It's a familiar action. It's a small reversal of my otherwise deteriorating condition.

---

112 May Okada was a Carleton faculty wife, then widow and employee, who lived next door to the Bonners when Jen and Tim were young. She was close to the family and often had Sunday dinner at their house.

113 The twelve-year-old son of a Carleton faculty member

114 People on the transplant list were placed in categories according to the severity of their heart failure. Entering the hospital for intravenous heart failure treatment moved Jen to a higher category and increased the chance she would be chosen if a suitable heart became available.

May wrote us the most wonderful letter a few days ago. Like the bird that flies off at the time of death with the soul, I feel like the bird brought us this letter. A last piece of May's soul.

10/13/88

Here I am in the hospital and it's not the same. I don't feel the same blind, happy faith in the doctors that I used to. I'm sad and I'm tired. They put a catheter and an arterial tap[115] in my arm and it hurts a lot and can't be moved. So I'm going to have to be very sleepy to sleep.

I'm depressed. I'm so sick. You know, I've been sick. But I never realized it. And everything hurts. The transplant—it'll only be worse. I'm scared of what could happen and scared of the pain if I get what I want.

—Sounds like a helicopter. Maybe they found me a heart.

It's 12:30 a.m. No one will call. They all think I'm sleeping. Maybe I should. Call off my pity party and give sleep a chance. I just have to restore some calmness to my mind. Remind myself all is not yet lost. My latest adorable doctor, Renaldo from Italy, says that I look better than he expected and that he expects the dobutamine to take care of my tiredness. My function is down, but my symptoms are not acute.

---

115 To administer intravenous fluids and check the oxygen content in Jen's blood

Mom says I've charmed him. He told them I was a very special young woman. I always feel old when I look into the doctors' eyes. Maybe that's what charms them: that I am beyond adulation and resentment.

He told me I should come have dinner at his house after I am better. "I want you to have a chance to taste something really good."

Oh, I sound all preachy and traumatized. I am. I'm sitting here feeling sorry for myself . . .

I wish Kurt would call. It would make me happy to know he was thinking about me. But I don't depend on him. I can get myself through this. I've gotten myself through worse. Just try to restore my old faith in the hospital. They have all the life support systems here if I need them. I'm not *that* sick.[116]

10/14/88

It's almost lunch time. I finished reading my *Calvin and Hobbes* book. They started my dobutamine drip, so I feel a lot better than last night psychologically. Just the idea that they're doing something to reverse my situation now, that I'm expected to improve, picks me up.

---

116 On her way to the hospital, Jen attended a hearing about her SSI application. The vocational expert for Social Security stated Jen could work at a full-time job. Rather than sending the usual medical statement, Dr. Braunlin appeared in person to describe Jen's disability. Jen's application was approved after two previous written denials.

Mom should be here soon. Jewelnel just called to say she would be by tomorrow.[117] I want visitors and flowers and candy and phone calls. You need the reassurance that you still have a connection with the outside world. I hope people call.

I'm feeling all shivery. I wonder if it's the dobutamine. Whee! How exciting.

I'm still scared shitless about the transplant, now that I'm thinking about it in terms of individual, ooky, painful things as opposed to one big resurrecting event.

10/15/88

My oxygen consumption is up 80 percent and my cardiac output has doubled. I have the energy to sit up and write letters again. The night is still a painful drag. I was even fussier last night. My nurses were kind of ditsy and I whined a lot.

Mom and Dad came up yesterday with two bouquets of flowers from John P., John R., and Jay, and two box-elder bugs in a jar. (It was a joke! I put that on the list as a joke!) I felt loved. And then Sue H. called last night and I called John P. and completely exhausted myself talking to them. Both plan on coming up today at about the same time and Jewelnel isn't here yet, so I'm wondering if I'm going to have a mob visit at 1:00 p.m. Mom

---

117 Jewelnel Davis, the Carleton chaplain

and Dad are coming up at 4:00 p.m. and then going to the Greg Brown concert. Kurt is coming up at 6:00 or 7:00 p.m.

Now it's 1:30 p.m. I just finished picking through lunch. Jewelnel called to say she hurt her back and couldn't come. Fred and S. came at 10:20 a.m., stayed until 11:00 a.m., and completely wore me out. I hope it was particular to their case (we kept the conversation going very well)—I hope John, John, and Jay don't wear me out so fast.

They said they'd be here early afternoon. I was trying to nap after Fred and S., but now I'm too excited, so I guess I'll just sit here and vegetate.

10:00 p.m. Dad just left, Kurt before. It's the first time I've felt empty after someone's left. Empty and frustrated. It's easy not to say what I wanted to say with Kurt. So easy to follow the conversation. Jen—if you assert yourself in the conversation, you won't always be wondering if you're subverting yourself around him. I get to resenting him—what makes him think he's so great, talking about this dorky stuff all the time instead of what I want to talk about?

I'm depressed that he's gone.

He was worried about me. I tried to be reassuring, but as I was crying with Dad just before he came, it was a little hard. I just said, "I *will* get the transplant soon."

Instead of it being this far off thing that would come as more of a favor than an outright necessity, it is essential to my survival, and like every other time, the hospital will come through. I really hoped it would come before I was sick enough to be in the hospital, but on the other hand, being sick now means it will have to come sooner.

Jay, John P., and John R. came with Rick and Sue L. It was great, but after an hour I was a wreck. Too much laughing and attempting to entertain. They brought me a Betty Boop "You Make Me Tingle" balloon. Normally this would be offensive—and perhaps they got it solely for the tackiness factor. But I was flattered—if a crowd of guys brings you a balloon with a sex symbol on it, it suggests they identify you with the sex symbol. Or am I being immodest?

Kurt hugged me good night for a long time. And made more than one vague reference to some post-transplant sexual activity that involved us. In a reference to us someday taking a shopping trip to Victoria's Secret: "We're doing a little stocking up for the future." But then said, "It was a joke! Okay, it was a bad joke, but it was a joke." Was he answering my raised eyebrows or pretending to talk to the people at Victoria's Secret?

10/16/88

I could hardly eat my Cheerios this morning. I listened to my heart with a stethoscope and it is big and beating fast and sounds *so* sick. I lay in bed last night and listened to it thonk around and thought about how glad I was to be in the hospital. I'm starting to wonder if I want to go home.

Midnight. All right, Kurt—just finished your Bible, *Illusions* by Richard Bach. Something about the way he has been quoting it all summer made me terribly skeptical. It was preachy and a little pretentious, a little who-the-hell-does-this-guy-think-he-is-anyway? But it did make me think. And since the overall message is "You are your own messiah"—essentially "Do what you want"—I guess it's harmless. But the urge to write it implies a certain condemnation of how other people live. The concept "Messiah" implies a hierarchy. More than that—it implies an enlightened minority. Fine—most of us have a desire to be in an enlightened minority. But the unenlightened you always have with you. The bad feeling I get in my stomach is that he is narrowing his eyes at these "less-advanced" masses. The Messiah attempts to understand everything about her/himself, which, if achieved, suggests a very balanced and together person. But then, to fulfill the task of Messiah, he or she sets out to tell others. In this, we have a pathology. And that's what makes me nervous about the book.

But then, why am I writing this? I do frequently dream of these diaries being discovered after my death and edited down (probably leaving out all my smiley faces and most of my references to getting laid). But I don't choose to call myself Messiah. I am an artist. It is an artist's job to record her art—*for her*—and then, perhaps, to sell it, to pay the rent. Artists, writers, we exist because people share. It is our gift, as human beings, this multitude of perspectives. If I hope to accomplish anything by what I write here, it would be to entertain, and possibly, by showing how I came to know myself, to affirm someone else's journey.

10/17/88

I write in here because I like discussing things with myself. I can work out how I feel about things and be more prepared to discuss them with others. The only reason I think about my diary someday being printed is because I've read other people's diaries and they've helped me, especially as a teenager, get ideas for how to get through my own life. The thing about *Illusions* is that it pretends to be An Answer. A diary is just there, take from it what you will. I'm not writing this entry with an audience in mind. I'm writing it because this argument is in my head and I want to work it out.

5:15 p.m. Kurt called. I told him I'd finished *Illusions* and he said, "Isn't it great?!" I said it was in some parts. I hate coming down on something somebody's really into. But these things bother me and when I water down my criticism I get mad at myself.

Remember the central tenet of the book: be true to yourself. If Kurt likes this book so much, he will appreciate my being true to this principle, even if it means criticism of the author.

What I didn't like about that book was the structure. The idea of the "Messiah's Handbook"—*rules*. I talked to Mom and she said she felt books like that were too simple. I agree. Like my first introduction to Taoism: nice ideas, but I rejected it because it was so unreal. The tenets are good to bear in mind, but a society run solely on them would disintegrate in a hurry.

My goals in life are to love and learn, not know and understand. The latter imply answers, gradients, quantitative amounts. They imply that life can be regarded as a test or game in which you succeed or lose. They bring it back to the contest or the race that I rejected long ago. There are no Answers I am looking for. I have no Task.

Even if this sickness got me now, I would be happy, because I have loved and been loved all of my life. In these last few days here, I have received love from so many people—it is proof to me that I am fulfilling my goal. Tim doesn't Know or Understand much of Life—much that he articulates, at least. But he's happy. Why do you have to be an Advanced Soul to have a truly worthwhile life?

Richard Bach talked about The River, but he talked about it with superiority. He talked about the Messiah being the only one floating free and everyone else—the "lesser masses"—clinging to the rocks, fighting the current. Oh give people a fucking break once in a while—we are *all* floating. We are *all* riding the river. Some may be trying to swim against the current—some may be trying to swim with the current, afraid they won't get anywhere otherwise—and some may be trying to get out. I'm sick of the idea that 99.9 percent of the people in the world don't know their ass from their elbow. There are jerks in the world and there are thoughtless people in the world—and sometimes it *seems* like they're 99.9 percent of the people in the world, but they're not. People do what they have to do to survive.

I have a lot of faith in humanity. I don't want to rise above it. I'm human. I want to enjoy being human. I'll rise above when I'm dead and go on to being whatever one is when one dies. If you're so "advanced," why do you feel compelled to reject what you are?

10/18/88

I'm home in the living room with the warm light and the Oriental rug over the hardwood floor. Mom has some beautiful Telemann horn music on the radio. I am wearing my magenta turtleneck and my teal blue sweater. Such a wonderful change from pastels and plastic.

I'm very tired—I might go to bed now (8:00 p.m.). It's odd, the first day home.

10/19/88

I did a lot more today. I'm still tired, but I'm getting my legs back at least.

Just reread my diary from last winter and am now feeling very sick of my writing.

10/20/88

It's 10:00 p.m., I've been in bed for 2½ hours already, but haven't slept. I can make it through the day if I stay in bed for at least twelve hours.

Kurt came by today. He brought my ticket for *Ghosts*[118] this weekend and a Taj Mahal record! He stayed for about two hours even though I know he's busy as hell. Jay and John P. had come by earlier and John P. was still there. So I got to introduce him to Kurt.

John left at 4:00 p.m. and Kurt stayed until 5:30 p.m. We sat on the couch and played the Taj record—it's better than the one I bought last year. He said he told his mom about three of my cards: the marriage proposal, "I didn't know you liked coffee," and "Kurt! I'm pregnant!" She laughed and said they were "priceless." *Quelle mere!* I told him if he wouldn't marry me, I'd marry her.

I was feeling good. I was saying whatever was on my mind. The trip to Victoria's Secret came up and I told

118 A play by Henrik Ibsen

him I thought that added a new dimension to the relationship. He said, "I could see that happening." I can't seem to draw the right smiley face to express my inner exhilaration at this. Oh, that's just what I wanted to hear. His feelings for me *are* growing. I am correct in my interpretation of his adoring looks and constant attention. I saw his eyes widen when I mentioned my black mini-skirt. I think right now we are mostly just very good friends. But it's wonderful to know that he will allow it to grow.

I'm in love.

10/21/88

Mom's starting to give me stress. I'm sick of her flopping down across the room from me and going on about "how tired we all are!" I am tired in my heart. That's it. I don't need anyone to remind me that I'm under stress. Why does she have to do this? Why can't she just let me deal? I know it affects her too, but it doesn't have to affect her so strongly.

10/22/88

"He seemed to be crushing scent out of the world with his footsteps. Crushing aromatic herbs with every step he took. Spice hung about him. He was a glance from God."

—Z.N. Hurston, *Their Eyes Were Watching God*

That's almost how I feel about Kurt. All day long I sit and listen to the Taj Mahal record he brought me and the Aretha Franklin tape I have.

Oh, it feels sublime to ease back in those love songs with the sweetness of feeling them exactly. So relaxing to think he could even love me back. Mom said today, "That boy thinks an awful lot of you. I can see it in his eyes," as we were listening to Taj this afternoon.

When I see his face in the door window, the sun comes up behind his head. And then he comes in, in his quiet way, and lets it grow. He doesn't pump it to the bursting point with giddiness or tease me into worrying. He just sits there until I'm convinced that even if he never does kiss me, I am blessed enough by our friendship.

"Ah been a delegate to de big 'ssociation of life."
—*Their Eyes Were Watching God*

Such a wonderful book. Much more about Knowing and Understanding than anything by Richard Bach. It's about what is important. Kurt and I talked about *Illusions* and seemed to reach some agreement without much argument. He still loves it, but he's much more of an introvert than I. It doesn't bother him so much that the "Messiah" doesn't have any friends.

Zora Neale Hurston and Toni Cade Bambara make me drunk with their writing. Someday I'll get to write like that, if Mom is right and I really should be a writer. I have no dialect to use. I have to force the poetry into my language. Or did Hurston do the same?—Could the people she wrote about really have spoken so beautifully every time they opened their mouths?

"You done hurt muh heart, now you come wid uh lie tuh bruise mah ears! Turn go mah hands!"

I talked with Susan today. I cried about how tired I was of the way Mom had been carrying on. But after the realization of my anger, I have nothing to do but accept. I can't change her. And bringing it up only brings a fight that solves nothing. So I'll just use the energy to add to myself. I support myself now. Build it into my wall so I can leave this house and be happy on my own. Take what comes from friends and hold myself up through the dry spells. Now I have Kurt to cry to, but last winter I didn't and I might not again.

But now he's lit a stick of incense inside me and it smells sweet every time I think of him.

10/23/88

Jay called me up tonight and said, "Hello, honey." Then he said, "What's this I hear about a guy from Olaf?" Then he said he and Kristen P. were going to start going out.

Whoa.

Well, I guess if he's got Kristen, I don't have to feel bad about him knowing about Kurt. I told him there wasn't much to tell about this guy from Olaf (yet).

I wonder if Jay's been checking me out all the same. He lets his knee rest against mine under the table and such. Maybe he liked us both and made the decision when he heard about Kurt. I wonder.

Kristen's a bit of a prude, but then so is Jay. I think they're very right for each other. Kinda weird, kinda brilliant, really nice—perfect. He termed it as an "alliance." I wonder how much actual *mashing* will take place?

Went to Kurt's play with Sean tonight. Stayed out for 4½ hours. Yay! I'm getting into a new rhythm.

Oh Kurt. I tried not to look at him too much tonight. I could see him in the light box all through the play. He looked so good—trim beard and black dress shirt. It's painful to think of. Now I'm so afraid, what if he never returns my love?

He could see it developing. Remember he said that.

10/24/88

Sue H.—finally I got to talk to her today. Oh, I miss girl-friends after a while.

When I see Kurt again I'm going to have to tell him what I thought of *Ghosts*. I was wishing in the middle of it that I could be reading it instead, so I could find out what Ibsen was really getting at. Well, the stage management was good. It was just the acting and the direction that weren't.

I must be feeling a lot better: I've been so horny ever since Kurt offered that bit of encouragement. Mom told me I was "resilient" today. It's so encouraging to know that I can gut my way through this, like I did last time. May gutted herself through 10 or more years. It's what I've inherited from her as my spiritual grandmother. Spirit.

10/25/88

Last night I dreamed up the most wonderful plan. I was worried that I might not get to live again with Sue S. this year, as I may be in the hospital most of winter term if I don't get the transplant by the time she gets back from Nepal. I was also bummed that her dog, Misty, just died. So I came up with a plan to apply for a grant next summer. Sue S. and I can get a dog as soon as I get the transplant and can start running with it. Then, after graduation, we can pack dog, camping gear, watercolors, oils, acrylics, six or so 3½' x 5' canvases, 10–20 2' x 3' canvas boards or stretched heavy paper, and several dozen smaller pieces of watercolor paper into the Dasher—along with our cowboy boots and Taj Mahal tapes. Then we'll drive southwest (by the Badlands and the Rockies, maybe) to the desert. There we will camp for awhile and I will do most of the large oil paintings of the rocks and the sky. Every day on the road I will do a watercolor at one of the truck stops we eat at and an acrylic wherever we camp. We'll bring the dog for peace of mind around strange men, and camp in real camp-grounds or stay in motels.

When I get home, I'll spend the rest of the summer translating the likelier paintings into prints. I told my folks about it tonight and they thought it sounded great. That was *very* encouraging. I wrote it all to Sue S. and will mail it tomorrow. I feel terrible to be the first to tell her about Misty, but I guess she has to find out soon-er or later. I just wonder if I shouldn't leave it until her boyfriend can be there to hug her when she hears. But she is 21.

Had cappuccino with Sue H. today. There was a guy there who was kind of cute in a Mr. Heintz[119] sort of way. He turned out to be bumming around on his bike, looking for work. He looked to be at least midthirties. Made me nervous a little—I had thought he was a prof at Olaf or something. He wants to be a nude model. He's probably harmless, but when you strike up a conversation with a stranger who turns out to be unemployed and camping in a friend's backyard and interested in nude modeling . . . it made me wish I hadn't been so friendly. But then

---

119 Jen's high school forensics coach

I don't want to act all paranoid. Sue smelled him differently than I did. Another good reason for a woman not to travel alone—some guys can look cute in that certain way that gets them by your weirdo-detectors.

I think I'm still awake from that espresso. And I'm hungry. Great! It's only midnight.

10/26/88

Rick came over today and we gossiped about everyone's love lives, including our own.

I'm reading *Sex Tips for Girls* again for encouragement. I so wish the transplant call would come tonight. I suspect Kurt has thought more than once about having sex after the transplant. If I could only get him to kiss me now. What is he waiting for? Is he not quite in love with me yet?

10/27/88

Kurt came over at 5:45 p.m. and stayed 'til 7:00 p.m., but we had a good dinner with margaritas and candlelight. I made chicken fajitas, which turned out pretty well. He didn't have time for dessert but is going to try to make a Kahlua-chocolate-cheesecake on Sunday, and wants me to come over. He hugged me so long and tight when he came and before he left. And when I opened the fridge to get him a drink, he came behind

me and rested his arms on my shoulders. I've occasionally touched him in little casual ways like that—maybe
three times. But that's the first time he's ever done it to
me. Since he's begun college, I no longer have that slight
worry 'round the edges that he's not quite old enough.
He's even starting to lose that freshman edge—he said
he was probably going to hang up the beef boycott this
winter for his Mom's chili.

10/28/88

I sat in Sayles and talked to people today. It was tiring
but fun. Traci, Nina, John R., and Andy. Maria L. wants
me to be the Art Editor for *Breaking Ground*.[120] What
she really wants is a censor, but I'll give it a shot. See if
they'll tolerate a non-angry feminist on their staff.

I want to do some more painting. I haven't worked in a
while. I'd like to finish the big painting from this summer. And I should stretch some more of that paper. I
need some more canvas. I liked the way I could put
washes on that big canvas on the Highway 3 painting.

I told Traci I was more in love with Kurt than I had been
with anybody else. She looked dubious. Talking with
Nina was much more fun. She wants her boyfriend to
take hormones so he can nurse their children. But he
doesn't want to. "He's so insensitive!" she wails.

---

120 A feminist journal published by members of the Carleton community

10/29/88

I just got back from Nina's Halloween party. I went as George Bush's "Thousand Points of Light."[121] Mom and Dad thought it was the greatest costume ever. I wore my black turtleneck and leggings and we taped little white Christmas tree lights all over me. Plugged in, it was *gorgeous*. I got a lot of compliments based on looks alone. But the people who got the joke were floored.

A thousand points of light costume

---

121 From George H. W. Bush's 1989 inaugural address, in which Bush described an image of community organizations "that are spread like stars throughout the nation doing good"

The party was fun, but I was too tired to do anything but sit in the La-Z-Boy. So I felt like more of a wallflower than ever. There were a lot of people there I didn't know. Most of the time, if people stare at me, I assume it's for positive reasons—tonight I looked way hot, so of course people were staring. But I was tired and feeling shy and small. So I felt pushed outside by their stares. But I had a good excuse. Next month, I'll be rowdy at parties.

I hope.

Went to Boliou and did some more work on the Hwy 3 painting. I think it looks a little better, but it's not quite done.

10/30/88

Big date with Kurt tonight. I'm so confused. Maybe it's because we were at his house. All the innuendo, all the physical contact, all of that unspoken momentum I felt everywhere else—*gone*. Was it because his Mom was upstairs? I don't understand. We sat in his kitchen, watching movies, and felt Just Friends to the core. The old distance was there. The vacuum that lately has been replaced by a slight electricity.

The weirdest thing is that *this afternoon*, I saw him at Dunvegan's and he was acting totally psyched, totally bouncy, and totally interested. He touched me on the shoulder. He was bouncing around the store.

Worst of all, I'm afraid he may think I tried to kiss him. We were hugging, before I left. I commented on how he smelled like cheesecake, as he had just taken a taste of the chocolate cheesecake. He blew in my face and I laughed and then turned to hug him straight on. He pulled away as I turned and said, "Oh my . . . !" I pulled away, instinctively going with the joke, "My goodness—whatever came over me?" But now I wonder if he really does think I tried to kiss him. Not that I would have minded, but I am very definitely leaving that up to him. He's the one who wasn't ready—he's the one who should say when we should move further.

There's only one thing worse than rejection and that is being rejected for something you didn't even mean to do.

10/31/88

I've been so pissed at him all day. It's easier on the heart than being confused. I feel toyed with. He knows I think he's wonderful, but doesn't think I need to hear it from him. I feel like he's just getting his ego gratification from me, but doesn't intend to do anything to return it. Last night pulled the rug out from under me. I don't know where I stand with him. He wants to stay here this weekend. Does he just want to be doted on?

If he's not ready to give me the love and respect I would like to give him, that's his loss. It makes me think he's a little less mature than I thought he was. But I'll go on, with my art and my friends and my life. And I could maybe even still be friends with him after a space.

I wanted to give him my soul, and all the sunshine in the world along with it. But he's smug and absorbing it all in. Well, not necessarily. He brought me Taj and the cheesecake. I can feel loved by his actions. If I could only understand his feelings.

I'm closing in myself again. I guess it's good to do that once in a while. Maybe Kurt saw me opening up and unconsciously warned me that he wasn't ready for it.

Maybe Sean can explain him to me tomorrow.

No Time is Wasted Time

11/1/88

Sean and I talked Kurt inside out and I feel close to Kurt
again. Sean couldn't tell me anything about our relationship or his intentions, but he had a lot to say from the
other side of his character. I said, "Sean, explain Kurt
to me," but it turns out I'd have a much better chance
of explaining Kurt to him. Sean's known him since 6th
grade, but didn't really start getting to know him well
until last year. And Kurt's opened up to me in ways he
just wouldn't with a guy. Or at least, he hasn't with Sean.
It was a great talk. Both of us love Kurt and desperately
want to get inside his walls a little more. Talking to Sean
made me realize how far I've gotten inside these walls.

It's no surprise Kurt is taking it slow if this is the closest
he's ever gotten to a non-family member, with the possible exception of his old girlfriend. And Sean doubts
that. And I'm sure he's still afraid to get too close, that
he'll lose me. Maybe that's why he seems to be waiting

until after the surgery. He's not the type to just be in it for sex. Unconsciously, though, he wants to wait until I'm out of such an obvious danger zone. I wonder.[122]

11/2/88

Talked to Susan, Mom, Jay, and John P. today. I feel good. Susan felt like an intellectual companion. Together we analyzed the philosophical aspects of my life. She gave me a good word that I hadn't thought of before. She said, "It's hard because people always *romanticize* your situation." That seemed to fit well.

Jay and John P. came over for the last of the cheesecake. They were sure up. I think Jay is definitely scoping me. The innuendo was flying! I told him about the letter I wrote to the *'Tonian*. He said he'd liked Beth S.'s article.[123] So I screamed at him about sexism and what was wrong with her article. He asked, "Women can enjoy sex?" I said, "Do you know a man who has multiple orgasms?" Well . . . ! I heard about that for the rest of the night. *Somehow*, he got the idea that *I* have multiple orgasms.

---

122 Years later, Kurt wrote and performed the play *Decaffeinated Tragedy* about his relationship with Jen.

123 Beth S. had written an opinion piece in the student newspaper saying the Carleton Women's Rugby Team used sexual themes and innuendo to sell its events. She argued that their behavior should be considered a form of sexual harassment and that "their characterization of themselves is unacceptable because it hurts all women." Jen's letter to the editor the following week made it clear she got the humor in what the rugby team was doing, and that women should be free to "talk about sex because they actually like it or (God forbid) wish to make a little joke." She concluded, "If we regard ourselves as powerful, sexually or otherwise, we are much harder to take advantage of. If we regard ourselves as powerless, we become not only victims of men, but worse, of ourselves."

Good grief. It would have been fine except for half the conversation, my mom was sitting in the other room. We also sat and sang all these great old songs. After they left, I went out to see if Mom would reproach me for such bawdy talk with the boys, but all she said was how sweet they were and how wonderful it was to hear us sing.

AROUND THIS TIME Jen let her parents know her Christmas list was on the dining room table. The Christmas holiday loomed large for Jen, since it also included her Christmas Eve birthday, and her holiday lists were serious endeavors when she was younger. The 1988 list encapsulated her actual desires within a matrix of family humor and shared understanding.

List of things I would like to have, possibly for Christmas

- A heart transplant
- New shoes (pumps)
- A camera
- Some nice underwear (nice = lace), mainly white, some black
- Black bra and/or camisole
- New clothes—easier to pick out myself—things involving outrageous amounts of $
- Bailey's Irish Cream
- OR some *real* alcohol that I really should learn to drink so Dad will stop laughing at me
- An apartment

- An 8-year-old diesel-engine station wagon with front-wheel drive and 4 speakers
- Fuzzy dice (but Jay is looking for some for me)
- Blank tapes and/or gift certificate at music store
- A saxophone—or maybe that should wait . . .
- New speakers for 8-year-old station wagon
- New contacts
- A calendar—the one with the quotes you got me last year is just the thing
- Godiva chocolate
- A scarf like Mom's new one
- Big silver earrings
- A Democratic President
- Good pens
- Watercolor pencils
- Socialized medicine
- Long black gloves and a little black hat to go with Mom's "flapper" dress
- No more than one book

11/4/88

Kurt's here again. My parents are gone and he's staying the weekend, but it is empty of that magical suspense now, because the suspense was only a torture and I had to ask him. The odd thing is that though I feel sad, I feel good too. Is it just numbness? I had out with all my feelings and he, his. He confirmed my worst fears: he didn't know anything about that electricity and couldn't remember saying anything like, "I could see that happening."

"Oh, I hate to lead you on," he said. "I still don't see my-self ever loving you—romantically," he said. "I really en-joy being friends with you," he said. The comfort is that the friendship that would have made our relationship so strong is as important to him as it is to me. I still feel just right when I'm with him. I just mourn those feelings of love I had about him.

11/5/88

Just had an amazing party with Kurt, Sue H., Rusty, Nina, and a few other friends. It's quarter to 2:00 a.m. I can't believe I'm still up. Sean came over to talk to me and Kurt. But when I got down from a midnight bath, Sean was almost asleep. He left at about 1:00 a.m. and Kurt and I talked for a while. Some of the innuendo from dinner carried over but it didn't mean anything. But at least he's mellow joking about it. I told him to bring me coffee in the morning and he asked me if I'd be shirtless.

I'm so glad we had the party tonight. I was bummed all day. I kept thinking of all the reasons why I had thought he liked me and wondering what happened to them all. All innuendo? All jokes?

Had a wonderful quiet day writing letters. I love having my parents gone. I wish I had the energy to move out now.

So do perfect men exist only in blue jeans commercials and will I never meet one?

11/6/88

I haven't slept in a week, so I don't know if it's physically possible to be in a good mood now, but I am bumming. Mom and Dad are back. Kurt is gone. We had a great dinner and all, but I was annoyed. I'd been listening to the Rolling Stones and Joni Mitchell—"Are you going to let me go there by myself? That's such a lonely thing to do"—all day and thinking of love.

No time is wasted time, in a good relationship, a bad relationship, or alone. You learn from it all. And I miss having a relationship. I want to set down this load in my heart. I want to feel safe, damnit! I feel so unsafe! I feel alone, so empty. I don't have the energy to run around tough and independent. I want security. I'm sorry if that's dependence. That's what my parents do for each other and that's what I want someone to do for me.

Kurt could do it, but only if he loved me. You can't make someone love you out of need. I can't get all my need filled from friendship, but maybe if I can stop thinking about my pain, I can appreciate the richness in our friendship that led me to think he felt more.

Oh, God—and I'm going in for a heart transplant soon. I need a vacation from myself.

Maybe if I get some sleep, I'll have the energy to go paint tomorrow.

11/7/88

I did, but it was only Elvis. Bleah. Well, it's pretty much done, at least. No more Art Prostitution.

Jen's Elvis

I'm feeling sharp and visual. Just going though *Vogue* to make Sarah's birthday card. I'm scared of the busy-work that stands between me and advertising, but I'm going to get my shit together and go for it. Half of my brain is *really* into it. I like to make decisions and think about visual and verbal punch. I could do it and I could be damn good. My posters are the best on campus and everyone is talking about my letter to the editor.

Felt better about Kurt today. Got up and put on green tights, red socks, my blue jean miniskirt, and magenta turtleneck. My mood could have gone either way, so I dressed to cheer myself up. Then I put on the Rolling Stones. After a few repetitions of "She's So Cold," which I lip-synched to in the living room and then played in the car all around town, I felt strong, free, happy, and on the loose. What I opened up, in hopes of giving to Kurt, I've gotten closed again. Fuck it. That's what the blues is all about. You Can't Always Get What You Want. Gotta go forward anyway, and you get water up your nose if you don't hold your head up.

Feeling too prepared right now, though. Something got slammed down a little bit wrong and I feel tense if I think about it. That's the trouble with being strong, free, and on the loose—it requires a certain amount of adrenaline, which is counterproductive to falling asleep. Future plans, future dreams, they all require hard-charging energy and guts. Now I need to find a way to curl up in me and provide my own shelter.

The blues gotta have that too. They can't be all about drinking yourself to sleep.

11/8/88

Dukakis just conceded the race to Bush. They interviewed Bush's adman. He said there are four things the
media wants: pictures, attacks, mistakes, and something else. Damn—I wanted to remember them. Well,
they were common sense. Someday I'll be there. I'll
show them that you can win with intelligence and style
and you don't have to be evil and lie outright.

Or maybe I'll run off to the desert and paint for the rest
of my life and not even come out to vote.

I'm depressed. I want to have energy. I want to get laid.
I want to kick the blues by dancing. Well, I've got my
second chance to look forward to. I'll never stop being
glad of that.

11/9/88

Mom and I saw our therapists today—we're real "Eight-
ies Ladies." It was a wonderful morning. I sat in the
Medical Arts Building in downtown Minneapolis and
drank coffee and wrote an extremely profound letter to
Sarah. I had another good talk with Susan. I like having that hour to think before I see her. We really have
interesting discussions. I've finally gotten past feeling
dumb when I talk to her. I suppose it's a hangup of our
society that we have to pay someone $75 an hour to get
this sort of conversation, but Susan and I focus on me in
a way that I am too modest to ask of a friend. And it'd

be exhausting to do that for another friend on a regular basis.

Now I feel that Susan likes me too. I may not have a lover, but I can get some sort of intimate emotional support from her. It's something. It helps. I feel cared for. I know I'm not alone with the monsters in my closet.

Kurt called me tonight. I'm afraid I may be a little too happy about this.

11/10/88

Today I painted. I'm working on a painting of me and J.B. Or, more exactly, an image of what I'm missing—the closeness, security, passion, and eroticism that I want right now.

Tomorrow I'm going to Hattie's[124] with Joseph. I think I'll stay there all day and paint. I love working. I love producing. I love thinking about what it is I'd really like to paint and then painting it. I've been sad that winter's coming, because the warmth is almost completely leached from the landscape. I suppose there is warmth in the browns left over, but I haven't found them yet. Today, though, I remembered what I craved to paint last year: coffee shops, diners, kitchens. Inside warmth. So, a whole new world is open to me. And tomorrow I will start.

---

124 A coffee shop

11/11/88

Cappuccino with Joseph was wonderful! We stayed there three hours talking about sex, death, religion, and philosophy.

He's probably the sort of friend Kurt thinks he wants to be to me. We like each other, find each other attractive, but have never dated and never gave it much more than a passing thought. This is *very* easy now, as Joseph is madly in love with his girlfriend. And we can talk about everything. He thinks Kurt is off his rocker and assures me I'm gorgeous. And he's so intense. We always go way off on some deep spiritual discussion about the Big Picture and Important Things. He's read *Illusions* and agreed and disagreed with it much the way I did. Joseph suggested that I have heart problems not because, as Richard Bach says, I crave excitement, but because dealing with mortality is something my soul has needed to do.

Hmm. That's a thought. Joseph also suggested that the Earth is an organism. I forget what this theory is called, but the rock is the body, vegetation is its growth cells, animals are the senses, and humans and higher life forms are its consciousness. So everything we do is contributing to a growing self-awareness of this organism.

There's a higher cause for you. Whoa.

11/12/88

Nine months. I've lost sight of the transplant again. I can't imagine it actually happening. I'm in a lower category now, since I'm out of the hospital, so it might be a while yet. Tonight I felt so normal anyway—sitting at the Big Steer for three hours with Kurt and Sean—it makes me forget how dark and long the night's been.

I realized, as I closed the garage door tonight, that millions of people think they've found love but lose, just as I have. I know it's obvious, but it wasn't until tonight that I really realized that True Love might not prevail. We were honest. We laid down our cards. And I lost. So now I wish we could go back to bluffing for a little longer. Though knowing Kurt, he'd never fold.

I tried to think of reasons not to love him, but tonight I couldn't find them. It was a fine time, while I was with him. But as soon as he was gone, I was sad, mad, and frustrated.

Saw Joseph again tonight. Maybe I couldn't date him. We're close, but we're just a little off. Maybe that is how Kurt feels about me.

11/13/88

I brought Jay and John P. some Hydrox cookies and talked with them about sex for a while. It was fun to hang out with guys who like me. Not that I have the faintest idea what's going on with Jay, but he did kiss me on the cheek. He's still going out with Kristen and I'm still in love with Kurt. At least the level of our feelings is closer to mutual.

11/14/88

Went to the Rueb with Jay, Matt, and Phil N.[125] Another student came down for a while. She didn't try to tell me how tired she was, though she did compliment Phil on having a non-population growth family.

It seemed like a lot of the other men in the Rueb were looking at me. There were hardly any women there and I was wearing a skirt, I guess. But I felt hot. I was so pleased to last until the end. We laughed *a lot*—I was really tired.

Jay and I had a talk this afternoon. He's moving out. He didn't tell me what the problem was between him and John P. He said it would help him if I could support John through some of this, as I was a mutual friend.

I lent Jay *Sex Tips for Girls* today. He loves it.

11/15/88

I'm tired and all I've done today is talk to Jay and John P. and write a letter to Sarah. Now it's 10:37 p.m. Kurt won't

---

125 Philip Niles, a Carleton history professor

call tonight. Didn't he say he'd call last night? Jay had dinner with me and Mom tonight. He's so sweet. He and Kristen are working again. But he still flirts with me. It's a puzzle but maybe we'll just be that sort of friends. Maybe we're both each other's second-best choice.

11/16/88

I called Kurt today. He forgot. He felt really bad about it, which reassured me as to his character. So we're going to go up to Victoria's Secret tomorrow and also eat somewhere. I felt odd on the phone tonight. We were so friendly and happy but underneath, I was so confused and annoyed.

11/17/88

Kurt and I had a good time this afternoon, despite the contradiction of shopping for horny underwear with a man who refuses to date me. He had a new definition of love that he wanted to try out on me. He said love is a stronger friendship based on insecurities. I called him on that. I told him that if he ever fell in love he would fight it every step of the way because he doesn't want to give up that control. He agreed. I told him (later) that if you lie back, you will float. And the current will carry you—swimming doesn't really make much difference and it just tires you out. He gave me the thumbs-up and said, "Taoism. Yeah."

We had a good talk. I feel good about him again. No love, but we can have deep and intense discussions about intellectual stuff.

I bought a garter belt. He bought a nightshirt-type thing for Megan. Negligee for his ex-girlfriend? Oh well, what can you do?

Went to transplant support group today and talked about car accidents again. I feel like a vulture. But why are vultures more maligned than predators? They don't hurt anybody. They aid in the natural process of decomposition. Why is it sinister to profit from a misfortune you didn't cause, while predators are considered valiant for doing others harm?

11/18/88

Went to the L&M bar in Dundas[126] this afternoon with Sue H. and other friends including Beth. We drank Coors beer on special. It was so relaxing and wonderful! The bartender was real nice to us and made us feel welcome even though we were college kids. I suppose five cute young women are five cute young women, wherever they're from. And we were polite and left a tip. It was so filling and nourishing. I felt alive again. I felt like I'd gone dancing. The beer tasted good and I felt in charge of myself, not like I was riding on anyone's coattails.

---

126 A small town near Northfield

It felt right, the way it did last spring, when I said I didn't need a boyfriend. There's something about drinking together that's richer than going for cappuccino, even though it's the same conversation and the same company. Maybe it's the different chemicals in the brain after alcohol, as opposed to caffeine. At Hattie's, we got real wired and talked about philosophy. In the L&M, we got all loose and giggly and talked about sex. There's more sit-back laughter and comfortable relaxing. We're going to do it every Friday we are able.

I'm torn in half by waiting. I want to have sex and wear my cowboy boots. I want to drive across the country, paint deserts, and go dancing. All these things I have to wait to do. But I don't want to put my life on hold. More and more, it seems there's just no way I'll get the transplant until I'm in the hospital. There are so many people waiting. There are so many things I want to do that take more energy than I have. So many ideas that are more concrete than just floating around in coffee shops and bars and doing the odd watercolor.

But still, I'm coming to think that the peak of human experience is sitting around in a coffee shop, a truck stop, or a small-town bar with a good group of friends. If you want to look at the Big Picture, you can hold hands and have a look, while still feeling secure and not lonely. But it's the small picture where you are that makes you feel cozy and feel like life is happy and worth living.

And sitting in the L&M feels just like dancing.

11/19/88

"My heart is so filled up with love, there's no part left to protest . . ."

—paraphrase from *Much Ado About Nothing*

With relief, the above line no longer describes my feelings for Kurt. He and Sean came for dinner tonight. Somehow I've made the switch. I've put him out of my head. Were he to change his mind, I'd still be his for the asking. But somehow I can tuck that feeling back inside my heart where it cannot hurt me every time I see him.

11/20/88

The Randy Travis song "Forever and Ever, Amen" is on. I love it now, ever since Jay told me he sang it to Kristen when it came on the radio out at the Big Steer.

Went to the Big Steer tonight with Kurt, Sean, and four others. Kurt is a real dork when he's with Sean, though. They are both so nice, but when they're together, they regress to Jr. High.

11/22/88

I had a huge migraine last night and felt goopy all day today. But I still managed to stay up until 1:35 a.m.

Susan said something really important to me yesterday. She suggested it's not only Kurt who may be unconsciously putting dating off until after the transplant. She suggested that I, too, am looking at it that way. I think she's right. Everyone's been so impressed with how much I have not put off, but still, there are a lot of things I'm holding back on. So I've been trying to think of my situation as just the way it is now, not a part of a future whole. As I'm always saying, I could die before I get to live with the new heart. So this is how I have to live now. I can't get a job. I can't move out. But I can date someone. I can paint. I can be myself.

11/23/88

Jay and Rick came by for goodbye coffee today.[127] Jay kissed me on the cheek and said, "Are you going to call me?" Well, I had to say yes. I adore Jay, but I don't love him. If he and Kristen are in love, I don't want to get in the way. But right now it doesn't matter anyway. For six weeks I will have the pleasure of corresponding with the two most intelligent men at Carleton: John R. and Jay. This, I am looking forward to.

Mom read in the paper today that the silicone implants she has have caused cancer in 20 percent of rats tested. Her doctor at Mayo said not to worry, but that's small comfort. I've felt all year that she was trying to appropriate my problem. Maybe it'll give her something to think about. But really, it wasn't bothering me *that* much.

---

127 Fall term at Carleton was ending.

Makes me believe in God. In a tough and exacting God. A God who knows what you need to learn and won't let you alone until you've learned it.

I still like the image of the Tao the best, but it does seem that in our lives, there's been something directing our course down the river so that we'll run into every learning experience on the way.

"The heavier the burden, the closer our lives come to the earth, the more real and truthful they become."
—Milan Kundera, *The Unbearable Lightness of Being*

11/24/88
I'm reading *The Unbearable Lightness of Being* now. It deals with a lot of crucial ideas about freedom and life that I prefer to the ideas in *Illusions*. And it keeps you thinking as it centers on a man who can't be monogamous, but isn't evil. The book resists, at its core, our immediate desire to divide its messages into good and bad, prevents you from relaxing and not thinking about each idea.

I think that our civilization is philosophically so far behind the Chinese, who have had the concept of Yin and Yang for four (?) thousand years. It is such a revelation in Western thought to come across a book that deals with an approximation of this idea.

11/25/88

It's 3:09 a.m. I just got back from movies with Sean. Kurt was there too but I didn't talk to him. Sean and I sat for two hours after the movies and discussed life, love, and Kurt. Sean told me Kurt was kind of dopey about a girl on his floor. I feel that old familiar kick in the stomach. Why is it that he generates a spark in me, yet I can't seem to catch his eye?

I wish I could lose him for good in my heart. Sometimes the open road of myself appears and I think of talks with Sue S. or other women. I think of my art and get a rush of independence and pride. It makes me feel good and centered in myself. But still I know that if Kurt wanted to give it a go, I'd say yes.

I wanted so badly not to be a J.B. to him, but I think that, for now, that's the best I could hope for. If I dated him now, there'd be no hope of being more than a learning experience. But still, I'd do it. Because no time is wasted time. Because everything in life is a learning experience and I'd rather get out there and experience than sit home and think. And it could end at any time. So you've got to take what life offers you when it offers it.

11/26/88

This is going to be a torturous weekend. Tomorrow Sean and Kurt and I are going out to celebrate Sean's birthday. Tonight I spent three hours talking to them to avoid the strange Japanese student who makes me nervous and keeps showing up in Northfield unannounced. (I can't decide if he's just insecure or a Japanese Axe Murderer—and being alone when he said he might drop by, I decided not to risk it.) Kurt appeared relieved that Sean had told me about the girl he likes. So we talked about it for a while as though it were no big deal. I was not quite as bouncy as I am when we discuss other things (say, waste management, euthanasia . . .).

11/27/88

I am closing up more day by day. I'm *almost* happy to be single again. I don't need a deep commitment anymore. I could be happy with friendly-dating Jay. I could play the field if he stays with Kristen. It's an exhilaration to be wide open, but such a safe relief when you're finally closed up.

11/28/88

Got a letter from Pat today, complimenting me on my letter to the *'Tonian* and asking about any Art Scandals. It was devoid of personal references, but I liked the letter. I'm glad I worked him into my circle of semi-permanent friends sophomore year. I can't bear his company for too long, now, but every few months I love to sit down and talk with him. Or get a letter. He is a good writer. He is an intelligent and artistic person, which is what I value from our infrequent contact. And it makes me feel so worldly to get a dry, intellectual letter from a former crush.

John P. and I had cappuccino this afternoon. We always talk about defects. Either we share personal anecdotes about being handicapped, which is fun, or we discuss character flaws in people we know. John seems unable to discuss the positive. I'm sure it's harder to socialize, being blind. Mrs. P. looks like she did her best to insulate John from harm and may have kept him out of the swing of things more than he should be.

11/29/88

"If you ain't lovin', you ain't livin' . . ." I know! I know! Actually, I'm feeling all right in my singleness right now. Kurt really is too young. I keep trying to make him over in my own image because he's still so unfinished. I don't know whether this is a general pathology, or a temporary aberration, but it should not be encouraged. I should date men who I do not have the constant urge to fix. I know I said I didn't want to change him when I was in love with him. Maybe you just can't know until afterwards.

11/30/88

I must be closed up pretty well. I have had a hard time opening up to Susan again. Oh well.

I'm kind of tipsy in my handwriting—I just had a beer and nachos with Dad.

Tomorrow Dad and I are going to be on WCCO (Ch. 4) on a human-interest spot about transplants. I'm going to try to sleep now while the beer's still got me slightly relaxed.

Let The River Carry Me

12/1/88

We did okay, Dad and I. We looked all right—not stunning—but all right. We sounded reasonable—not sparkling and witty—but intelligent.

The odd thing about being on the news is that it reminds me how "abnormal" my life is. Normal people don't get on the news. As I watched myself, I found myself slipping into news-watch-phase: this mild shock mixed in with sympathy for whomever was being shown with whatever problem or tragedy. I came upstairs thinking "Heart transplant! God, that'd be hard; what in the world would it be like to live with that?"

So which reality is real? My reality allows for it all to be relative, but that reality says it's all concrete. The newscasters are normal. I am abnormal. The man who interviewed us was happy. We are tragic. Putting us on the news like that builds a wall between our experience and theirs. We are outside normal people's experience.

What a small and confining reality "normal" experience is. It is the reality I remember from high school. Maybe some of my classmates have seen outside of it, but I'm sure some—most?—haven't. I don't look down on that, but it makes me sad. There is so small a margin for error in that reality.

I had the most magical dream last night. I dreamt that I was a fish and that I swam in the ocean to a new place. I climbed out on to the beach, naked, holding onto a baby girl's hand. I felt so pure and clean and full. There was all sorts of stuff afterwards about Matt, Bryce, Devin, Kris, and other people at school. We were all on this beach/island and it was very festive—perhaps a dreamscape spring term.

Maybe the transplant will come over winter term or spring break. I can't help hoping that the white sand symbolized snow and that it will come in time for winter term.

12/3/88

I'm back in the hospital for more dobutamine. I feel great already. This morning and afternoon, though, I felt as though my energy had been reduced to a thin shell. I would sit and feel fine, get bored, get up to do something, and then tire out just trying to get there. I had absolutely no reserves. There was no bath I could take, no tea I could drink, to give me strength.

Now I'm feeling fortified. I feel electric and tingly all over. But still I can't wait for night to quiet this place down so I can get some sleep.

On the way up, in the car, I started thinking that I've had a full life. I feel like I've begun to comprehend my life. I'm beginning to make peace with the way I fit into the world. People die all the time for senseless reasons. There is no justice in the sense that we learned in school. If we are reincarnated, perhaps there is in some grand over-view sense. But there's no reason I should or shouldn't die. People get so vehement about life and death: capital punishment, abortion, euthanasia. But still we die all the time. People accept the inevitability of death in statistics, yet fight to preserve this sense of power over it.

I no longer see it as important. I would like to go on living. I would like to do a lot of things. But if I die, it will not be "unjust." I do not "deserve" to live to a certain age. I am lucky to have lived at all.

A man who was a cuter, younger version of Fred just came in and in Fred's quiet, hesitant way, told us that they might have a heart for me.

They won't know for a few more hours whether the person is a donor or not. Right now, we are waiting for someone to die. I'm not thinking about that, anymore than I am thinking about the possibility of really and truly getting the transplant tonight. I came into the hospital, which increased my chances of getting the transplant. Someone's accident has increased my chances even more. But nothing is for certain and I won't think about it. I won't get my hopes up.

And I won't think about the other family somewhere in the hospital, hoping and praying even more fervently than I that this person won't die, and that I don't get my transplant tonight.

Dr. Shumway came in from her Yo-Yo Ma concert to don her scrubs. It is a definite go.

Now is the time—still can't think about it, don't want to worry—to offer up my prayer of thanks to the universe for letting me get this far. Now I'll lie back on that stretcher and let the River carry me on to the future.

The Big Association of Life

As Jen had wished, she is "dry-eyed and practical" when the transplant materializes. She removes her ring and hands it to Barbara before taking leave of her parents. Then she climbs on the hospital gurney for her journey to the operating room. The moment Jen has been dreading—going under anesthesia—is soon to arrive. Sara Shumway is about to become the third surgeon to enter her chest. Would that we could pause here a little longer. But heart transplants are done under the pressure of time, with only a handful of hours to place a precious donor heart. Along with the Bonner family, the transplant team, and the unknown donor family, we must move on.

Jen's heart anatomy, unusual since birth and distorted further by surgery, presented unique challenges to the surgeons. Scar tissue drew her heart close to her breastbone, and Shumway ran into complications right after opening Jen's chest. Only after managing massive bleeding and a series of technical problems could Shumway remove the weary organ that served Jen for nearly twenty-two years. The actual transplant, placing the donor heart, was the smoothest part of the operation.

But the long-awaited normal heart struggled against the

pressures in Jen's lungs. To give the heart a chance, Shumway turned to a portable heart-lung bypass machine called ECMO, an acronym for extracorporeal membrane oxygenation. At the time, ECMO was used mainly in infants. Jen was transported to the intensive care unit, where ECMO could oxygenate her blood for a time, and let the new heart rest.

Shumway spoke plainly with Bob and Barbara. They understood the transplant had not gone well but remained hopeful that Jen would come through as she had every time before.

Over the next thirteen days, Jen returned to the operating room three more times so Shumway could control bleeding and try to take her off ECMO. Friends found the Bonners in the hospital at almost any hour. In Northfield, Tim was unaware of Jen's peril, though he doubtless noticed his parents' absence.

Despite the respite ECMO provided, the transplanted heart couldn't function effectively in Jen's body. Her other organs failed along with her new heart. Bob and Barbara watched Jen retain more fluid and become less recognizable with each trip to the OR. They gradually realized that she would not survive and their resolute wait became a vigil.

Jen never regained consciousness after she went under anesthesia for the transplant. She was shielded from the hospital days that were so excruciating for her parents.

Stuart Jamieson, once thought to be the man who would save Jen, came to the ICU when one of his lung transplant patients was readmitted. He stopped to see Jen and told the Bonners her situation was "precarious." By then, they knew that was not quite the right word. On December 15, Jen showed signs of brain death. Neurologic tests confirmed that her ebullient personality and unconventional intelligence were no more. On

December 16, ECMO was stopped and, two minutes later, the body of Jen Bonner died.

THE NORTHFIELD COMMUNITY, diminished by the absence of students, was laden with grief. Scattered by winter break, most students could not attend Jen's funeral on December 19. Many were only vaguely aware of how sick she was, and others just assumed the transplant would be successful. Her death shocked them.

Losing Jen was perhaps hardest of all on Tim. Bob and Barbara hadn't figured out how to tell him that Jen was in the hospital and that she might die. Before her funeral, they explained to him what happened. He refused to believe it. With every attempted explanation, he cried out, "Don't say that!"

Bob says, "He just rejected the notion that she was dead. For months he wouldn't look at pictures of Jen or even mention her name."

In January, a celebration of Jen's life packed the Carleton chapel. As friends and family rose to speak, they left their tears in the pews. Bob delivered the eulogy, a speech he had prepared for over the past two decades. "I have known in my bones that I would bury her, but she never knew that . . ."

He portrayed their family life as a kind of fiction, "not a lie . . . but the product of realism and faith . . . One primary fiction as parents was our decision to treat Jen as a normal child with some particular limitations . . . Barbara and I presented views of life and of ourselves to our baby daughter that were conscious fictions, and then lived them as fully as we could . . . We probably became better people as we tried to live up to what we had presented to her."

Especially in her last year, Jen approached her life as a work of art, ". . . living each day with full consciousness. . . . She accepted her essential vulnerability. She accepted that death is part of life, and that we live within limits not of our own choosing. . . . Her prose and her art entered an ascending spiral of creativity. . . . We will never know if she could have sustained life on those terms. . . . She was always so conscious of what she was doing, so determined to find the meaning."

Bob quoted Tennessee Williams in his closing: "snatching the eternal from the desperately fleeting is the great magic trick of existence." Then Jen's father said simply, "Now you see her. Now you don't."

As JEN WROTE in her diary, "Time always seems continuous in retrospect. It fools us into thinking that it is continuous in the future too." Though she was sick when she entered the hospital, she was not near death. Once again, it appeared she was in the right medical center at the right moment when, on the day of her admission, a heart became available and was a match for her.

The television station that interviewed Jen and Bob a few days earlier learned that the transplant had occurred. But when the station found out that Jen was not doing well, they declined to do a follow-up to their human interest story. No one wants to hear about a heart transplant gone wrong. That's not the way this story was supposed to end.

Jen had borne her physical limitations with buoyant optimism. When she occasionally sank into a low mood, she popped out of it by the next day. She felt more lucky than not. In some ways, her life had been idyllic. She had spent most of it within the limits of a town she loved—the Small Picture that she embraced while drinking beer with friends at the L&M.

In the Big Picture, the one she could bear to look at only once in a while, she was tumbling through a relentless cascade of medical what-ifs all her life.

CHANCE EVENTS WORKED to both shorten and lengthen Jen's life. Her story invites speculation about what might have been and appreciation for what actually occurred.

A decade before her birth, the University of Minnesota was on the stimulating frontier of heart surgery. Along with the promise for cures, new surgical procedures brought learning-curve danger to the first patients. Mistakes, surprises, and failures, first in the surgery labs and then in the operating rooms, preceded the later happy endings.

Jen entered the world at the U of M when there was just enough knowledge to keep her alive. Aldo Castaneda, who became one of the greats in open-heart surgery, happened to be her surgeon during the early prime of his career. He successfully employed the Waterston shunt, a new procedure designed for a young infant.

This type of shunt was used for a time, but the medical community recognized that the Waterston sent unregulated blood flow to the lungs and damaged them. Surgeons abandoned it in favor of other approaches, including a modified Blalock-Thomas-Taussig shunt, which is a preferred shunt today.

U of M cardiologist Ray Anderson watched and waited and chose the next moment to intervene when he referred Jen to Mayo. There, surgeon Gordon Danielson and the cardiology team used all their skill to keep Jen going during her time in and out of the hospital.

And finally, Sara Shumway was given the difficult, maybe

impossible task of successfully transplanting a heart into a young woman with ruined lungs and a battered heart encased in scar tissue.

When Jen was admitted on December 3, she was due for a heart catheterization. This test would have revealed the high pressures in her lungs and disqualified her from receiving the transplant. But the sudden appearance of a suitable donor heart put the transplant in motion before the catheterization could be accomplished.

Today, the transplant community still grapples with the problem of how to distribute scarce donor hearts in the most beneficial way. People who need new hearts far outnumber the hearts that become available. Heart transplants in the US have plateaued at under three thousand per year. Should a heart go to the sickest patient or to someone with a better chance of long-term survival? Should time on the waiting list be a factor?

The majority of people who need a new heart developed heart disease during their lifetime, rather than being born with it. For these patients, often a transplant is their first major cardiac operation. Survivors of congenital heart disease like Jen present many more technical problems, largely because of their previous operations.

On average, today's transplanted heart delivers ten to fifteen additional years of reasonably healthy life. The age cutoff for recipients has risen to seventy or so. Though guidelines are in place, chance and the press of time create a scramble to get a donor heart to the person who needs it the most.

Despite reassurances to the Bonners fifty years ago, an artificial heart has been a long time coming. A partial artificial heart, known as a ventricular assist device (VAD), was approved by the FDA in 1994. A VAD may serve as a bridge to transplantation or as a longterm treatment in itself.

A new human heart still provides the best results, as photos of former vice president Dick Cheney and baseball great Rod Carew attest. Though their bridge VADs had worked, both grew visibly healthier after receiving new hearts.

One day we may be able to grow perfect new hearts in the lab using stem cells, but that day is far off.

INSTEAD OF A BRIEF existence measured in weeks or months, Jen enjoyed almost twenty-two years. The love her parents felt for her as a baby became deeper with their detailed appreciation for the person she became. When physicians fend off death in children, added time is especially precious, as young individuals unfold and become themselves.

Jen attained that bright sliver of early adulthood when, without reservation, she wanted to understand herself and to be understood. Her diary catapults us into the mind of a fully articulated human being. She could animate almost any topic. And she is knowable. She learned who she was and how to be at ease with that person.

She let the story of her last year flow unfiltered onto the page. Readers meet a young woman in extremis who considered her life normal enough to look for a new boyfriend, and who endearingly kept looking. Here is an ambitious painter who aspired to Mozart-like greatness, yet acknowledged some of her work as "crap." Readers can know her with the satisfying particularity that defines real relationships.

For Jen, her diary promoted personal growth as it documented her life. Her honesty with herself recalls Joan Didion's classic essay about self-respect—"Self-respect is a discipline, a habit of mind that can never be faked but can be developed, trained, coaxed forth."

Sitting down with her notebook each night, Jen developed that discipline. The intimacy of her own handwriting on the page warded off the temptation to posture for others. She confronted the great questions of life, yet remained expressive and funny, never ponderous, never mean, and never taking herself too seriously.

Diary pages

Powerful themes dominated her everyday thoughts. How could she give herself to another yet retain her own identity? "I hate being in love and feeling like I have to fit inside someone." How she fought the pull of love, yet friendships made her feel "light and free." How her vocation contained her: "It made me feel whole to do some Art. . . . Artists exist because we share."

And finally, how her late-night self accepted her mortality, writing that death is like the ocean, ". . . huge, terrifying, uncontrollable. I have to learn to be comfortable in all that deep water."

One of Jen's dominant traits was her optimism—"Whatever is lying in wait for me, it won't get me right now." She possessed the same emotional hardiness that many medical pioneers shared. They all believed the best outcome was possible.

Jen's last conscious thoughts almost certainly revolved around hope. As the Bonner family's minister said, she looked at the void and found the River.

LOSING JEN SHOOK the stalwart marriage of the couple who met in the shadow of the Medicine Bow mountains. Bob and Barbara mourned jointly and individually, and a decade passed before they regained their equilibrium. Both sought new challenges while they pried away the fingers of grief's stranglehold.

Bob served as Carleton's Dean of Students for three years and taught the history of the American West. Returning to Wyoming for historical research, he wrote *William F. Cody's Wyoming Empire*, a book about Buffalo Bill's attempts to develop real estate in the Big Horn Basin. He became a transformative board member at Laura Baker.

Barbara edited the book *Sacred Ground*, writings about home and homelessness. She took art classes and painted. Some things didn't change. The Bonner household still declares that Barbara, Jen's Queen of Color, lives there.

Months after Jen's death, Tim and his parents put together a photo album of Jen. He finally acknowledged that he used to have a sister, but didn't anymore. Tim remained at Laura Baker, where he eventually got his own room in a cottage shared with five other residents. He carefully chooses the music, movies, books, magazines, and companions that fill his day. As always, he makes a weekly trip to the library.

Kurt Hartwig earned a PhD in folklore and remained active in theater. Twenty years after Jen's death, he premiered his one-man play *Decaffeinated Tragedy: A Love Story That Never Was* at the Prague Fringe Festival. This meditation on memory, loss, and his relationship with Jen included excerpts from her diary and some of her art.

Kurt wrote, "We came together on mortality. Neither of us knew many other people who had experienced mortality in the ways we had . . . Jen faced her death. I faced others'. She learned that we don't have a lot of time. I learned that people leave you."

He addressed their relationship directly. "I did let Jen down. I couldn't have asked for a more generous, or understanding, or patient friend. And none of that absolves me of the fact that as good a friend as I tried to be, I wasn't up to the job. I think she forgave me, sort of constantly, which is a mild consolation. It's hard to forgive myself though. Not that I think I did a bad thing. I did the best I could . . . You can't choose to love someone—why do we choose who we choose? I know why I ran."

ALDO CASTANEDA RETIRED from Boston Children's Hospital in 1996 and returned to Guatemala to establish a children's cardiac surgery hospital. Stuart Jamieson left the University of Minnesota the year after Jen's transplant. He became the head of cardiothoracic surgery at the University of California in San Diego and still practices there. Sara Shumway has had a distinguished career at the University of Minnesota, where she has helped the heart transplant program excel at performing complicated transplants for patients like Jen.

EVERY MOTHER'S DAY, Barbara receives flowers from three of Jen's friends. Jen can't send flowers herself, yet she is still here for anyone who reads her diary.

Jen describes her future as an artist on the road or alone in an urban apartment, as a bride who gets lots of teddies at her shower, and as a woman who can dance and have children. That future is a fiction, one that extends the mirage of endless well-being Bob and Barbara built for their family, and that her physicians maintained for as long as they could. It is an illusion that readers willingly share. We know Jen is gone. Yet the mirage shimmers each time a reader opens this book, where by Jen's own hand, she remains very much alive.

Self-portrait

Acknowledgments

For early drafts of the manuscript, Susan Fraker provided sustained and invaluable editorial support. I also received advice and encouragement from other early readers including Jane Hamilton, Margo Tolins-Mejia, Tim Mennel, Marcia Cushman-Perkins, Josie Rawson, Kirsten Johanna Allen, Kristin Henning, Susan Schultz, Judy Lutter, Penny Wheeler, Ginny Hustead, Susan Sencer, Judy Stark, and Sue Mahle.

William Boggess was a steadying editorial hand at a midpoint when I had drifted from the best course for the project.

Corey Pulju and Loretta Springer printed manuscript drafts for review, and Heidi Eyestone reproduced Jen's art for publication. Toni Easterson advised on a crucial design element. Suzanne Savanick Hansen, Naomi and Jeff Goldenberg, and Kurt Hartwig shared images of Jen's art that they own. Kurt also sent the script for *Decaffeinated Tragedy* and generously commented on my manuscript.

At Wise Ink Creative Publishing, Laura Zats guided the project to publication, with help from editors Jessie Bowman and Erik Hane.

Charlie Quimby, my spouse since our Carleton days, kept me going with his personal tonic, which is equal parts critique and appreciation. And finally, Bob and Barbara Bonner made this book possible. They raised a remarkable human being, offered up their family story, shared insights about their daughter's medical journey, and trusted in the long process of bringing Jen's work to print.

Selected Bibliography

Bonner, Barbara and Robert. *Personal communications* 2013–2017.

Bonner, Jennifer. *Diaries* 1977–1988.

Bonner, Robert. "A Father's Words." *The Carleton Voice* 54, no. 2 (1989) 30–32.

Cooper, David K.C. *Open Heart: The Radical Surgeons Who Revolutionized Medicine.* New York: Kaplan Publishing, 2010.

DeBoer, Arthur. "The Waterston Shunt: A Commentary." *Annals of Thoracic Surgery,* 44. no. 3 (1987) 326–327.

DiBardino, Daniel J. "The History and Development of Cardiac Transplantation." *Texas Heart Institute Journal* 26, no. 3 (1999) 198–205.

Dunn, Rob R. *The Man Who Touched His Own Heart: True Tales of Science, Surgery, and Mystery.* New York: Little Brown and Co., 2015.

Kantrowitz, Adrian. "America's First Human Heart Transplantation: The Concept, the Planning, and the Furor." *American Society for Artificial Internal Organs Journal* 44, no. 4 (1998) 244–252.

Kubo, Spencer H. "Trends in Patient Selection of Heart Transplantation." *Journal of the American College of Cardiology* 21, no. 4 (1993) 975–981.

Hartwig, Kurt. *Decaffeinated Tragedy: A Love Story that Never Was.* World premiere, Prague Fringe Festival, 2009.

McRae, Donald. *Every Second Counts: The Race to Transplant the First Human Heart.* New York: G.P. Putnam's Sons, 2006.

O'Connell, John B. "Task Force 1: Organization of Heart Transplantation in the U.S." *Journal of the American College of Cardiology* 22, no. 1 (1993) 8–14.

Shumway, Norman. "Present Status of Heart Transplantation in Man." *Proceedings of the American Philosophical Society* 115, no. 4 (1971) 267–270.

Slovut, Gordon. "The Complex Case of Dr. Jamieson." *Star-Tribune*, November 7, 1988 1A.

Thompson, T. "A new and disquieting look at transplants." *Life*, September 17, 1971, 56–70.

About The Authors

Jennifer Bonner was an art major at Carleton College and a dedicated diarist. Born with severe heart defects, she nevertheless lived a full and joyful life with her parents, Bob and Barbara, and her brother, Tim. After waiting most of 1988 for a heart transplant, she died at age twenty-one, soon after the transplant took place.

After working as a medical writer, **Susan Cushman** attended medical school at the University of Minnesota, where she also completed her residency. She practiced as an ob-gyn in the Minneapolis metro area for more than twenty years. With her husband, novelist Charlie Quimby, she lives in Minnesota and Colorado.